# THE LANGUAGE
# OF
# LOVE AND GUILT

## Mother-daughter relationships
## from a cross-cultural perspective

Ruth Wodak
*University of Vienna*

Muriel Schulz
*California State University, Fullerton*

JOHN BENJAMINS PUBLISHING COMPANY
AMSTERDAM/PHILADELPHIA

1986

**Library of Congress Cataloging in Publication Data**

Wodak, Ruth, 1950-
  The language of love and guilt.

(Benjamins Paperbacks, 3)
Bibliography: p.
Includes indexes.
1. Mothers and daughters -- Cross-cultural studies. 2. Sociolinguistics -- Cross-cultural studies. I. Schulz, Muriel. II. Title.
HQ755.85.W63    1986    306.8'743    85-30674
ISBN 0-915027-45-3 (US)/90 272 2022 0 (European) (hb.:alk. paper)
ISBN 0-915027-44-5 (US)/90 272 2023 9 (European) (pb.:alk. paper)

*For our Mothers and Daughter*

*Marian Hill Ripley*
*Alison Kathleen Schulz*
*Erna Franziska Wodak*

# THE LANGUAGE OF LOVE AND GUILT

BENJAMINS PAPERBACKS

3

BENJAMINS

BP

PAPERBACKS

# PREFACE

In May 1978, we met for the first time. Muriel was in Vienna with her husband, who was on a Fulbright, and Ruth was working on her Habilitation. We talked about many things: women in Austria and the U.S., family life, mothers, discrimination in general. At that time Muriel was a wife, a daughter, and a mother of a daughter; Ruth was a daughter (and, since then, has become a wife and also a mother). We talked about our own lives, about our diverse roles and role-conflicts.

At another meeting, in Osnabruck, Germany, in April 1979, we both gave papers on sex-specific language: Muriel talked about Motherese, and Ruth about the woman's search for linguistic identity. And, in the following April, Ruth told Muriel of a research project dealing with the mother-daughter relationship in Vienna which had been influenced by Muriel's paper the previous year. The design interested Muriel, who proposed that they work together to try an interdisciplinary, cross-cultural study: she would replicate the Viennese research in Los Angeles, and both would interpret the results and write the book together.

And so we started, not guessing how exciting, complex, and also trying the process would be. (This is the first time, to our knowledge, that such a study has been attempted in sociolinguistics.) In the first place, we completely underestimated the difficulties consequent upon working at such a distance from one another. We could neither drop in on nor telephone each other whenever we wanted to discuss a point. We had to write. Letters came and went, always slowly — some never arrived. Gradually, however, we completed our research and gathered our statistics.

Writing the book at such a distance would have been even more difficult. Fortunately, however, we received a grant from the Rockefeller Foundation and were able to spend a month together in 1982 at the Foundation's Study and Conference Center in Bellagio, Italy, where the book took shape. We are extremely grateful to the Rockefeller Foundation and to the staff of the Villa Serbelloni, for giving us this opportunity. The peace and atmosphere of the Villa made the impossible possible: in roughly five weeks we had a completed draft of the book.

When we started talking about the manuscript and searching for a publisher, we were intrigued by reactions we encountered. Responses to our design made clear that we had touched areas of taboo, guilt, and anxiety. We were asked if we had daughters and were interrogated about our relationships with them and with our own mothers (although we have written on schizophrenia, suicide, rape and crime without being asked whether we have experienced them). We were surprised to find that ours was rarely categorized as a female book about female topics; the mother-daughter relationship, after all, affects everyone — if only indirectly. Our study is for everyone who is interested in relationships, in communication, in family life.

We would like to thank the Jubiläumsfonds (Vienna), the Wissenschaftsministerium (Vienna) and the Partners-in-Excellence Fund of the California State University System (Fullerton) for grants in support of our research. We cannot name the teachers, administrators, and students who participated in the study, but we are deeply grateful to them and to the mothers and daughters who participated in our research.

In addition, Ruth would like to thank Dr. Ursula Hamberger for interviewing and for help in analyzing the tests; Mag. Karl Zolles for doing the Austrian statistics; and Ms. Tanja Haase for editing parts of the typed manuscript. Special thanks go to her husband Günther, who supported her in every part of the research and writing, and to her son Jacob, who sometimes sleeps, permitting her to do the final editing.

Muriel wishes to thank Robert Dilligan, of the University of Southern California, for sharing with her the computer expertise necessary for the preparation of the manuscript and the analysis of the results of our research; Les Perleman for assistance with the statistical program; Lynette Turman for selecting classrooms; and her three children — Alison, Gavin, and Evan Schulz — for helping to type the book into the computer. Most important, however, are thanks for the loving support of her husband Max, who took her to Austria, introduced her to all of the supportive friends mentioned here, and, always, urged her forward.

# TABLE OF CONTENTS

1. INTRODUCTION . . . . . . . . . . . . . . . . . . . . . . . . . . . 1

    1.1 Formulation of the Problem . . . . . . . . . . . . . . . . . . . . 1
    1.2 Current Problems . . . . . . . . . . . . . . . . . . . . . . . 3
    1.3 Our Study . . . . . . . . . . . . . . . . . . . . . . . . . . 5
    Notes . . . . . . . . . . . . . . . . . . . . . . . . . . . . . 5

2. THE RELATIONSHIP BETWEEN MOTHER AND DAUGHTER . 7

    2.1 Introduction . . . . . . . . . . . . . . . . . . . . . . . . . 7
    2.2 Psychoanalytical Concepts . . . . . . . . . . . . . . . . . . . 7
        2.2.1 Differences in Early Male and Female Development . . . 7
        2.2.2 The Daughter's Struggle for Individuation . . . . . . . . . 9
        2.2.3 The Symbiosis between Mother and Daughter . . . . . . . 10
    2.3 Sociological Concepts . . . . . . . . . . . . . . . . . . . . . 12
        2.3.1 The Stereotypical Mother . . . . . . . . . . . . . . . . . 12
        2.3.2 The Impact of Feminism . . . . . . . . . . . . . . . . . 13
    2.4 Linguistic Concepts . . . . . . . . . . . . . . . . . . . . . . 15
        2.4.1 A Cognitive Theory of Text Planning . . . . . . . . . . . 18
        2.4.2 Schematic Theory . . . . . . . . . . . . . . . . . . . . 19
        2.4.3 Schematic Theory and Writing . . . . . . . . . . . . . . 21
    2.5 Conclusion and Hypotheses . . . . . . . . . . . . . . . . . . 22
    Notes . . . . . . . . . . . . . . . . . . . . . . . . . . . . . 23

3. MOTHER-CHILD DISCOURSE . . . . . . . . . . . . . . . . . 25

    3.1. Introduction . . . . . . . . . . . . . . . . . . . . . . . . . 25
    3.2 Varieties of Caretaker Talk — Terminology . . . . . . . . . . . 26
    3.3 The Characteristics and Stages of the Caretaker Register . . . . 27
        3.3.1 Characteristics of Caretaker Talk . . . . . . . . . . . . . 27
        3.3.2 Stages in Caretaker Talk . . . . . . . . . . . . . . . . . 29
    3.4 Motherese: Its Functions . . . . . . . . . . . . . . . . . . . 29
        3.4.1 Introduction: Establishing the Primary Relationship . . . 30
        3.4.2 Symbiotic Language . . . . . . . . . . . . . . . . . . . 31
        3.4.3 Instrumental Speech . . . . . . . . . . . . . . . . . . . 33

3.4.3.1 Expressions of Power and Control: Differences
between Mothers and Fathers . . . . . . . . . . . .  34
3.4.3.2 Indirect Control and Its Consequences for the
Child's Emotional and Cognitive Development .  35
3.4.3.3 Indirect Control: A Model of Feminine Discourse. 37
3.4.4  Indirect Control — Conclusions . . . . . . . . . . . . . . . .  38
3.5  Pedagogic Language Functions . . . . . . . . . . . . . . . . . . . . . .  39
3.5.1  Cognitive Consequences . . . . . . . . . . . . . . . . . . . . . .  39
3.6  Mother-Daughter Discourse  . . . . . . . . . . . . . . . . . . . . . . .  41
3.6.1  Qualitative and Quantitative Differences in Mother-
Daughter Interaction . . . . . . . . . . . . . . . . . . . . . . . . .  41
3.7  The Impact of Motherese on Female Development . . . . . . . .  45
3.7.1  The Effects of Symbiotic Language . . . . . . . . . . . . .  45
3.7.2  The Effects of Instrumental Language . . . . . . . . . . .  46
3.7.3  The Effects of Pedagogic Language . . . . . . . . . . . . .  47
3.7.3.1 Socialization into Different Cognitive and
Emotional Worlds  . . . . . . . . . . . . . . . . . . .  50
Notes  . . . . . . . . . . . . . . . . . . . . . . . . . . . . . . . . . . . . . . . . . .  51

4.  SAMPLE, METHODOLOGY, AND COLLECTION OF DATA . . 53

4.1  Introduction . . . . . . . . . . . . . . . . . . . . . . . . . . . . . . . . . . . .  53
4.2  Methodological Considerations: Qualitative and Quantitative
Methods in Sociolinguistics . . . . . . . . . . . . . . . . . . . . . . . .  53
4.2.1  Analysis of Essay Content  . . . . . . . . . . . . . . . . . . .  54
4.3  The Design of the Empirical Study  . . . . . . . . . . . . . . . . . .  57
4.3.1  The Cross-Cultural Comparison . . . . . . . . . . . . . . . .  57
4.3.1.1 The Austrian Design . . . . . . . . . . . . . . . . . .  59
4.3.1.2 The U.S. Design  . . . . . . . . . . . . . . . . . . . . .  60
4.3.2  Collection of the Data . . . . . . . . . . . . . . . . . . . . . . .  60
4.3.3  The Ethical Dilemma and the Observer Paradox . . . . .  61
4.3.4  Analysis of the Data . . . . . . . . . . . . . . . . . . . . . . . .  63
4.4  The Empirical Investigation . . . . . . . . . . . . . . . . . . . . . . . .  63
4.4.1  Description of the Austrian Sample  . . . . . . . . . . . . .  63
4.4.1.1 Sociological Factors in Austria . . . . . . . . . . .  63
4.4.1.2 The Austrian Schools Chosen  . . . . . . . . . . . .  64
4.4.1.3 The Nature of the Austrian Sample  . . . . . . . .  64
4.4.2  Description of the U.S. Sample . . . . . . . . . . . . . . . .  65
4.4.2.1 Sociological Factors in the U.S. . . . . . . . . . . .  65

4.4.2.2 The U.S. Schools Chosen . . . . . . . . . . . . . . 66
4.4.2.3 The Nature of the U.S. Sample . . . . . . . . . . 67
4.4.3 The Selection of Categories for Analysis . . . . . . . . . 68
Notes . . . . . . . . . . . . . . . . . . . . . . . . . . . . . . . . . . . 69

5. DEFINITION OF THE CATEGORIES . . . . . . . . . . . . . . 71

5.1 Introduction . . . . . . . . . . . . . . . . . . . . . . . . . . . 71
5.2 The Schema of the "School Essay" . . . . . . . . . . . . . . . 71
5.3 Text Categories . . . . . . . . . . . . . . . . . . . . . . . . . 72
     5.3.1 The Category of TEXT TYPE . . . . . . . . . . . . . . . 72
           5.3.1.1 Reflective Texts . . . . . . . . . . . . . . . . . 73
           5.3.1.2 Unreflective Texts . . . . . . . . . . . . . . . 74
     5.3.2 The Category of COHERENCE . . . . . . . . . . . . . . 74
           5.3.2.1 Consistency . . . . . . . . . . . . . . . . . . . 76
           5.3.2.2 Illogicality . . . . . . . . . . . . . . . . . . . 76
           5.3.2.3 Contradictions . . . . . . . . . . . . . . . . . 77
     5.3.3 The Category of CLICHES . . . . . . . . . . . . . . . . 77
     5.3.4 The Category of LENGTH . . . . . . . . . . . . . . . . 77
     5.3.5 The Category of SEMIOTICS . . . . . . . . . . . . . . . 78
     5.3.6 The Category of PARTICLES . . . . . . . . . . . . . . . 79
5.4 Sociological Categories . . . . . . . . . . . . . . . . . . . . . 80
     5.4.1 The Category of SELF-IMAGE . . . . . . . . . . . . . . 80
     5.4.2 The Category of MOTHER ROLES . . . . . . . . . . . . 80
     5.4.3 The Category of SELF-ASSESSMENT . . . . . . . . . . . 81
     5.4.4 The Category of EDUCATIONAL STYLE . . . . . . . . 82
     5.4.5 The Category of QUALITY OF SANCTIONS . . . . . . 82
5.5 Psychological Categories . . . . . . . . . . . . . . . . . . . . 83
     5.5.1 The Category of MOTHER RELATIONSHIP . . . . . . 83
     5.5.2 The Category of AFFECTIVITY . . . . . . . . . . . . . 83
     5.5.3 The Category of RELATIONSHIP TO THE RE-
           SEARCHER . . . . . . . . . . . . . . . . . . . . . . . . 84
Notes . . . . . . . . . . . . . . . . . . . . . . . . . . . . . . . . . . . 85

6. SOCIOLOGICAL-PSYCHOLOGICAL PARAMETERS OF
   THE MOTHER-DAUGHTER RELATIONSHIP. SOCIO-PSY-
   CHOLOGICAL VARIATION (SPV) . . . . . . . . . . . . . . . . 87

6.1 Introduction . . . . . . . . . . . . . . . . . . . . . . . . . . . 87

6.2 Sex-Related Socio-Psychological Variation . . . . . . . . . . . . . 87
    6.2.1 The SPV MOTHER ROLE . . . . . . . . . . . . . . . . . 88
    6.2.2 The SPV SELF-IMAGE . . . . . . . . . . . . . . . . . . 89
    6.2.3 The SPV EDUCATIONAL STYLE AND RULES . . . 89
    6.2.4 The SPV SELF-ASSESSMENT . . . . . . . . . . . . . . 89
    6.2.5 The SPV RELATIONSHIP WITH THE MOTHER . . 90
    6.2.6 The SPV AFFECTIVITY . . . . . . . . . . . . . . . . . . 90
    6.2.7 The SPV RELATIONSHIP TO THE RESEARCHER . . 91
6.3 Cultural Differences in Socio-Psychological Variation . . . . . . 92
    6.3.1 Social Class and Ethnicity . . . . . . . . . . . . . . . . . 92
6.4 A Socio-Psychological Theory of Text Planning (SPTT) . . . . . 93
    6.4.1 Sex and the SPTT — Macrotextual Level . . . . . . . . . 93
        6.4.1.1 The Textual Variable TEXT TYPE . . . . . . . . 93
    6.4.2 Sex and the SPTT — Microtextual Level . . . . . . . . . . 95
        6.4.2.1 The Textual Variable COHERENCE . . . . . . . 95
        6.4.2.2 The Textual Variable CLICHES . . . . . . . . . . 96
        6.4.2.3 The Textual Variable LENGTH . . . . . . . . . 98
        6.4.2.4 The Textual Variable SEMIOTICS . . . . . . . . 99
        6.4.2.5 The Textual Variable PARTICLES . . . . . . . . 99
6.5 Conclusions about Gender and the SPTT . . . . . . . . . . . . . 100
6.6 Essay Analysis . . . . . . . . . . . . . . . . . . . . . . . . . . . . 100
    6.6.1 Essay A — Austrian Girl . . . . . . . . . . . . . . . . . . 100
    6.6.2 Essay B - Austrian Boy' . . . . . . . . . . . . . . . . . . . 102
        6.6.2.1 Comparison of Austrian Essays A and B . . . . . 103
    6.6.3 Essay C — U.S. Girl . . . . . . . . . . . . . . . . . . . . 104
    6.6.4 Essay D — U.S. Boy . . . . . . . . . . . . . . . . . . . . 106
        6.6.4.1 Comparison of U.S. Essays C and D . . . . . . . 107
    6.6.5 Comparison of Austrian and U.S. Texts . . . . . . . . . . 107
6.7 Influence of the Schools — Vienna and Los Angeles . . . . . . . 108
6.8 Sex and Gender — The Effect of Feminism . . . . . . . . . . . . 110
    6.8.1 Feminism and Sex-Specific Differences in Writing . . . . 110
6.9 Concluding Remarks: The Socio-Psychological Theory of
    Text Planning . . . . . . . . . . . . . . . . . . . . . . . . . . . . 110
Notes . . . . . . . . . . . . . . . . . . . . . . . . . . . . . . . . . . . . 111

7. SELF AND OTHER ASSESSMENT . . . . . . . . . . . . . . . . . . 113

7.1 The Administration and Analysis of the Interviews and the
    Giessen Tests . . . . . . . . . . . . . . . . . . . . . . . . . . . . . 113

7.1.1  Introduction  . . . . . . . . . . . . . . . . . . . . . . . . 113
7.1.2  Methodological Remarks  . . . . . . . . . . . . . . . . . . 114
7.2  Interviews  . . . . . . . . . . . . . . . . . . . . . . . . . . . . 115
7.2.1  Procedures  . . . . . . . . . . . . . . . . . . . . . . . . . 115
7.2.1.1 Interviews with Daughters — Procedures  . . . . . 115
7.2.1.2 Interviews with Sons — Procedures  . . . . . . . . 116
7.2.1.3 Interviews with the Mothers — Procedures  . . . . 116
7.2.2  Interviews — Contents . . . . . . . . . . . . . . . . . . . 117
7.2.2.1 Interviews with Daughters and Sons — Contents . 117
7.2.2.2 Interviews with Mothers — Contents  . . . . . . . 118
7.3  The Giessen Tests . . . . . . . . . . . . . . . . . . . . . . . . 119
7.3.1  The Test . . . . . . . . . . . . . . . . . . . . . . . . . . . 119
7.4  Summary of the Most Important Results of the Analysis of
Combined Data From Interviews, Essays, and Giessen Tests  . 120
7.4.1  Comparison of Data Sources . . . . . . . . . . . . . . . . 120
7.4.2  The 30 Austrian Mothers — Data Analysis . . . . . . . . 121
7.4.2.1 The Austrian Mother Interviews — Tendencies
and Significant Results . . . . . . . . . . . . . . . 122
7.4.2.2 Correlation of Giessen Traits with Mother-
Daughter Relationships  . . . . . . . . . . . . . . 123
7.5  The Giessen Clusters: A Typology of Mothers . . . . . . . . . 125
7.5.1  The Correlation of Mother-Types with Daughter Variables  . . . . . . . . . . . . . . . . . . . . . . . . . . . . 126
7.6  Cross-Cultural Comparison of Mother and Daughter Responses. 127
7.6.1  Satisfaction with Being a Woman . . . . . . . . . . . . . 127
7.6.1.1 Father-Daughter Relationships  . . . . . . . . . . 130
7.6.2  Relationship Between Mother and Daughter  . . . . . . 131
7.7  Interview Contents — Cross-Cultural Comparison  . . . . . . 132
7.7.0.1 Social Class, Ethnicity, and Future Expectations . 132
7.7.0.2 Austria — U.S. — Sex Instruction  . . . . . . . . 132
7.7.1  Wish to Marry . . . . . . . . . . . . . . . . . . . . . . . 137
7.7.2  Privacy and Taboo  . . . . . . . . . . . . . . . . . . . . 138
7.8  Form of the Verbal Data from Mothers and Daughters  . . . . 141
7.8.1  Comparison of Text Types  . . . . . . . . . . . . . . . . 141
7.8.2  Comparison of a Mother-Daughter Text  . . . . . . . . 142
7.8.3  Concluding Remarks about the Comparison  . . . . . . 145
7.9  The Mother-Daughter Relationship . . . . . . . . . . . . . . . 145
7.9.1  Sex-Related Differences in the Mother-Daughter
Relationship  . . . . . . . . . . . . . . . . . . . . . . . 145

7.9.2  Cross-Cultural Similarities . . . . . . . . . . . . . . . . . . 146
7.10 Cross-Cultural Differences in Mother-Daughter Relationships . 148
7.10.1 A New Ideology in the U.S. . . . . . . . . . . . . . . . . . 148
7.11 Suggestions for Further Study . . . . . . . . . . . . . . . . . . .
Notes . . . . . . . . . . . . . . . . . . . . . . . . . . . . . . . . . 151

APPENDIX I — THE CASE HISTORIES . . . . . . . . . . . . . . . . 153

APPENDIX II — TABLES . . . . . . . . . . . . . . . . . . . . . . . . 189

APPENDIX III — THE GIESSEN TEST . . . . . . . . . . . . . . . . 207

APPENDIX IV — ORIGINAL VERSIONS OF 8 AUSTRIAN
    ESSAYS . . . . . . . . . . . . . . . . . . . . . . . . . . . . . . . 211

REFERENCES . . . . . . . . . . . . . . . . . . . . . . . . . . . . . . 220

INDEX OF AUTHORS & NAMES . . . . . . . . . . . . . . . . . . . 248

INDEX OF NAMES . . . . . . . . . . . . . . . . . . . . . . . . . . . 249

# 1. INTRODUCTION

## 1.1. *Formulation of the Problem*

On May 4, 1770, Maria Theresa addressed her famous daughter Marie Antoinette with the following words.

> Madame my dear daughter, So now you are in the place assigned to you by Providence. In view of your circumstances you are the luckiest of your sisters, indeed of all princesses. You will find a tender father who, if you desire it, will also be your friend. To give him your full confidence will involve no risks. Love him, obey him, try to anticipate his thoughts as much as you can. . . . Of the Dauphin I say nothing. You know my delicacy on this matter. The woman is subject to her husband in everything, and she should have no other occupation than to please him and do his will. The only true happiness on earth is a happy marriage: I speak from experience. Everything depends on the woman, (on whether she is flexible, good, and amusing). . . . I recommend, my dear daughter, that you reread my letter on the 21st of every month. I beg you, be true to me on this point. My only anxiety concerns negligence in your prayers and readings . . . . Bestow affection on your family, your aunts, your brothers-in-law and sisters-in-law. Allow no bickering; you can silence people or avoid it by moving away. . . . Do not forget a mother who, although far away, will be thinking about you till her last breath. I give you my blessing and remain always your true mother.[1]

Apart from the social standing of the two women and their style of correspondence, which is typical of their time, this is a perfectly normal communication (in Western cultures) between mother and daughter. The letter is full of direct and indirect exhortations, orders, and advice on various aspects of her daughter's life. At the same time, it gives the daughter a very normative conception of the role of a woman, a superego which still exists today (though in a mitigated form), especially in Europe: "Marriage and family are a woman's greatest joy; the woman should be subject to her husband in every respect, and should not lead an independent life or have needs of her own" (Bonner 1973; Kurthy 1978; Wagner, Frasch and Lamberti 1978; Keller 1979). Although the daughter is a married woman, and thus is separated from Maria Theresa, to her mother she remains the child who must be supervised and who ultimately still "belongs" to her. Maria Theresa has not acknowledged the separation; the symbiosis continues to exist.

Marie Antoinette replied to her mother (12 July 1770):

> I will tell you then that I get up at ten o'clock or nine o'clock or nine-thirty and, having dressed, say my morning prayers, then breakfast; after which I go to my aunts' apartments, where I generally find the king. I stay there until ten-thirty; at eleven I go to the hairdresser. Before noon I receive; anyone can come except common people. I put on my rouge and wash my hands in front of everybody; then the men leave, the ladies stay, and I dress before them. Mass is at noon; if the king is at Versailles I go with him and my husband and my aunts to mass; if he is not here I go with the Dauphin, but always at that time. After mass we dine....[2]

Marie Antoinette attempts to take refuge in plain descriptions of her everyday life, reporting a wealth of irrelevant details to satisfy her mother's curiosity, without explicitly mentioning her mother's instructions and without answering her questions. The mother's probe and the daughter's evasion illustrate the fixed communication patterns described by Halpern (1976), who speaks of them as "songs and dances" (German *Tanzlieder*), the stabilized, habitual communicative rituals which develop between parents and children and which come to characterize their interaction. For example, a certain kind of question or remark from the mother (such as the telephone greeting "How come you never call?") inevitably triggers a certain kind of answer from the son or daughter ("I've been busy, Mom"), and the exchange marks the beginning of a conflict between them. It is very difficult to break out of such circles — which express reproach and guilt, dominance and submission — because they symbolize the relational patterns which hold between parents and children.[3]

Children of both sexes become involved in communicative circles with their parents. We assume that the ritual exchanges of mothers and daughters will differ from those of mothers and sons and will reflect specific aspects of their relationship. Thus, although the style of the correspondence between Maria Theresa and her daughter is typical of a certain historical period and social class, the content transcends historical boundaries as an instance of mother-daughter communication. Can we imagine Maria Theresa [or any woman] addressing a similar letter to one of her sons? Such a close relationship extending even to the intimate sphere of marriage seems typical and possible only between mother and daughter; they share a very special type of communication, full of expectations, orders, taboos, rivalry, conflict, jealousy — and at the same time symbiotic love.

## 1.2. Current Problems

In recent years, a great many publications have examined the mother-daughter relationship (books by Neisser 1973; Hammer 1975; Dally 1979; Friday 1977; Franck 1976; Grasso 1979; and Rich 1979, for example, as well as articles in *Newsweek* [19 February 1979], *Time* [26 February 1979], and *Der Spiegel* [22 May 1980] and newspaper coverage in the *New York Times Magazine* [13 May 1979], and *Die Presse [Vienna]* [11 July 1980]). This increased interest can be explained in several ways.

The social changes affecting women in the past decades (such as improved household technology, increased job opportunitities, smaller families, and the women's liberation movement) have led to a re-examination of and modifications in the traditional roles of the sexes (Bernard 1981). Consequently, one would expect present mother-daughter relationships to reflect strongly not only the usual conflicts resulting from the the daughter's difficulty in achieving separation and individuation, and from the generation gap between them, but also added conflict deriving from the current social changes in how women appraise themselves and evaluate their femininity. Today much of a mother's life style — if she still lives according to traditional values — must be rejected as the main female model for her daughter if the daughter is to create a non-traditional role for herself.

Most descriptions of the mother-daughter relationship have been written by daughters who have — apparently — not been able to cope with their ambivalence towards their own mothers and have not gained a perspective which enables them to consider objectively the social factors contributing to their conflict.[4] Therefore, many of their discussions have been negative and extremely biased. When they have difficulties, such daughters blame their mothers, overlooking the degree to which social pressures have determined the nature of their conflict.

Only recently have feminist scholars begun to investigate the role of the mother (Chodorow 1974 represents the first major discussion of the question). Argumentation concerning the mother-daughter relationship has frequently been undifferentiated, failing to accommodate the irony that on the one hand it is the patriarchal structure of society which is responsible for women's status, while on the other it is often the mother herself who passes on to her daughter a negative appraisal of the female role. Moeller-Gambarov (1977), who discusses the attempts of four intellectual women to create new life styles for themselves, and Grasso (1979), who studies the sexual development and relationships of thirty women, were the first to consider both sides of this problem from the feminist perspective in their search for alternatives. However, even their work fails adequately to consider, on the one hand, the uniqueness of the interpersonal relationship between mothers and daughters and, on the other, its historical and socio-cultural aspects.

The uniqueness of the mother-daughter tie derives from the fact that the daughter participates not only in the anaclitic (emotionally dependent) relationship of the child with its mother, but also from the fact that both mother and daughter are of the same sex. Our culture, while it encourages boys to become independent of their mothers at an early age, sanctions — and in fact encourages — continued dependence in girls. That the girl is expected to develop a gender identity as a female compounds that dependence. Even in bourgeoise western societies of the sort we are investigating, the boy has limited access to the model presented by his father. As a result boys receive their socialization chiefly from age mates and from adults in the outside world. Girls, on the other hand, first learn their gender roles at home in the world of their mothers (Chodorow 1974, 48-57). In this way social norms of the female role are translated and reproduced, the mother embodying the role with which the daughter identifies primarily and to which she relates emotionally most strongly in a preoedipal bond. A mother passes on to her daughter the social evaluations of her own role as a woman, beginning in the primary mother-child dyad (Anthony and Benedek 1970; Spitz 1970; Lorenzer 1972). During this period the daughter develops a closer identification with her mother than does the son, and the mother identifies more closely with her, often experiencing the daughter as an extension of herself. This generates between them a unique bond, in which each feels the other to be part of the self. Thus Jung (1969, 162) remarks, "Every mother contains her daughter within herself, and every daughter her mother...."

The mother-daughter relationship figures in questions of speech acquisition, of sex-specific socialization, of identification, of cognitive and emotional development, and of psychological development. We regard the relationship between mother and daughter as a central interface of important interdisciplinary facts which manifest themselves above all in their communication. The mother's discourse serves as:

1.    a model for the child's acquisition of linguistic and pragma-linguistic competence;
2.    an important source of emotional, cognitive, and communicative socialization;

3. a model of sex-specific speech behavior;
4. an instance of the super-ego (imparting moral values and norms);
5. the channel for a relationship, the dynamics and alteration of which make possible the development of the child's identity following symbiosis and individuation. This relationship is, so to speak, the model for all the subsequent object relationships which will be formed by the daughter.

## 1.3. *Our Study*

An interdisciplinary topic requires an interdisciplinary approach. This study therefore attempts to accommodate the range of issues noted above, using a combination of textlinguistic, sociolinguistic, psycholinguistic, sociological and psychoanalytic theories and categories in a framework similar to that which Wodak (1981a) used to analyze discourse in crisis intervention therapy. Our purpose is to present a quantitative and qualitative analysis of essays written by 12 year-old school children in Vienna and Los Angeles on the subject "My Mother and I." We are interested in sex-specific differences in the quality of the mother-child relationship and in the expression of this relationship at a textual level. We have selected our sample from 12-year-olds in order to be able to observe the daughter's responses to the mother at that point in her life when separation is just getting under way. We chose the topic "My Mother and I" in order to be able to see how the texts of girls and boys differ, given an emotionally charged subject, whether by culture, social class, ethnicity, type of school, or sex of writer. We assume that sex, class, and culturally specific socialization processes affect the cognitive and emotional structuring of reality of children, manifesting themselves at the language level. We also analyze interviews with the girls, comparing their written and spoken texts and comparing their language choices and attitudes with those of their mothers, also recorded in interviews.

## NOTES

1) Quoted in Gooch (1965) 122-23.

2) Quoted in Mayer (1968) 32-33.

3) A therapist, Halpern suggests ways to cope with such conflicts and describes cases where patients *have* succeeded in changing the patterns (only after they have confronted their feelings and altered their inner relationship toward their parents) by using metacommunicative strategies ("Why do you ask?" or "I'm old enough to do as I please" or "If you don't stop nagging, I won't call at all"), thus refusing to join in the usual interaction.

4) This failure is evident in the work of most psychoanalysts, as well. For a review of current theories of the mother/daughter relationship and a discussion of the limitations of the psychoanalytic model, see Hirsch (1981).

# 2. THE RELATIONSHIP BETWEEN MOTHER AND DAUGHTER

## 2.1. *Introduction*

Our study deals with psychological and social influences upon the mother-daughter relationship and with the possibile correlation of these with linguistic behavior. In order to see the interaction of these factors, we draw upon concepts from psychology, sociology, and linguistics.

## 2.2. *Psychoanalytical Concepts*

Preoedipal development has only recently attracted much attention, but already Freud stated that a girl's relationship with her mother is of vital importance to her development as a woman. Although we are conscious of the feminist criticism of Freud's views and of the psychoanalytic theory of motherhood, we argue that a study of mother-daughter relationships must incorporate psychoanalytic theory, while bearing in mind this judgment by Mitchell (1974):

> The greater part of the feminist movement has identified Freud as the enemy. It is held that psychoanalysis claims women are inferior and that they can achieve true femininity only as wives and mothers. Psychoanalysis is seen as a justification for the status-quo, bourgeois and patriarchal, and Freud in his own person exemplifies these qualities. I would agree that popularized Freudianism must answer to this description; but . . . a rejection of psychoanalysis and of Freud's works is fatal for feminism. However it may have been used, psychoanalysis is not a recommendation *for* a patriarchal society, but an analysis *of* one. If we are interested in understanding and challenging the oppression of women, we cannot afford to neglect it (xv).

### 2.2.1. *Differences in Early Male and Female Development*

Although both girls and boys have to separate from their primary love object (the mother), girls have an added burden. They must transfer their libidinous feelings to the other sex (initially the father) in order to develop as heterosexual beings (Chodorow 1974). Simultaneously, they must identify with the mother in order to accept the female role she represents. Every identification process entails love and admiration, and every separation conflict is accompanied by feelings of hatred and guilt. Thus are born the girl's ambivalent feelings for her mother.

> When we survey the whole range of motives for turning away from the mother which analysis brings to light — that she failed to provide the little girl with the only proper genital, that she did not feed her sufficiently, that she compelled her to share her mother's love with others, that she never fulfilled the girl's expectations of love and, finally, that she first aroused her sexual activity and then forbade it — all these motives seem nevertheless insufficient to justify the girl's final hostility. Some of them follow inevitably from the nature of infantile sexuality; others appear like rationalizations devised later to account for the uncomprehended change in feeling. Perhaps the real fact is that the attachment to the mother is bound to perish, precisely because it was the first and was so intense; just as one can often see happen in the first marriages of young women which they have entered into when they were most passionately in love. In both situations the attitude of love probably comes to grief from the disappointments that are unavoidable and from the accumulation of occasions for aggression.
>
> (Freud, Female Sexuality, 1931)

We do not entirely subscribe to Freud's theory — in fact, essential concepts such as "penis envy" have been revised considerably[1] — but we should bear in mind his comment that anger and aggression result from the process of separation. This anger has important consequences for both sexes, but especially for the girl, who must continue to identify with the mother during the process of individuation. While many of the socializing effects of this early stage may be extinguished as the girl matures, still she must continue to deal with ambivalent emotions in her relationship with her mother. Dinnerstein (1977) argues that children associate female qualities both with the mother and with childhood dependence, including the pain associated with separation from her. Boys can act out their renunciation of the mother's model in a socially sanctioned way: they renounce the qualities in themselves that they consider to be feminine. Girls have to deal with the pain of separation without the liberating act of renunciation. The resulting ambivalence remains central to the daughter's relationship with her mother for the rest of her life. Chodorow (1974) reminds us:

> The development of a girl's gender identity contrasts with that of a boy. Most important, femininity and female role activities are immediately apprehensible in the world of her daily life. Her final role identification is with her mother and women, that is, with the person or people with whom she has her earliest relationship of infantile dependence. . . . Feminine identification is based not on fantasied or externally defined characteristics and negative identification, but on the gradual learning of a way of being familiar in everyday life, and exemplified by the person . . . with whom she has been most involved (51).

In this sense, the sex-role development of a girl in modern societies is more complex than that of a boy. A daughter must separate herself from the mother, but she cannot create her own identity as an antithesis to that of the mother, as the son can. Furthermore, though the boy is expected by the culture to repudiate the mother as a role model, the girl is not. The daughter must simultaneously develop her *personal* identity, separate from that of her mother, while accepting *the mother* as a model for her own *gender* identity. Thus, the process of separation and individuation pushes her away from the mother, even while the development of a gender identity pulls them closer together.[2]

### 2.2.2. *The Daughter's Struggle for Individuation*

The preoedipal relationship between mother and daughter is not ended by the attraction towards the father. To the contrary, the form, intensity and ambivalence of the relationship with the mother influence all other object relations the girl will have. More recent theoretical approaches to psychoanalysis (Mahler 1972; Mahler, Pine and Bergmann 1975; Bergmann 1980) stress the vital role of the first two years of the mother-daughter relationship in the development of the girl's sexual identity. Bergmann lists four factors involved in early female development which are decisive for the process of separation and individuation and for the development of an identity:

1.   the girl's perception of the difference between the sexes;
2.   the crisis of rapprochement, during which the daughter struggles to venture out into the world and yet also to return to the security offered by the mother;
3.   the daughter's identification and de-identification with the mother;
4.   the mother's attitude towards her own femininity and that of her daughter.

The experiential quality of these developmental phases determines important facets of the daughter's identity. Bergmann (1980) characterizes the four phases as follows:

> The girl notes the anatomic differences between the sexes at a very early age. This happens at a time when the sense of separation has not yet been developed strongly, i.e., at a time when the child still expects the mother to conjure up solutions. Re-established nearness to the mother helps at the beginning of the rapprochement period but the rapprochement crisis

demands that the girl de-identify from her mother sufficiently to become a separate individual and ensure that she is not swallowed up again. Only then can she identify with her mother's characteristics. The mother's attitude to the female child has a major effect on how the girl copes with this task. The mother's attitude is affected by her perception of herself as a woman and the importance of the female child to her. In her relationship to her daughter, the mother probably re-lives important events of her own separation-individuation experience (15-16).

The daughter's problems are complicated even further when she goes to school. On the one hand, school prepares its students for life in a complex society, but on the other, schooling for girls is really a sort of "pseudo-training," in that it is not expected to interfere with the training for the woman's "real" roles — as wife and mother (Chodorow 1974, 55). Studies show that teachers encourage dependence in girls (Serbin, O'Leary, Kent and Tonick 1973) and judge most positively girls with sex-appropriate behavior (Vreogh 1968; Serbin, O'Leary, Kent and Tonick 1973). Yet girls who score high in femininity and dependence have lower IQ scores and a greater incidence of maladjustment than their more androgynous sisters (Baumrind 1980). The preference for feminine behavior in girl students is reported as early as the first grade, and may contribute to our understanding of why the girls with the highest IQ do not excel in school (Coleman 1961). The studies cited here suggest that teachers may be exerting upon girls a pressure against achievement by rewarding feminine behavior rather than scholarly ability. The tendency increases in adolescence, when the discrepancy between ability and achievement in girls increases as a result of peer pressure not to surpass boys (Coleman 1961). As blunt as our initial statement may seem, it still is the basic message of many in-depth psychological treatises (cf. discussions in Lee and Stewart 1976).

### 2.2.3. *The Symbiosis between Mother and Daughter*

An intense relationship between the girl and her father depends upon the girl's having established an intensive relationship with her mother. In searching for new objects to love the girl not only has to drop the primary love object (the mother), but also has to change the sex of the object (from female to male). An emotional separation and break from the mother (and from women) is a necessary result of development; but like any separation, it is accompanied by ambivalent negative feelings. Deutsch (1944, I) speaks about the mother's double relationship with the daughter as it is represented in the framework of the "bisexual triangle" which characterizes the adolescence of the girl:

It is erroneous to say that the little girl gives up her first mother relation in favor of the father. She only gradually draws him into the alliance, develops from the mother-child exclusiveness toward the triangular parent-child relationship and continues the latter, just as she does the former, although in a weaker and less elemental form, all her life. Only the principal part changes: now the mother, now the father plays it. The ineradicability of affective constellations manifests itself in later repetitions (209).

Although we do not agree with Deutsch's theories on the passive (or masochistic) nature of women, this citation is of central importance. The ambivalence of the mother-daughter relationship begins during the process of separation and continues through adolescence (Blos 1962), when the girl completes the development of her identity. In her attempt to establish a stable ego, a boundary between the mother and herself, the adolescent daughter projects what she defines as bad onto her mother and tries to take that which is good onto herself. Such an arbitrary defense mechanism cannot break the underlying psychological unity of mother and daughter, or solve the problems associated with it. If, as often happens, the adolescent daughter selects another woman as a role model, it is difficult for the mother not to see her daughter's behavior as a repudiation, and the ensuing crisis generates distress and anger on both sides. Few mother-daughter pairs escape strife at this time (Rheingold 1964) and few mother-son pairs suffer it (in a study of university students, Ausubel [1954] found that only *women* regularly reported extended struggles with their mothers during adolescence). For those who are unable to resolve the conflict, there are at least four possible outcomes (although one of these relationships may change to another, from time to time): the first involves an unacknowledged rejection of the mother and difficulty in dealing with her in any socially sanctioned way; the second involves a break with the mother, accompanied by reproach on one side and guilt on the other; the third involves a life-long re-enactment of the familiar "songs and dances" — mother attempting to control and daughter attempting to resist; and the fourth involves a life-long symbiosis — widely reported in studies of marriage, in which the husband, the wife, and her mother form a triangle dominated by the female relationship (Cohler and Grunebaum 1981). The difficulties of individuation may be mitigated or aggravated by the type of mothering the girl receives (Graber 1973; Dally 1976; Halpern 1976; Brody and Axelrad 1978; Grasso 1979) and by the mother's own personality and attitude towards her femininity (Mahler 1980). Nevertheless, the process can be expected to produce similar pressures upon the mother and daughter in any case (Mussen and Rutherford 1963; Anthony and Benedek 1970; Freud 1976).

## 2.3. *Sociological Concepts*

### 2.3.1. *The Stereotypical Mother*

In addition to psychological problems of maturation, we are interested in sociological factors influencing the relationship between mothers and daughters. That relationship must be understood in its wider social setting, including the cultural values and norms that define the roles of the sexes. The family cannot be considered as an autonomous social sub-system, nor can the division and definition of roles within the family be regarded as independent of social conditions. We take an interactionist perspective which argues that role definitions, conflicts, and conflicting norms are central in our society, and that power struggles are responsible for maintaining a society which is not static, but, rather, changeable (Krappmann 1972).[3]

There is scarcely another female role that is so heavily conditioned by social appraisals and precepts as the role of the mother. Bolognese-Leuchten-müller says (1981):

> The reasons why the role of the mother must at present be understood and interpreted mainly as ideological glorification of a social function may be found in the traditionally ambivalent male attitude towards women. As a result of biased upbringing, the woman has been viewed as existing only in two functions artificially opposed to each other — as sexual object or as de-sexualized Other (144-45).

She goes on to add:

> The tendency to equip the role of the mother with more or less professional qualities and even understand it as a "profession" confirms on the one hand the desire to continue to define functions concerning household and up-bringing of children as exclusively female affairs and on the other hand a trend trend towards increasing rationalization of the mother-child relationship at the cost of its spontaneous-emotional character (147).

The role of mother demands yet other qualities. In analyzing the concept of "mother" in German school books, Kummer (1978) finds that the characteristics of motherhood reinforced are self-sacrifice, extensive care for the well-being of the child, and complete devotion to the needs of the family. There is no emphasis on the mother's need to have her own interests or her own personality: the "ideal" mother sacrifices herself to her family. While it should be obvious that most women are unable to fulfill such demands, many women suffer from their inability to conform to the model. As a result they suffer from a variety of psychic symptoms, noted in another study of children's books (Dunedin Collective for Women 1973), which shows that while the mother is represented as the "paragon of devotion to her family" admired in myth, she is also "often cross, nags, and is almost obsessed with neatness and cleanliness." The tensions between the maternal ideal and the reality later become important factors in the depression and suicide of women (Wodak 1981a).

### 2.3.2.  The Impact of Feminism

In response to studies like those cited above and pressure from feminists, U.S. publishers have established guidelines to assure that the sexes will receive equal treatment in textbooks, and publishers have provided new models in children's books (Tibbetts 1975a and 1975b; Klein 1975). Since such changes should affect children's perceptions of the female role, we are interested in examining the differing impact of feminism upon these assumptions and upon children in the two cultures.

Another concept undergoing change is the persistent belief that either a career or the fulfillment of individual needs is incompatible with the role of a mother (Scanzoni 1975). Lehr (1979) reviews recent studies on the impact of the profession of the mother on the development of her children, noting that earlier studies often neglected equally important variables, such as attitude of the husband, the family situation, the quality of the mother's profession, and, especially, the mother's satisfaction with her role and the subjective meaning to her of her professional life. Several of these variables have been addressed in research by Douvan (1966); Etaugh (1974); Hoffman (1974a and 1974b); Marantz and Mansfield (1977). These researchers conclude that whether mothers work or not, because of their own attitudes, women satisfied with their roles will usually have a positive influence on the development of their children.

Many publications have dealt with the changing perception of parental roles within the family (see especially Bonner 1973; Lehr 1979; Cater and Scott 1977; Scharmann and Scharmann 1979; Schmalohr 1979; Bolognese-Leuchtenmuller 1981). All are concerned with the impact of the maternal and paternal roles — of both their caretaker roles and their professional lives — on the development of their children, especially of their daughters.

In view of the existing social discrimination against women in employment opportunities, salary potential, and chances for promotion to higher positions, of the low economic value placed on mothering (Bernard 1974), and of the prejudices and stereotypes which still partially define the female role (that girls may be more frivolous, but should be better behaved and more industrious than boys; that girls should be quiet and demure, that family and career are incompatible; that women are irrational and primarily interested in social relationships, etc. [Wagner *et al* 1978]), it is understandable that the mother often continues to have a negative perception of her own role, and to transmit that perception to her children. The father's role in the process of socialization has been ignored until relatively recently (Lynn 1974; Lamb 1976 and 1977; Scharmann and Scharmann 1979), but the belief that the incorporation of a sensible balance of both male and female roles and norms is essential for both sexes is slowly gaining ground. Chodorow (1974) after comparing mothering practices in widely divergent cultures suggests:

> Daughters and sons must be able to develop a personal identification with more than one adult, and preferably one embedded in a role-relationship that gives it a social context of expression and provides some limitation upon it. Most important, boys need to grow up around men who take a major role in childcare, and girls around women who, in addition to their child-care responsibilities, have a valued role and recognized spheres of legitimate control (66).

We assume that today, particularly, there will be an increase in uncertainty among young women as a result of the social changes under way and the variety of choices available to them. This situation will contribute to the conflict between mothers and daughters, when mothers represent the traditional norms and values, while daughters strive for liberation. Two factors — sexual freedom and economic independence — seem especially relevant. These have led to new possibilities for women, even while increasing their uncertainty about which models to follow. Old roles, norms, and values have been rejected, but new styles (including new male roles) have not yet been clearly defined, and society as a whole has not kept up with the changes. The child's identification with and response to the mother will also be conditioned by ethnic and class norms and values. Since Austria remains relatively stratified socially, we consider social class to be an important factor in Vienna.[4] In the U.S., where there is a greater social mobility and stratification is difficult to define (Nichols 1980), we use ethnicity as a comparable social variable. Although class-related differences may occur, we do not begin with an assumption that working-class families are generally repressive, that sanctions are not verbalized in their homes, or that norms and roles are neither flexible, explainable or internalized in such families. We simply analyze our texts in terms of the child's class or ethnicity in order to see whether any differences emerge. If values and expectations differ by class or ethnicity, we expect to find differences in child socialization correlating with those factors (as Lynn 1979 suggests).

2.4. *Linguistic Concepts*

The mother-daughter relationship occupies an important place in research into the socialization of children and their language development. Various sociolinguistic, psycholinguistic and textlinguistic disciplines deal with different aspects of these fields. We draw upon research from the following:

1.   *Research into Speech Acquisition and Development.* Researchers have described in detail many aspects of language development. Several of these are relevant to the variation that occurs in the language of children and, hence, to our study.

2.   *Descriptive Studies of Adult-child Interaction.*
     Unfortunately, these studies often fail to consider the child's sex or the interaction of the parental figures, and they do not extend to the emotional level of communication. We draw upon this research, always bearing in mind that the quality of the affective relationship between caretaker and child is the most important aspect of their interaction (Spitz 1972; Klann-Delius 1979).

3.   *Studies of Sex-linked Differences in Child Language.*
     There are some studies dealing with sex- and class-specific factors in Caretaker Talk, but there are few based on the "Motherese" model dealing with the speech of school-aged children. These studies, too, often neglect the affective quality of the interaction observed. We are interested not only in sex-specific differences in the use of expressive language, but also in the quality, quantity, and range of those differences in the two cultures we study.

     We have chosen an essay topic designed to evoke an affective response from the boys and girls, in order to test the failure of Keseling (1978) to find anticipated sex-linked differences in the cognitive and emotional levels in the writing of 14-year-old school children. He expected to find sex-specific differences in emotive language, since boys are educated to restrict their emotions (except for aggression), whereas girls are permitted to express openly their feelings of love, guilt, fear, and sadness. Possibly Keseling's failure to find the expected differences in expressivity resulted from the neutral subject on which the students wrote. In his study, students read a short story and were asked to retell it in a few sentences and to discuss several questons about it.[5] Neither the story nor the topic assigned would, in itself, evoke emotions from the students. We believe, however, that an emotion-laden topic *will* evoke sex-specific differences in the transparent expression of feelings and emotions. At an adult level, such sex-linked differences have been shown to exist. In a study of crisis intervention therapy sessions, Wodak (1981a, d, e) found statistically significant differences in the capacity to express emotions during conversations. Men (especially those from the middle-class) tended to present their problems in a very neutral, descriptive, impersonal manner, and the impact of the problem (a suicidal crisis) was *not* transparent in the course of their verbalization. On the other hand, all women (except those from the lower middle-class) were able to express their feelings very well. This — as other research on sex-specific socialization suggests — has its roots in childhood socialization and education. Girls learn earlier to give free rein to their feelings and to verbalise them — something which is much more difficult for boys (and sometimes even forbidden by the traditional male role).

4.    *Class-specific Differences in Expression.*
It is not the intention of this study to enter into general details of speech behavior specific to class and sex. However, it is worth mentioning some of the findings of research into speech socialization and variation as they relate to the process of socialization. These may throw some light on the issue in question: the mother-daughter relationship and its manifestation at a textual level.

Klann-Delius (1979) investigates the widespread stereotype that girls and women are verbally superior to males, a stereotype which would suggest that there should be qualitative differences in speech socialization between the sexes. In an exhaustive study of psychological, sociological, neurolinguistic, and linguistic papers, she arrives at the following conclusion, focused on possible genetic differences (assuming that only differences which are evident in the first years of life can be thought to be genetically specified):

> No sexual differences have so far been found in the basic ability of verbal cooperation and communicative coordination. However, differences are possible in the degree of differentiation of communicative coordination and communicative orientation (7).

If she is correct (see also Macaulay 1978), sex-specific differences in linguistic behavior appearing later must derive from language socialization processes, and not from "natural" differences.

Klann-Delius argues convincingly that existing studies on sexual differences in the speech acquisition of children do not permit sex-linked generalizations for several reasons:

1. There is a lack of longitudinal studies.
2. The number of samples is insufficient.
3. The type of linguistic model used affects the nature and possibility of the results.
4. There is no theory explaining correlations between sex, speech acquisition, and general psycho-social development.[6]

To this we would add another:

5. Studies generally fail to consider such class-specific aspects of socialization as the influence of educational quality and the method of issuing of orders and prohibitions (liberal-restrictive, verbal-non-verbal, etc. [Bernstein 1970; Oevermann 1970; Robinson and Rackstraw 1973; Cook-Gumperz 1973]).

The study of male/female language differences in the last ten years has changed considerably our views of sex-specific linguistic variation (see Kramarae 1981 for an overview). Although studies have confirmed the tendency of speakers to develop sex-specific differences in stylistic ranges in childhood, research which has attempted to describe how these differences come about have been limited and have not included other essential information such as speech situation, functions of the speech acts, the family structure, and other important parameters. Most studies lack exact qualitative analyses of the style-range of the speakers, and neglect situational parameters which have an important impact on classs and sex-specific variation.[7]

Micro-studies of individual speaker strategies in closely defined speech situations with unchanging subject and with due consideration for other sociological and psychological variables can provide the basis for correlating speech socialization, class and family structure with certain psychodynamic processes which we wish to examine. On the basis of these findings, Dressler and Wodak (1982) and Wodak and Moosmuller (1981) have proposed a theory of "*Socio-psychological Variation*," which asserts that 1) analysis on the socio-phonological level can only be valid when it includes parameters of a sociological and psychological nature, in a well-defined situation, taking into consideration the topic of the discourse and its communicative function, and 2) that studies of variation must be done both quantitatively and qualitatively, ideally using a large data base accumulated through the use of different field techniques.

### 2.4.1. *A Cognitive Theory of Text Planning*

Previous research on language variation has focused largely on spoken language, on individual words at the phonological and morphological level, and only rarely on extended discourse. However, an analysis of conversation in a therapeutic setting (Wodak 1981a) distinguished at least three kinds of text (scenic, narrative, and descriptive) in which the realization differs significantly and predictably by class and sex. Although on topics taken from the public sphere women and men showed no class-specific differences in text types used, in discussing the private sphere such differences existed for both sexes. Specifically, she demonstrates (in a study of 1134 problem presentations in crisis intervention groups) that text types were predictable according to topic, sex, and class of speaker.

Considering these empirical results, we believe an adequate theory of the process of text planning should be extended to include written discourse, and must consider socio-psycholinguistic factors, since sociological and psychological parameters seem to affect the realization of text types.[8] Such a theory, based on the practices of the cognitive school of text planning, assumes that a text-thematic deep structure (a macrostructure) will be realized by specific text types, depending upon the sex, class, or ethnicity, etc. of the speaker or writer.

Researchers from a variety of disciplines have investigated the problem of text production and text comprehension. They have attempted to explain the verbalization of cognitive concepts, and to understand, describe, or simulate the transformation of a cognitive plan into a linear text (Freedle 1977, 1979; Shank and Abelson 1977; Kintsch and van Dijk 1978; Beaugrande and Dressler 1980, 1981). Freedle and Duran (1979) suggest that it is possible to find a correspondence between cognitive terminology and sociolinguistic terminology, and that text production may depend strongly and systematically on sociological and psychological parameters of the speaker. Wodak

(1981a) provides empirical evidence in support of their hypothesis, evolving a *Socio-Psychological Theory of Text Planning (SPTT)* which explains and predicts linguistic features of the text (discussed fully in Chapter 6).

### 2.4.2. Schematic Theory

In analyzing the essays of the boys and girls from a text linguistic point of view, we will concentrate on two levels: the *macrotextual* and the *microtextual*. The macrotextual dimension considers the text as a whole, including the form chosen by the writers. The microtextual includes semantic, syntactic, or semiotic linguistic indicators occurring within the text. We assume that a text-thematic macrostructure (Gülich and Raible 1977, 266; Kintsch and van Dijk 1978) can be realized in alternative text types, the type being triggered by the sex and class of the speakers or writers. We assume, as well, that sex specific socialization processes are responsible for a different verbal structuring of cognitive experience by girls and boys. Techniques used in text planning and production are acquired during socialization and are formed by cultural and social norms (Freedle 1977, 1979), so that *SCHEMATIC STRUCTURES* (conventional forms used to order and verbalize cognitive experiences) depend on the social and emotional environment of the speaker/writer. This means, according to our hypothesis, that gender role stereotypes will be reflected in the text type chosen to express a given thematic macrostructure, and that these role-stereotypes influence cognitive and emotional experience and the acquisition of specific *SCHEMAS* to organize it.

Because schematic theory has been used by researchers from such disciplines as sociology, psychology, linguistics, and computer science, terms have been used for very different phenomena, often with overlapping boundaries that have rendered them imprecise or vague (Tannen 1979 reviews the history of the use of schematic theory terminology). We have elected to use the formulations of Beaugrande and Dressler (1981), for which they have specified precise distinctions in meaning for use in text linguistic analysis.

*Schematic theory* derives its name from the word *SCHEMA*, first used by Bartlett (1932) in research on memory processes:

> Schema refers to an active organization of past reactions or of past experiences, which must always be supposed to be operating in any well-adapted organic response (201).

The term is sometimes used to refer to linguistic concepts and sometimes to psychological ones. For our purposes, *schema* means

> a global pattern of events or states in ordered sequences linked by time, proximity, and causality (Beaugrande and Dressler 1980, 90).

Another schematic structure used in talking about texts is the *FRAME*, a chunk of knowledge about some central concept upon which one draws in producing or understanding a verbalization of it:

> Frames state what things belong together in principle, but not in what order things will be done or mentioned (Beaugrande and Dressler 1980, 90).

We have mentioned *schema* first because the term antedates *frame* historically and is the central concept in schematic theory. However, in the cognitive theory outlined by Beaugrande and Dressler and used by us, frames are *unordered* chunks of knowledge about a concept and schemas are *ordered*. This distinction, important to our discussion of text production, implies that a frame of information may, during the cognitive process, become a schema when a chunk of knowledge with only associational links is given causal, spatial, or temporal order. By way of illustration, there may be a "Lecture Frame" consisting of the expectations activated by the announcement of a lecture: there will be a speaker and an audience; they will be separated and facing each other; the speaker will be expected to talk without feedback for a length of time; and so forth. There is a "Ticket Buying Frame" containing knowledge concerning how to go about getting tickets, and this may contain several schemas, such as one ordered set of actions to be taken if there is a box office and another if tickets must be ordered by phone.

Specific schemas ("Tuesday Book Club Lecture Schema") may contain a sequential order of events customary at those meetings, and for any *specific* lecture, there are *SCRIPTS*:

> stabilized plans called up very frequently to specify the roles of participants and their expected actions (Beaugrande and Dressler 1980, 91).

In talking about a specific lecture schema, then, the script may identify *the* speaker and refer to "*the* audience" or "*the* woman selling tickets" without ever having specified that there *was* a speaker, an audience, or a ticket seller present, these being givens of the schema.

Frames, schemas, and scripts exist as chunks of stored knowledge about reality as it has been experienced in the past, and the information contained constitutes general knowledge about experience shared by a great many people. To produce a text, the speaker or writer chooses elements from these chunks in accordance with a goal, or *PLAN*:

Plans differ from the schemas in that a planner (e.g., a text producer) evaluates all elements in terms of how they advance toward the planner's goal (Beaugrande and Dressler 1980, 91).

The goal of the specific discourse (to communicate, inform, or persuade) is central to the formation of a plan and will, therefore, influence the choice of a frame (Ochs 1979; Levy 1979; Freedle and Duran 1979).

### 2.4.3. *Schematic Theory and Writing*

We assume that in our student essays we are dealing with the product of just such a discourse process. There is a *schema*, "The School Essay," which activates student expectations on the basis of previous experiences of writing of essays in class. Included within the schema are "*Essay Frames*," which specify what form an essay takes, "*Writing Schemas*," which specify how one proceeds, and so forth. Each classroom will have developed its own *script*, and these scripts will vary from classroom to classroom, from school to school, and from culture to culture. In analyzing differences in writing, then, we examine within a single school the essays produced in two classrooms differing only in teacher (the U.S. sample); essays from different schools within the same city (both samples); essays from schools with an urban-rural difference (U.S.); and essays from schools in different cultures.

We assume, furthermore, that *PLAN, FRAME, SCHEMA* and *SCRIPT* are cognitive concepts, directly related to the storing and retrieving of knowledge. On the linguistic level, we have the topic, which evokes a *plan* from the student (to communicate, argue, or persuade). The topic and plan determine macrostructure ("*expository form*" is the term used in rhetoric; Beaugrande and Dressler use "*text type*"). Information about what each form comprises is stored as a *frame* on the cognitive level. The student chooses a form, retrieves knowledge about the topic, and then arranges the material in a *schema* (or *developmental pattern*) compatible with point-of-view, attitude, and so forth — one that determines how the form will be developed (whether by example, illustration, comparison, contrast) and ordered (whether temporally, causally, or otherwise). Finally, the child produces the *script* (or *essay*), filled out with specific participants and experiences.

Because we hypothesize that girls and boys are socialized very early into different cognitive worlds and world-views, we expect that the sex of the child will determine some of the choices made during this process of reducing information to a linear text and that differences will result from different material stored in memory and retrieved for the topic "My Mother and I."

The social and psychological experiences stored in memory provide girls with one set of frames, schemas and scripts, and the boys with another. The goal (the communicative function of the essay and the child's point of view) will also differ, according to sex: consequently, the choice of linguistic schemas will differ, as well. We expect to find linguistically definable sex-linked differences in the essays of boys and girls. There should be cultural differences, as well, since all of the chunks of knowledge upon which the child is drawing have been acquired during the course of acculturation. Exactly this evidence leads us to our Socio-Psychological Theory of Text Planning (our SPTT). We assume that boys and girls will handle the topic of the essay differently in form and content, because of sex-specific social patterns. We also assume that the culture will have an impact on the modes of socialization, as do attitudes, values, norms, and ideologies.

Research into the correlation between the quality of the mother-child relationship and textual variation within one sex is especially relevant. Only with such data will it be possible to evaluate the effect of psychological factors upon the determination of general sex- and class-specific speech differences. We are concerned not only with the quantitative recording of variation, but also with determining the qualitative style range of that variation when the subject and the speech situation are held constant. Only in this way can we attempt to postulate the relationship between psychodynamic processes, socialization processes, and speech behavior; only this kind of approach will enable us to investigate different types of relationships between mothers and daughters and the different manners of solving (or not solving) the separation conflict that arises between them.

### 2.5. Conclusion and Hypotheses

On the basis of theoretical considerations and the study of existing literature on the mother-daughter relationship, we have formulated several hypotheses to be tested in the course of our empirical investigation.

1.  The structure of the mother-child relationship shows cultural, ethnic, and class-specific differences, as do the educational and cognitive worlds of children and the emotions they express in discourse.

2.  The relationship between mother and daughter differs significantly from that between mother and son, and emotions generated within the relationship differ significantly in boys and girls, a difference which will be manifested in sex-specific language behavior.

3.    The structurally necessary conflict between mother and daughter tends to manifest itself in an aggressive (depressive) and ambivalent emotional structure.

4.    The quality of the mother-daughter relationship may be affected by such social factors as the marital status of the mother, the ages of brothers and sisters, the number of children in the family, the mother's occupation, and the parental figure in the afternoon.

5.    Such psychological variables as the type of up-bringing, the quality of commands and prohibitions, and especially the mother's personality, her attitude toward her femininity, and her contentment with life will influence the quality of the relationship of the daughter with the mother.

6.    The daughter's values and role concepts differ significantly from those of the mother; class-specific differences play a role in the variation that occurs.

7.    A confrontation of self- and other-assessment (how girls perceive their mothers and how mothers perceive their daughters) will allow insight into different types of relationships. The quality of the mother-daughter relationship should be reflected significantly in the speech behavior of both.

8.    As human relationships develop, are integrated, and manifest themselves in language, sex- and class-specific speech differences in the form and content of language develop. A study of the effect of these variables will strengthen the basis for the formulation of a "Socio-Psychological Theory of Text Planning."

## NOTES

1) Freud has been misunderstood in two ways: first he did not reduce the mother-daughter relationship and the development of femininity to the concept of "penis envy" (this is clear in the reference cited). Secondly, Freud emphasized that every human being is bisexual, but that socialization and identification processes make the child adopt one sex identity. This has also been noted by Helene Deutsch.

The concept of penis envy has been revised considerably since the early days of psychoanalysis. Karin Horney and others in the thirties concluded that since the girl discovers her own sexual organs, penis envy must be interpreted as a metaphor for a social phenomenon (Horney 1928; Mack-Brunswick Ms.). Current discussions accept penis envy as a metaphor for envy of the social values accorded to men. Also, we should not forget that Freud conceptualized his theory at a time when he was considered to be a revolutionary; he was the first to concern himself with the child, with children's sexuality, and with women (the first to consider them seriously). His theory should be considered in context of the limitations of the time during which it was developed.

2) Our chief concern here is with the emotional consequences of the contrasting socialization of boys and girls. There are cognitive consequences, as well, as we will discuss below.

3) We disagree with Parsons (1968), who argues that existing roles, norms, and values are *functional* for maintaining the existing society (which is viewed as good).

4) Social class in the Austrian sample is assigned on the basis of the education of both parents, on their professions and incomes, etc., using the scale developed by Oeverman (1972).

5) The story was *An der Nähmaschine*, by E. Langgasser.

6) Klann-Delius is addressing her criticism to American descriptive studies of child language. Dressler and Wodak (1982) find similar shortcomings in studies of variation.

7) Dressler and Wodak found that it was important to distinguish between professional women and housewives; between emancipated and conservative women (young women opposing traditional values often adopt dialectal forms; [see also Chesire 1974]). Professional women tend to use more standard forms than housewives, even middle-class housewives, who should — according to theories of language change — use standard forms (see also Ammon 1973; Nichols 1978). Daughters involved in a conflict with their mothers tend to use a reverse register to mark their separation, whereas sons adopt the same style as their mother. Therefore, only an exact qualitative analysis of certain situations, taking into account all of the above factors, allows generalizations on sex- and class-specific variation (see also Wodak/Moosmüller 1981).

8) Neglect of sociological and psychological parameters leaves text planning otherwise unexplained (for a long discussion and review of the literature, see Wodak 1981a, 112ff).

# 3. MOTHER-CHILD DISCOURSE

## 3.1. *Introduction*

Children experience very little of the world first-hand. Most of what they know, they learn through the speech addressed to them by others in their social network. Most of that speech comes from the primary caregiver, typically the mother in Western cultures, whose importance in the oral transmission of culture can hardly be exaggerated. She does not simply provide information to the child; she interprets it — by her attitudes, her behavior, and her language choices.

The origins of sex-specific behavior can be found in the primary socialization of the child, a socialization that occurs in the early years almost entirely through the channel of language and chiefly in the mother-child dyad. The vocabulary appropriate to social roles and the attitudes taken toward different forms of social behavior are transmitted to the infant in the course of social interaction between the mother and the child. This is especially critical in the socialization of the daughter. Because they share the same sex, the daughter accepts the mother's interpretation of reality more readily than the son, who very early turns away from the mother's model and creates an identity in opposition to it. Whether the daughter eventually imitates or rejects the model presented to her, her mother remains an initial point of reference. In a paper analyzing consequences of child-rearing practices in different cultures of the world, Chodorow (1974, 43) argues that "a crucial differentiating experience in male and female development arises out of the fact that women, universally, are largely responsible for early childcare and for ... later female socialization." The ways in which mothers socialize their daughters has been little studied, partly because that socialization occurs in everyday discourse, samples of which are difficult to obtain. (See Circourel 1978 for a discussion of the defensiveness of parents who know they are being observed and their self-conscious efforts to stage acceptable dialogues.) In this chapter we propose to look closely at the register addressed to young children by their caretakers, considering what it is, why it occurs, and what purposes it serves in the child's maturation. We are specifically interested in those characteristics of Caretaker Talk and Motherese that contribute to the emotional, cognitive and social (cultural) education of the child. As we have argued above, the uniqueness of the mother-daughter relationship and its specificities emerge very early, starting in the first months of the life of the female child. We wish to investigate and explore communication strategies which evoke and stabilize the expected structures and patterns of behavior — and the girls' responses of love and guilt.

## 3.2. *Varieties of Caretaker Talk - Terminology*

During the 1970's, a systematic study of the linguistic input to infants demonstrated that the register used by adults in speaking to children is not the "haphazard sample" suggested by McNeill (1966, 36). It is, rather, a highly specialized register, used throughout the world by speakers of all ages, in addressing language-learning children.

Several labels have been applied to the speech variety addressed to infants. In first identifying it as a specialized register, Ferguson (1964) chose the term *Baby Talk* (German *Kindersprache*), both because the register is addressed to babies and because some of its features imitate the way babies speak. However, because *Baby Talk* has customarily denoted the speech produced by language-learning children, another term, thought to be less ambiguous, was coined: *Motherese* (German *Ammensprache*). That, too, has proved to be problematical. It suggests that the register is used only by mothers but, in fact, they have not proved unique in their ability to modify their speech in the regular ways characteristic of the style used in talking to children (Snow 1972). Nor is Motherese necessarily sex-linked. When it is the mother who is the primary caretaker, and both parents are living with the child, the father's speech diverges from the mother's in predictable, even complementary, ways (Gleason 1975; Rondal 1980). But when fathers take on the caregiving role, their speech develops many of the characteristics associated with the nurturant, maternal role (Gleason 1975; Lamb 1977; Noller 1980). Even children as young as four have demonstrated an ability to produce qualities of *Motherese* when roleplaying the caretaker (Andersen 1977) or when talking to infants (Shatz and Gelman 1977). Since the register is associated with the caregiving role, a third term has been devised, *Caretaker Talk*, a term unmarked for sex or age. The register is elicited when a speaker (of any age or either sex) becomes an infant's caregiver, and it is conditioned by the specific needs which the caretaker is called upon to fulfill for the child.[1]

Although there appear to be some universals in Caretaker Talk, features of the register and the frequency of their use vary in different languages

(Ferguson 1964), in different dialects of the same language (Drachman 1973), among different members of the family (Ferguson 1977), or according to the social class and and intellectual aspirations of the parent and the intellectual development of the child (Rūķe-Draveṇa 1976). Even different members of a family develop different versions (Ferguson 1977). Jocic (1978) suggests that the kind of Caretaker Talk produced correlates with the emotional tie between the adult and child: the greater the tie, the more the adult adapts her speech to the child's communicative competence.

It would be convenient if we could use the term *Caretaker Talk* for all discussions of features of the generalized register, but it is impossible to do so. Although there are many varieties of Caretaker Talk, most of the research has focused solely on the mother's output. Some of the characteristics have been observed in the mother's behavior and assigned to the register without specifying whether or not the features occur in *all* adult-child registers. Since our interest is in specific characteristics of the mother's speech which differentiate it from that of other adults, we will attempt to distinguish between the two varieties, using the term *Motherese* when referring to specific characteristics differentiating the mother's speech from that of others who use special registers with the child. In referring to general adult-to-infant registers, we will use the term *Caretaker Talk*.

### 3.3. *The Characteristics and Stages of the Caretaker Register*

### 3.3.1. *Characteristics of Caretaker Talk*

The caretaker register is not the product of conscious strategies. No one teaches speakers to use it; children, in fact, learn it by imitation (Gleason 1973). Adults are unaware of many of its characteristics (Brown 1977), aside from elements like the high pitch, exaggerated intonation, and special lexicon that are familiar because they occur commonly in affected imitations of baby talk used by children to mock one another, or as part of the "sweet talk" sometimes exchanged between lovers. The features of Caretaker Talk which clarify and simplify, or those which serve to gain and hold the child's attention, are produced unconsciously by adults and seem to be elicited by specific difficulties occurring in communicating with infants (Snow 1972; Halliday 1976; Brown 1977; Oksaar 1977; Schieffelin 1979; Jochens 1979). Speech addressed to babies is at once simpler and more complicated than ordinary adult speech. Adults must complicate the conversational input to children by adding information about the context and by making all linguistic relationships explicit in order to negotiate with the child the shared understanding of meaning necessary before communication can take place (Ervin-Tripp 1980). But, at the same time, they must simplify, deleting non-essentials if the message is to be short enough so that the child can process it and respond within the limited attention span available. And most important, perhaps, they must charge it with affect, if it is to gain and keep the child's attention.

Since getting the child's attention is the first step in engaging an infant in social interaction, adults load their early Caretaker Talk with attention-getting devices. Expressive (affective) features — those which seem primarily to express the speaker's feelings toward the addressee — set the message apart, marking it as language addressed to the child.[2] Child language research has made clear that infants acquire language through social interaction, and that they hear a great deal of speech around them which they ignore and from which they learn little or nothing (Shipley, Smith and Gleitman 1969; Snow 1979). It is the speech which actively engages them that facilitates their learning of the language. Thus, caretakers invariably find ways of marking the register as Caretaker Talk. Eventually they can do so verbally, by saying the child's name at the beginning of an utterance, by repeated greetings addressed to the child, or by using such formulas as "Listen to this" or "Look here" (Jochens 1979). But with the preverbal child, adults use special paralinguistic features (Blount and Padgug 1976), nonverbal signs (Bruner 1978), and vocatives (Gleason 1975) to mark that speech which they address to young children as a special register.

Other features develop in response to the child's limited understanding of the language system. Generally, for instance, Caretaker Talk limits itself to the "here and now", selecting as its topic an object or person physically present or an action appropriate at the time of the discourse. This provides the child with an immediately available situational and referential redundancy (Messer 1980) as a substitute for the linguistic and contextual redundancies yet to be mastered. Restricting conversation to the "here and now" also makes it possible to touch or point to things present, supplying gestural redundancy to the verbal communication. The caretaker can and does model desired behavior (Garnica 1977), or mark a referent by pointing or by moving her line of regard from the baby to some object (Collis and Schaffer 1975). As the child masters the linguistic system and is able to use its context, the caretaker is able to withdraw many of the kinesic redundancies supplied in early caretaker talk, gradually moving from dependence upon nonverbal clues to the use of linguistic ones (Cook-Gumperz 1977; Jochens 1979).

### 3.3.2. *Stages in Caretaker Talk*

What we have in the variety identified as "Caretaker Talk" may very well be a combination of registers: 1) an *expressive* register used with lovers, pets, and babies, designed primarily to communicate affect; 2) a *clarifying* register addressed to people who have difficulty in understanding the message, such as large audiences (Broen 1972) and non-native speakers (Ferguson 1975); 3) a *pedagogical* register (some features of Caretaker Talk, such as "test questions" and slow, careful articulation, disappear as the child grows older but reappear in "Teacher Talk" [Delamont 1976]); 4) a *social* register used for eliciting speech from others (Ervin-Tripp 1978, 363); and 5) an *authoritative* register adopted by people in positions of power (Crumrine 1968).

Speakers adjust the complexity of Caretaker Talk to the linguistic capabilities of the child throughout the language-learning period. As the child grows older, the register becomes more like adult-adult speech: caretakers begin to use a lower pitch, a more abstract vocabulary, fewer repetitions, a faster rate of speech, more function words, and more complicated syntax (Phillips 1973; Fraser and Roberts 1975; Gleason 1977; Ringler 1978; Snow 1979). Affective features diminish more rapidly than any of these (Remick 1971). It is possible that the mother indirectly encourages the child's growing autonomy by suppressing affective devices and that the child expresses an urge for autonomy by rejecting them.

Because it is the mother's version of Caretaker Talk that provides a model for the daughter learning language, we will analyze details of that register in the next section. By looking closely at how the mother's register differs from others in the child's network, we can see how Motherese fosters the child's feelings of love and guilt. And we can see how it becomes the daughter's model for feminine discourse.

### 3.4. *Motherese: Its Functions*

Motherese serves three principle functions: *affective*, *instrumental*, and *pedagogic*.

1. It provides the child with warm, loving interaction.
2. It becomes the primary means of controlling the child's behavior.
3. It is the channel through which the parent teaches and socializes the young child.

### 3.4.1. *Introduction: Establishing the Primary Relationship*

The family network in which they participate can be expected to influence children's developing language behavior (Milroy 1980; Milroy and Margrain 1980). However, the family network is hierarchical, in that some relationships are more vital than others. Although an infant's growth may be enhanced by the presence in the network of parents, brothers, sisters, aunts, uncles, or grandparents, some of these potential relationships may be empty with little detrimental effect. But the role of the nurturant primary caregiver is one necessary to the well-being of the child. Whoever serves in that role plays an important part in promoting the child's cognitive abilities and emotional stability (Yarrow 1963; Beckwith 1971; Lewis and Goldberg 1969; Hatano, Miyake, and Tajima 1980; Belsky 1981).

Although another woman, or the father, or several people, or even a child can fulfill the role of the primary caretaker, it is usually the biological mother who does so. The mother takes practically complete charge of the social interaction with her language-learning infant. Because of the child's interactional limitations, early parent-child "conversations" are carried out entirely by the adult, who performs the roles of both the speaker and the listener. Even with preverbal children, the mother poses questions to the child and then answers them, acting out the child's conversational participation as well as her own. She sets the topic, interprets the meaning of the child's actions, decides which of the child's acts will be interpreted as social acts (Richards 1974) and which sounds will be accepted as constituting "talk" (Ryan 1974). By selectively responding to the sounds emitted by the child, the mother legitimizes certain sound combinations and assigns meaning to them, reporting to others the childs' "first word", for example, along with its "meaning" (although there is no possibility of verifying that the child even intended to utter a word [Ryan 1974; Oksaar 1977; Derwing 1977]).

Such "dialogues" do not merely serve as interactive and pedagogical devices, however. They require — and express — a symbiosis between the mother and the child. Inspection of the texts of dialogues between caretakers and children makes clear that mothers must struggle to interpret the sounds of children's utterances accurately, search for the semantic connections that have led the child to produce the utterances that occur, assign meaning to them, and — finally — attempt to repeat, expand, and elaborate upon whatever the child has said, in order to keep the interaction going. It is hard work, and the burden falls mainly on the shoulders of the primary caretaker (the mother).

More than others in the network, mothers provide the child with *mutuality*, which Schaffer and Crook (1979, 76) argue is "the keynote in the relationship between mother and even the very youngest infant." Mutuality involves the mother's willingness to suppress her own identity and try to take the point of view of the child. The mother and infant establish an "interlacing" system of behavior and feedback so well tuned that it becomes "an organized system with its own rhythm and flow" (Thoman 1981, 193). Schachter *et al* (1979, 123-25) call Motherese "alter ego speech", hypothesizing that it reveals the "underlying structure of self-other (speaker-listener) differentiation" between mother and child. Initially that differentiation is slight, and it is possible to see in the development of motherese a reflection of changes occurring in the symbiotic tie between mother and child. Of the three types of conversation used by the mother in training her child in how to carry on dialogues with others (factual exchange, focus-centered communication, and emotionally regulated dialogue), Jochens (1979) hypothesizes that it is the latter which is especially significant in evaluating the mother's contribution to the child's development. She says:

> this type of communication requires special psycho-dynamic processes on the part of the mother. In her close tie with the child, the mother, in phases of regression, reactivates archaic object- and self-conceptions from her own childhood, enabling her to mobilize empathic capacities. Because of this ability to identify, the mother is capable of discovering the significance for the child of objects such as the teddy bear, the corner of an eiderdown, etc., and of supporting the child's use of these objects. These things characterized by special qualities (such as softness), are to the child "transitional objects" (Winnicott 1953) aiding the child's development from pure subjectivity to objectivity (127).

Although all members of the infant's network develop the ability to interpret imperfect attempts to communicate, none other than the mother usually develops such linguistic rapport with the child. The mother's superior intuitive skill in understanding the speech of infants even transfers to non-related children (Weist and Kruppe 1977).

### 3.4.2. *Symbiotic Language*

It is not surprising to find that the mother is better able to understand and accommodate to her child's verbal limitations than others in the network. She spends more time with the child than do the others, so much time in fact that she matches her own state with that of her child. A remarkable set of photographs printed by Sylvester-Bradley and Trevarthen (1978) show

how a mother expresses a rhythmic harmony with her child by elaborate "mirroring" of the infant's nonverbal behavior: imitating gestures, facial expressions and body positions. This sort of empathy finds linguistic expression in the mother's use of the inclusive first person plural pronoun *we* or *us* in interacting with the child:

1.     We wouldn't want to hurt the kitty, would we?
2.     It's time for our medicine now.

The use of *we* blurs the distinction between the speaker (*I*) and the addressee (*you*) (Wills 1977). Since *we* perfectly expresses the inseparability of the child and the alter ego (the mother), it has quite properly been called the *symbiotic pronoun* (Friday 1977, 68).

Few of the characteristics of maternal speech are so sex-specific as the use of *we*. In Hungarian, Jocic (1978, 162) found that it occurred only in the Caretaker Talk of female relations close to the child. It is only used downward (Ervin-Tripp 1976), occurring regularly in the discourse of teachers, nurses, doctors, and mothers — groups of people (primarily women) charged with the care of people who are either physically or mentally unable to choose what is best for themselves. In fact, its use attributes a degree of incompetence to the addressee: *We wouldn't want to hurt the kitty, would we?* suggests that the person addressed does not realize the danger implicit in whatever activity is under way. *It's time for our medicine now* expresses the nurse's responsibility for seeing that the right medicine is taken at the right time, a responsibility not to be entrusted to the patient.

Although the occurrence of this feature in maternal speech may be prompted by the helplessness of the child, it serves affective functions, as well. Like the tag question, it invites confirmatory participation or agreement ("Shall we go to the store now?") and expresses the mother's affiliation with the child (Wales 1978). It is supportive, implying that the speaker will cooperate with the child in carrying out whatever action is requested, even though help is often patently impossible (*Let's see if we can eat all of our cereal* really means *I want you to eat all of your cereal*).

The symbiotic *we* has a relatively short life in maternal speech. After a certain age children perceive that *we*-directives are patronizing (Tanz 1980) and dislike receiving them. Another factor in its disappearance may be its overt expression of mother-child symbiosis: it denies the separateness of mother and child. In fact, the mother's assumption that the child is an extension of herself frustrates the separation the child is struggling to achieve.[3]

Even while they resist the mother's use of the symbiotic pronoun *we*, girls adopt it as part of their own speech. The language recorded by Goodwin (1980) shows boys using the first person singular and the second person pronouns (*I, mine, you*) in peer interaction. Girls, who played more cooperatively as a rule, used the symbiotic first person plural (*we*) throughout their dialogues. Here we see at a very early age the imitation of a maternal speech pattern even while the girl is struggling against its use. Opposed to her rejection of the mother's symbiosis is her attraction to the mother and to her positive qualities. So at the same time that she is developing an identity separate from that of her mother, the daughter is identifying and internalizing something of the model the mother presents to her. In this we probably see a meeting of the psychological and social forces at work in shaping the girl's behavior. First, she has the model before her of an often altruistic mother — subordinating her own convenience, interests, and comfort to those of her child. As a beloved figure, the mother represents a desirable model. In addition, the daughter is pressured by society to conform to that model — to develop the nurturant and emotional qualities valued in the mother. Thus, at an early age girls exhibit more empathy and altruism, and are more sharing and helpful than boys (Maccoby 1980, 223; 345-46; 219-20).

### 3.4.3. *Instrumental Speech*

Although parental authority is, as Goffman (1976, 4) points out, only temporary and is exerted "in the best interests" of the subordinate child, still parents come as close as anyone does to having absolute power over other human beings. During the early years, the child is completely dependent upon adults for care and affection. Goffman describes the price paid for that dependence as being

> subjected to various forms of nonperson treatment. He is talked past and talked about as though absent. . . . Teasing and taunting occur. . . His inward thoughts, feelings, and recollections are not treated as though he had information rights in their disclosure. (5)

Speier (1970) gives a remarkable example of the degree to which mothers may control the discourse of their children and treat others as nonpersons. In this example, a boy rings the doorbell at the gate. When the mother comes to the door, she cannot see him because of a tunnel-like entrance between the gate and the door (nor can he see her).

1.    Mother:   Who's there?
         Boy:      Can your son come out?

| Mother: | What? |
|---------|-------|
| Boy: | Can your son come out? |
| Mother: | What do you want? |
| Boy: | Can your son come out? |
| Mother: | (Pause) Who is it? |
| Boy: | Jerry. Can your son come out? |
| Mother: | No. No he can't come right now. (Closes front door) |
| Boy: | When do you think he could come out? (When there is no answer, the boy leaves.) (193) |

The mother in this scene treats both her son and the visitor as non-persons: she speaks for her son without consulting him and she closes off the conversation with the boy without a farewell and with no apparent concern for his feelings. While this is not an unusual scene, neither does it typify maternal behavior. In fact, middle-class mothers generally behave in a less overtly authoritarian way.

### 3.4.3.1. *Expressions of Power and Control: Differences between Mothers and Fathers*

Parental power devolves almost exclusively upon the primary caretaker, who is usually the mother, and it is instructive to see how she goes about masking her power in parent-child discourse. Several observers report that the mother's speech appears to be less controlling than the father's (Greif 1980; McLaughlin, Schutz and White 1980; and below), and some qualitative differences have been recorded which help to account for those perceptions. When playing with their children, mothers are reported to be more likely than fathers to allow the child to initiate the type of activity they will engage in (Engle 1980); they display more indices of close parent-child relationship in their speech (Stein, reported by Gleason 1975, 290); and they engage the child in more interaction (McLaughlin, Schutz and White 1980). These studies found fathers to engage in more independent play (without involving the child at all), to issue more directives, and to be generally less responsive to what their children were saying. Schaffer and Crook (1979), after studying the directive techniques used by mothers of 15- and 24-month-old children in a laboratory situation, concluded that although much of their speech had a controlling *function*, mothers strove to regulate the child's behavior subtly and indirectly, basing their actions in part on a sensitivity to the child's ongoing behavior. Mothers avoided an overload of imperatives by timing their directives so that the probability of compliance was high, and they used a variety of nonverbal behaviors to direct the actions of their children.

Commands issued by mothers are likely to differ from those of fathers. In Gleason's (1975) study, mothers used fewer threats and directives with imperative syntax than fathers.[4] Bock and Hornsby (1981) found that mothers more often phrase a directive as a question, a form which is more compatible with a mitigation such as *please* or *dear* than is a command. And, of course, the *we*-imperatives (discussed above) serve as mitigated commands, *suggestive* rather than *directive*.

### 3.4.3.2. Indirect Control and Its Consequences for the Child's Emotional and Cognitive Development

Medinnus (1969) reviews research demonstrating that although they are aware that their mothers manipulate them covertly, during the early school years children rate their mothers more favorably than their fathers, citing (among other factors) her less domineering behavior. (Of course, her indirect controls have the power to trigger enormous guilt, as we will discuss further below.) The child often feels helpless anger against the unacknowledged command implicit in the "request" or "suggestion" — helpless (and guilty) because there is nothing explicit in the formula to justify that anger. This evidence relates directly to our discussion of educational style, its impact on the socialization of children, and our assumptions about cultural-, ethnic-, class- and sex-related differences. The use of direct and indirect control, and its linguistic markers and strategies, are of specific interest when considering the emotional development of the relationship and tie between mother and daughter—especially for the development of our concept of love and guilt.

Greif (1980) and Borker (1980) both argue that indirection occurs because mothers are less willing to demonstrate power openly than are fathers. They see in the mother's use of indirect means in controlling her children evidence of the woman's discomfort with the superordinate position of power which is available to her as a mother, but not elsewhere in her life. However, several researchers have demonstrated that powerlessness correlates with role, not sex (Erickson, Johnson, Lind and O'Barr 1978; Brown 1980; O'Barr and Atkins 1980; Smith 1980; Bernard 1981). Since the mother's role vis à vis her child puts her in a position where power can be exercised over a long period of time, there is every reason to assume that she should be learning gradually to exercise power in a more direct, controlling way, if indeed discomfort were the initial cause of her behaving differently from the father.

And yet the opposite occurs. It is, perhaps, necessary that mothers find some way to mitigate the powerful thrust of their directives. As primary caretakers, they must issue a great many commands (more of them all the time, as the children grow older, according to Clarke-Stewart 1973). And yet mothers have been found to use *fewer* imperatives with time (Broen 1972; Snow 1972; Bellinger 1979). In fact they have evolved techniques which couple features signifying high dominance with high affiliation as delineated by Argyle (1969), strategies which permit them to dominate without appearing to be domineering (Rogers-Millar and Millar 1979). To use direct commands would place them perpetually in a relationship of low affiliation with their children, one likely to interfere with the attachment necessary to the child's emotional well-being and self-esteem (Loeb, Horst, and Horton 1980; Belsky 1981). Their avoidance of direct imperatives appears to be important to the child's cognitive development, as well. Several studies have shown the mother's avoidance of imperatives to correlate positively with the child's cognitive development (Kagan and Freeman 1963; Hess and Shipman 1968; Ringler 1978). Endsley, Hutcherson, Garner and Martin (1979) found authoritarian mothers less likely to interact with their children positively or to orient them to explore novel materials, two behaviors correlated with the child's curiosity measure. Hatano, Miyake and Tajima (1980) found the mother's warmth a positive predictor of IQ and her directiveness a negative predictor of the child's later achievement on a conservation test. And Maccoby (1980, 286-88) reports on several studies showing that parents who use suggestive rather than directive controls have children who are better able to resist distraction and who have internalized a locus of control.

Although the ideal middle-class mother attempts to control her children by indirection, mothers have evolved oblique ways of signaling to their children that a directive is meant more seriously than its surface structure suggests. Metaphorical code-switching (a switch from one register to another [Blom and Gumperz, 1972]) is a method frequently used. Bilingual Mexican-American mothers tend to reprimand their children in Spanish (Redlinger 1976). American mothers can convey seriousness by switching from a diminutive name to the child's full name (Cook-Gumperz and Gumperz 1978, 10). Norwegian mothers move from their local dialect into Standard Norwegian to emphasize a command (Larson 1978). And Black mothers cite proverbs (Smitherman 1980 calls it "addressing the walls").

We seldom have an opportunity to observe how the child feels about the mother's use of indirect controls, because indirection denies the child a chance to respond (Maccoby 1980, 285, speculates that the child eventually perceives the manipulation that is occurring and is resentful). When people refuse to acknowledge openly that we anger or bore them, or that we strain their patience, they deprive us of the opportunity to deny their claims or to justify our behavior. We can only feel angry or guilty or both. Toni Morrison provides an example of how the child feels in this situation. In her novel *The Bluest Eye* Pecola, a child who has been given refuge by the family, is fond of drinking out of the Shirley Temple cup and, consequently, has consumed an enormous quantity of milk. The mother complains "to the walls":

> 'Three quarts of milk. That's what was *in* that icebox yesterday. Three whole quarts. Now they ain't none. Not a drop. I don't mind folks coming in and getting what they want, but three quarts of milk! What the devil does *any-body* need with *three* quarts of milk?' Ashamed of the insults that were being heaped on our friend, we just sat there. . . . My mother's soliloquies always irritated and depressed us. They were interminable, insulting, and although indirect (Mama never named anybody — just talked about folks and *some* people), extremely painful in their thrust. She would go on like that for hours, connecting one offense to another until all of the things that chagrined her were spewed out. Then, having told everybody and everything off, she would burst into song and sing the rest of the day. But it was such a long time before the singing part came. In the meantime, our stomachs jellying and our necks burning, we listened, avoided each other's eyes, and picked toe jam or whatever. (37)

The situation of the children in this passage is a familiar one. The mother refuses to engage them directly, but she succeeds in conveying her message, nonetheless. The children feel guilty — in fact they are made to share the other's guilt — but they have no opportunity to argue their innocence or, in fact, to respond at all.

3.4.3.3. *Indirect Control: A Model of Feminine Discourse*

Children continue to perceive their parents as fulfilling stereotypical roles, according to which the father occupies the instrumental and the mother, the expressive role in the family, even when their own parents do not match the stereotype. Since the mother is usually the primary caretaker, the actual amount of time in which her behavior is instrumental is likely to exceed that of others in the child's network (Brim 1959).[5] And yet children do not perceive her as occupying this role. Kohlberg (1966, 99) reports that American children perceive their fathers as being "more powerful, punitive, aggres-

sive, fearless, instrumentally competent, and less nurturant than females",
and daughters of working mothers hold the conventional domestic conception
of femininity. Children's role-playing demonstrates the stereotypes of parental roles they have internalized. "Mothers" are more polite and use more
endearments, while "fathers" demand (and are treated with) more deference,
tending to be authoritative and forceful, sometimes pouring out directives,
apparently as a way of establishing a power relationship with the child (Andersen 1977).

Children notice and imitate the changes that occur in the mother's
instrumental language. Researchers have found that directives develop in
the speech of children in much the same order as they evolve in Motherese
— from direct commands to more indirect means (Garvey 1975, 1979,
studied American children and Hollos and Beeman 1978, Norwegian and
Hungarian children). Girls, especially, seem to be internalizing their mother's
model at an early age. Larson (1978) found metaphorical code switching
used as a means of control by mothers but not fathers. Similarly, its use
became sex-linked in children's speech, as well. Girls (ages 5 to 14) use it
more often and more distinctly in negotiating for control than boys. Ervin-
Tripp, O'Connor and Rosenberg (1984), in a study of children's control acts,
found that boys and girls (maximum age, 8) had developed different strategies
to avoid compliance with control attempts by other children. Boys refused
outright more than girls, who used a wider range of strategies to avoid compliance. Both girls and boys rejected control attempts about equally, but
girls *appeared* to be more cooperative and less resistant to the control acts of
other children than boys, although they were not.

### 3.4.3.4. *Indirect Control - Conclusions*

Summarizing the evidence and arguments above, we believe that strategies of indirect control will induce stronger responses and greater problems
for daughters than sons. Since daughters separate from their mothers more
slowly, they are submitted to more of these communication strategies than
sons. Their own separation patterns create more situations in which the
mother may feel required to use indirect methods of control. And, finally,
in identifying with the mother and learning the female's role (of which being
a mother is a central one), the daughter consciously or unconsciously acquires
many of these strategies, which she will use herself as a woman and as a
mother (the "songs and dances" of Chapter 1), even though she may not
want to do so or to acknowledge that she does so.[6]

## 3.5. *Pedagogic Language Functions*

### 3.5.1. *Cognitive Consequences*

As the primary caretaker, the mother is the child's principal language teacher (Jochens 1979). Her philosophy determines what her language input to the child will be and, consequently, what the child's linguistic output will be. For example, several researchers note a difference in the degree to which different societies treat children as conversational equals. Guatemalan mothers do not think of themselves as influential upon the child's language acquisition, and do not provide the analytical features found in English Caretaker Talk (such as slow enunciation or exaggerated intonation [Harkness 1976]). Blount (1973) and Ochs (1980) report similar attitudes and differences in the speech of Luo and Samoan mothers. Blount adds that in the United States young children are allocated "conversational peer status" and are pushed toward early conversational facility, in contrast with Japan, where the dependence of the child is indulged and children's errors are overlooked. As a result of their different attitudes, Japanese mothers are more in favor of baby talk and continue to use it longer; they talk less to their children, and their children talk later (Fischer 1970).

Similar differences have been observed within a single culture. Schachter, Marquis, Shore, Bundy and McNair (1979) noted that a greater *quantity* of speech was the one characteristic that most strikingly differentiated their middle-class and working-class mothers. A reason for this kind of difference is suggested by research finding that mothers who judged prelingual children incapable of understanding them made fewer attempts to engage their infants in verbal interaction (Tulkin and Kagan 1972; see also Bingham 1971, cited in Brown 1977). Both Ward (1971) and Clarke-Stewart (1973) found that Black mothers in the U.S. spend more time caring for the child's needs and less time talking or playing with them than white mothers, who emphasize educational aspects in interacting with their children. Ward says of the Black community she studied, "adults do not regard children as people to talk to" (71). They are more concerned about behavior than about conversational skills. Clarke-Stewart hypothesizes that both sets of mothers may be socializing their children appropriately for the lives they will face.

Whatever philosophy dictates their behavior, middle-class mothers in the United States pride themselves on the verbal precocity of their children. While it is true that Caretaker Talk cannot properly be called a "teaching language" (other functions are more important than instruction) still features which Brown and Hanlon (1970) have called "training variables" do occur regularly in Caretaker Talk throughout the world (Rūķe-Draveņa 1976), and some of its pedagogical features (like exaggerated intonational contours, slow delivery, and the use of test questions) constitute markers of the "Teacher Talk" addressed to primary school children (Delamont 1976).

Cultural expectations, transmitted by the mother, shape the linguistic output of children in other ways. For example, Ann Peters (1977) points out that though there is probably a continuum along which children can be arranged according to whether their approach to processing information is primarily *analytic* or *gestalt*, in western societies a gestalt response is generally rejected systematically in favor of an analytic one. Nelson notes (1975 and 1977) that although some children are clearly oriented toward the interpersonal functions of language, while others incline toward the ideational, language pedagogy in western cultures is biased toward the ideational. Analytic language is used and elicited in naming situations (like reading or describing); expressive language is evoked by social, interpersonal situations. The pedagogic functions of language encourage the development of analytic language; informal, naturally-occurring social interaction develops expressive language; and instrumental functions may involve both (Nelson 1981).

This evidence forms a central issue of our argument about the consequences of different kinds of socialization. Boys and girls (and children of different social classes, ethnicities, and cultures) are socialized into different emotional and cognitive worlds, worlds which are evaluated differently within the society (Labov 1970, and Leodolter 1975a found different patterns, related to ethnicity and class, respectively, used in coping with a given verbal situation, one more highly valued than the other). Thus, although alternative modes of communicative strategies may emerge, in western cultures the middle class male pattern (analytic) is the more highly valued one. The fact that children master their first language whether their approach to it is primarily analytic or gestalt has obscured the existence of developmental differences which may persist both cognitively and linguistically. (We will discuss the cognitive consequences more fully below, in our consideration of mother-child social interaction.) Linguistic evidence of persistent cognitive differences is appearing in an increasing number of studies of both language variation and second language acquisition. For instance, recent research in language variation suggests that despite surface similarity in output, adult speakers may produce language by different sets of underlying rules (Fillmore, Kempler, and Wang 1979). Krashen, Seliger and Hartnett (n.d.) review considerable research indicating that there are two kinds of second language learners: those who learn most efficiently by the traditional analytic, deductive method of instruction (rule plus practice) and those who learn better with a conversational, inductive approach. And Winterowd (1979) identifies two kinds of writers: propositional (writers who are facile with deductive structures and logical syllogisms) and appositional (writers whose approach is gestaltist, holistic).[7] It is not surprising, considering the bias toward analytic thinking in our society, that both second language instruction and writing instruction have stressed the analytic approach.

### 3.6. *Mother-Daughter Discourse*

Sometimes socialization occurs in mother-daughter interaction as a result of deliberate efforts by the mother, when she nourishes certain behaviors in her daughter; sometimes it occurs unconsciously, when she is unaware of it — even when the daughter attempts to resist it. The characteristics of speech specific to her roles as a woman, a wife, and a mother, as well as those specific to her interaction with her daughter, provide the daughter with her first definition of femininity. Characteristics of Motherese arise from the three functions it serves: the symbiotic function (used for constituting an emotional environment and relationship); the authoritative function (with its strategies of indirect control); and the pedagogic function (used for teaching language and training children in social norms and roles).

In the following sections, we will show relationships between the evidence given by studies on sex-specific socialization and the communicative patterns developed by the mother, thus focusing on the mother-daughter relationship and its impact on female development. In summarizing this evidence, we will propose our own theory of sex-specific language acquisition, recurring to the three functions of Motherese mentioned above and to theories of cognitive and emotional socialization into different modes of structuring reality — preparatory to outlining our theories of *Socio-Psychological Text Planning* and *Socio-Psychological Variation* at the text linguistic level.

### 3.6.1. *Qualitative and Quantitative Differences in Mother-Daughter Interaction*

A great deal of research is available showing that the mothering of daughters differs consistently from the mothering of sons. When, for example, researchers have found different quantities of vocalization between mother and child, varying according to the sex of the child, the greater quantity invariably is directed toward the daughter, at least after the first few months (N'Namdi 1978 and Greif 1980, who found no differences, are recent exceptions).[8] Gunnar and Donahue (1980) report a higher rate of vocal social interaction by girls with their mothers at six, nine, and twelve months; Goldberg and Lewis (1972), more mother-daughter than mother-son vocalization at one year; both Lewis and Cherry (1977) and Stoneman and Brody (1981), more verbalization by mothers to daughters at two years; and Halverson and Waldrop (1970), more words in longer interactions with daughters than with sons in assisting their two-and-a-half year-olds in taking developmental tests. Mothers and four-year-old daughters in the study by Bates (1971) were more verbally responsive to one another than were mothers and their sons of the same age. Noller (1978) found that mothers of three-and-a-half to five-year-olds interacted more with girls than boys. In a study by Endsley, Hutcherson, Garner and Martin (1979) mothers of daughters interacted more with their preschool children than did mothers of sons. Only in the school years do researchers begin to report mothers directing more verbalization to sons than to daughters (Cicirelli 1978).

A great many factors may influence the quantity of speech addressed to children. One is the verbal form used. Lewis and Cherry (1977) observed that mothers of two-year-olds in a free play laboratory situation habitually addressed more questions to their daughters and more directives to their sons. Since questions were longer than directives framed with imperative syntax, some difference in quantity probably resulted from the syntactic form used. Another variable is the context in which language is used. Daughters in the Lewis and Cherry study were most often spoken to in helping or conversational situations — contexts fostering social interaction — and sons were addressed while they were engaged in independent play. Thus conversation directed to the son was disruptive, as opposed to conversation directed to the daughter, which was usually integrated into the activity under way. One can predict more turnovers in the conversations occurring as part of an ongoing activity than in those interrupting one.

The mother's expectations about the child's behavior will also influence the number of vocalizations she attempts. Cherry (1975) proposes that if parents expect their daughters to excel in verbal competence — and they do, according to her own study and to Friedlander, Jacobs, Davis and Wetstone (1972) — their verbal behavior will be shaped accordingly. Both of these factors help explain why Lewis and Cherry (1977) found that mothers addressed more *conversation-maintaining* devices to their daughters: mothers expect greater conversational reciprocity from their daughters and, consequently, model more conversational devices for them.

The child's behavior may also influence the amount of verbal interaction occurring between mother and child. Boys in the Lewis and Cherry (1977) study tended (in a laboratory or waiting room setting) to rove more and to play farther from their mothers than girls (cf. also Lewis and Weinraub 1976). Since it is easier to engage in verbal interaction with someone nearby, the proximity of the daughter to the mother may affect the quantity of vocalization in the mother-daughter dyad (Cherry 1975 suggests this as a possible explanation for such differences). Similarly, Maccoby (1980, 221-22) describes boys as more demanding at ten months, less willing to enter into reciprocal interaction with parents at one year, naughtier at one and two, and less obedient at four or five. She cites a cross-cultural study by Edwards and Whiting showing girls more likely to approach their mothers sociably, wanting to play, as opposed to boys who approached their mothers with ego demands. The behavior of the child is an important factor inadequately considered in much mother-child research. It is difficult to judge the *direction* of influence in observing mothers with their children. Lieven (1978) provides interesting evidence of this in a discussion of two children, Kate and Beth, who used language quite differently. Since their mothers responded verbally to them in different ways, the researchers were inclined to attribute the girls' behaviors to differences in mothering. However, the researchers began to notice that they, themselves, responded to the girls in ways identical to those of the mothers. This suggested to them that the girls' own behaviors determined the kind of language they received from others.

Finally, it is possible that research finding daughters more sociable or more responsive to their mothers is distorted by the sex of the caretaker. Spelke, Zelazo, Kagan, and Kotelchuck (1973) found that one-year-old children vocalized more with the same sex parent. Lewis, Weinraub and Ban (1972) found that one-year-old boys look more at their fathers than mothers. McLaughlin, Schutz and White (1980) report that parents use less complex language with same-sex children. Lamb (1976a, 8) reports that boys more consistently than girls prefer playing with their fathers. Rebelsky and Hanks (1971) observed that fathers vocalized more to their sons than to their daughters by the time the children were three months old, the number of vocalizations decreasing for daughters over the period studied. And Block (1976, 73, updated 1981) found "specific, consistent, sex-of-parent and sex-of-child effects" in a review challenging the findings of Maccoby and Jacklin

(1974). It is possible, then, that some of the effects recorded as superior responsiveness in girls or a greater degree of interaction between mothers and daughters may be the result of the same-sex effect (discussed more fully under "Effects of Symbiotic Language" below).

One difficulty in assessing the relationships between language input and sex of child is that sex is a variable that often depends upon the presence of other variables for its effect. For example, all studies of verbal differences between boys and girls should control for birth order, since maternal differences relating to the order of birth are often reported, and these frequently interact with sex of child (Jacobs and Moss 1976 discuss this research; see also Maccoby 1980, 398). Cultural norms may also account for differences. In societies where it is customary for punishment to be administered by the same sex parent it is likely that the mother will be more severe with her daughter than with her son, or that parents will exhibit more negative verbalization to same-sex children (Baumrind 1971; Noller 1980).

Another factor that may account for some of the differences in (and contradictory reports of) sex-linked behavior is the mother's satisfaction with or conception of the woman's role. Apparent contradictions in research on whether mothers are more severe with their daughters or with their sons can often be explained by looking at specifics of the mother's situation. Her position in the social network or expectations for her children may influence her behavior toward them. Minturn and Hitchcock (1963) and Harper (1969) report that Rajput and Havik Brahmin mothers are less severe with their daughters than with their sons. Both explain this by saying that the mothers feel sorry for the daughters, knowing that when they grow up and marry they will have to leave home and live under the domination of a mother-in-law (the situation the mothers presently find themselves in). Therefore, they treat their daughters more gently and kindly than their sons. Kunkel and Kennard (1971) found, on the other hand, that Black mothers in the South were more *severe* with their daughters because they expected more would be required of them than of their sons (cf. also Lewis 1975). Clearly, one must scrutinize the contexts in which exceptional mother-daughter behavior is reported, noting the class of the parent, her own life style, her concept of herself as a woman, and the values of the culture to which she belongs.[9]

### 3.7. The Impact of Motherese on Female Development

### 3.7.1. The Effects of Symbiotic Language

Whatever the cause, the vocal interchanges between mothers and daughters appear to have, at a very early stage, both quantitative and qualitative differences from those between mothers and sons. The origins are partly physiological. Generally, boys suffer more discomfort and are less consolable than girls during the first few weeks of life. During this period, mothers' interactions with their sons tend to be more frequent but less successful than with their daughters. From the very beginning daughters respond more sociably to their mother's caretaking and quite early they establish social interaction with the mother unrelated to caretaking chores (such as looking, smiling, and touching). Significantly, Thoman (1981) calls this early mother-child interactional pattern *affective communication*, a precursor of propositional communication. It is also a precursor of the symbiotic functions of Motherese, discussed above.

As a result of the quantitative and qualitative differences in mother-daughter interaction, the daughter develops a stronger affective and social dependence upon the mother than does the son (Magrab 1979). Chodorow (1974, 62) argues that females in Western middle-class families continue to exhibit an "immature dependence" upon their mothers in adulthood, unlike women in matrifocal societies, who achieve a "mature dependence" in their mother-daughter relationships (she quotes Guntrip's 1961 definition):

> *Mature dependence* is characterized by full differentiation of ego and object (emergence from primary identification) and therewith a capacity for valuing the object for its own sake and for giving as well as receiving; a condition which should be described not as independence but as mature dependence (291).

In matrifocal societies women spend their child-rearing years much in the company of other women. Because they have ongoing social relationships of their own, and because they have an opportunity for exercising some power and authority in their own cultures, such mothers find it easier than do Western mothers (often raising their children in isolation from other adults) to permit their daughters to achieve individuation and separation. The Western mother has less power, less self-esteem based upon her role as housewife and mother, and less societal support in raising her children. Although, on the one hand, she feels social pressure to break the symbiotic tie with her children, to cease seeing them as extensions of herself, on the other she — as the single caregiver — is held responsible for their behavior and development (Slater 1970). If her children do not achieve separation, she is blamed. If they do not behave appropriately, she is blamed. The guilt, as inevitable as the love and anger intertwined in the mother-child relationship, is stronger with respect to the daughter, and exerts more pressure on her, because the symbiosis between them is stronger and because the mother's definition of "appropriate" behavior is likely to be more precise for the same-sex child.

### 3.7.2. *The Effects of Instrumental Language*

Whether children develop their gender roles as a result of social learning (Mischel 1966), cognitive development (Kohlberg 1966), or identification (Chodorow 1978), parents — and particularly mothers in Western societies — are the children's earliest and most visible role models. Since the acquisition of adult modes of action evolves through a constant restructuring of the model in light of new experience, later experience with other adults inevitably modifies the child's initial conception of appropriate role behavior. However, in the process of development, children generally incorporate some aspects of each parent into their personalities. This is most evident when a daughter becomes a mother. Women have little knowledge of or preparation for parenthood other than that acquired at home by observing their own mothers. The mother's version of the maternal role is the one they have had the greatest opportunity to observe, both in public and in private. They have, in fact, participated in its enactment (as daughters) and, significantly, they have experienced it in a same-sex relationship. It is inevitable that their own maternal role will include aspects of their mothers' behavior — often, in fact, features that they have deplored.

> There are times when I sound just like my mother . . . it's like I was a child again, and I can hear my mother yelling at Betsy and myself, and then going cold and ignoring us when we didn't do what she wanted. I find myself doing the same things with Billy and Susan, though I try and stop myself . . . but it's just like with my mother, when I get angry with people, and can't let them know it, it's like all my feelings freeze up inside me, and I sort of close up inside myself . . . and get that hard, sort of icy tone in my throat and know that my mother is there inside me.
>
> (Cohler and Grunebaum 1981, 17)

This rueful acknowledgment that daughters repeat their mothers' actions is commonly heard when women discuss their experiences as mothers and daughters. The knowledge that they are repeating the experiences of their own mothers is perhaps most painfully evident in verbal similarities when the daughter speaks with her mother's voice or utters her mother's words. The woman expresses guilt, too, of course. As a mother, she is behaving in ways that she detested as a child (children cite irritability and scolding as the traits they most dislike in their mothers [Medinnus 1969, 385]). She recognizes that behavior because it reminds her of something in her own mother she was determined to reject. But like the power mechanisms described above (the strategies of indirect control mothers use) a variety of maternal verbal behaviors are unconsciously internalized even while they are being consciously rejected.

### 3.7.3. The Effects of Pedagogic Language

Because of the richer language environment mothers provide for their daughters, one should expect girls to show superior verbal skills during the language learning phase as a result of nurture enhancing nature. Several studies have demonstrated that children of mothers who provide them with a rich verbal mode exhibit better language performances than children without that language environment (Elardo, Bradley and Caldwell 1977; Newport, Gleitman and Gleitman 1977; Clarke-Stewart 1980; Masur and Gleason 1978), and that the quantity of speech addressed to children correlates positively with their cognitive and linguistic development (Gordon 1969; Clarke-Stewart 1973; Schachter, Marquis, Shore, Bundy and McNair 1979; Moerk 1980; Fowler 1981). Nevertheless, after reviewing the enormous body of literature dealing with children's verbal skills, Klann-Delius (1981) concludes that current research neither proves nor refutes beliefs that preschool girls acquire language more rapidly or have a higher rate of verbal productivity than boys.

Several explanations for the failure to establish sex-linked differences suggest themselves. For instance, studies which identified class differences in linguistic competence relating to maternal input may have overlooked crucial differences in mothering which could account for variations in language facility. The measures used to quantify linguistic competence might possibly be biased toward middle-class norms. Or the sample may just not yet be large enough. As Klann-Delius notes in her 1981 review, the number of subjects involved in child language research to date is extremely small.

On the other hand, the greater quantity of interaction between mothers and daughters, to the extent that it exists, may have other than verbal consequences for the development of the child. The mother is modeling and reinforcing social roles for her daughter. Clearly, some of the qualitative sex-related differences noted in parental speech have this effect. Noller (1978), for example, discusses a situation in which modeling by both parents occurs. She studied the leave-taking behavior of mothers and fathers toward their nursery school children. Fathers engaged in more affectionate interaction with daughters than with sons, although mothers behaved similarly with both. Noller speculates that sons in a situation like this are learning that males are less affectionate than females and that male affection is directed more toward females than toward males. Girls observe these differentials, as well, of course, and both girls and boys are learning that females express and receive more expressions of more affection than males. Although Greif and Gleason (1970) found no sex-related differences in parental *training* of children in politeness routines (both parents equally urged their children to behave politely), there were differences in parental *modeling*. Mothers in the study exhibited significantly more polite behavior than fathers. And, in a study of sex-related differences in parent-child conversation, Greif (1980) found that fathers interrupted their children's speech more than mothers, and that both parents interrupted the daughter more often than the son (Bronstein-Burrows 1981 found a similar pattern in a study of parent-child behavior in a small city in Mexico). Greif hypothesizes that parents are modeling appropriate speech behavior (i.e., that males have more conversational rights than females, and adults more than children). A comparison between Gleason's (1975) study of fathers' speech to young children, which shows boys receiving few endearments from their fathers (who are more likely to use gruff address terms, like "Tiger" or "Fruitcake"), and the role-playing data reported by Andersen (1977) supports the assumption that such learning is taking place. Children aged four to seven, using hand puppets, role-played mother, father, and child. They appear already to have internalized sex-linked assymetry of usage: while all girls used endearments when role-playing, boys avoided them, even when role-playing the "mother" or "father."

Asymmetry in affectionate behavior results both from modeling and deliberate reinforcement. N'Namdi (1980) believes that fathers withhold affectionate responses to their sons in order to reinforce unaffectionate, independent behavior, and Block (1976) finds considerable evidence that *both* parents encourage their sons (more than their daughters) to withhold the expression of affect. Moss's 1972 study of parents' attempts to evoke smiles or babble from their seven-week-old infants and to get them to watch a moving object or grab at a bell illustrates the effect of gender stereotypes upon parents. No time limit was specified in the experiment, and although the children showed no sex-linked differences in their performance of these tasks, both parents spent more time encouraging girl babies to smile and vocalize than boy babies. Moss hypothesizes that parents were prompted by a stereotype holding that girls are, or should be, more sociable than boys and suggests that sex-linked differences may be "amplified over time through the stereotyped sex-role attitudes of parents, which evidently are present and functioning when the infant is young" (162). In a related finding, Tauber (1979) reports on a study showing that parents of children (average age, 8-1/2) are more likely to engage their daughters in sociable play and their sons in active play. This pressure may not increase the sociability of the daughter (according to the measures used by Maccoby and Jacklin [1974] it does not), but it *does* correlate with a higher degree of prosocial behavior, such as helping, sharing equally and offering help, or expressing affection to others (Abramovitch, Carter and Pepler 1980; Maccoby 1980, 217), and (as we have seen) with the development of expressive rather than analytical speech.

Whenever consistent differences occur in the quantity or quality of interaction between mothers and their daughters or sons, gender role instruction is occurring, whether voluntarily or involuntarily. For example, mothers are encouraging their daughters to remain dependent upon them by engaging them in social interaction, while fostering independence in their sons by encouraging them to move away and play alone. Brooks-Gunn and Matthews (1979) cite two observations (which happen to be sex-linked) from the reports of the Educational Testing Service's Infant Laboratory illustrating how this occurs:

> Baby walks away from his mother, trips and falls. Baby returns to his mother, fretting. Mother touches baby and baby touches her. Mother takes out plastic ring, shows it to baby, rolls it across the room, saying "See the ring! Bring the ring to mommy! Can you get the ring!" Baby looks, smiles and walks toward the ring.

> Baby walks away from her mother, trips and falls. Baby returns to mother fretting. Mother picks up and hugs baby. Mother, still holding baby, offers baby a stuffed animal (86).

Actually, we may see in examples like this nurture reinforcing nature. Mahler, Pine and Bergmann (1975) suggest that girls naturally show less interest than boys in exploring their environments and argue that there is a connection between the girls' timidity and their awareness that they lack a penis. Of this timidity, Cohler and Grunebaum (1981), after refuting the notion of penis anxiety, go on to say:

> While Mahler's preference for an object-instinctual explanation may be questioned, the phenomenon she notes is of critical importance in understanding the relationship between women and their mothers in our society. Already during the second year of life, a pattern is beginning to emerge that will shape the future of the relationship between adult women and their own mothers. In contrast with the little boy, who is already beginning autonomous exploration of the environment that, in time, will lead to relatively greater psychological differentiation, the little girl is beginning to show the pattern of continued closeness to her mother in which issues of dependency and attachment on an anaclitic mode and continued lack of separateness become the basis for the subsequent adult relationship between women across three and even four generations within the American modified extended family (20).

This close interactional pattern prefigures the divergent courses the socialization of girls and boys will take. The boy must free himself from his identification with the mother (and, consequently, his dependency upon her), but the girl is encouraged to preserve both. Belotti (1975, 56-65) identifies two psychological factors which contribute to the prolongation of symbiosis between the daughter and her mother: *imitation* of and *identification* with the mother. The very real dangers which lead parents to restrict the freedom of their adolescent daughter assure that she will be developing her own sex-role attitudes at a time when she is still close to her mother, subject to these two forces. Many of the differential behaviors noted during the school years (greater compliance of girls, lesser independence, and less exploratory curiosity about their environment) have their roots in the bonding, established very early, between the mother and daughter (Cohler and Grunebaum 1981, 20-23). Baumrind (1980) argues that the different course of socialization of boys, in which they work out an identity in accordance with a hypothetical rather than a real model, contributes to the development of their analytic powers, since they must create their role model themselves by *abstracting* elements from the behavior of males in their environment.

### 3.7.3.1. *Socialization into Different Cognitive and Emotional Worlds*

In Chapter 2, we have given evidence for different cultural and sex-specific modes of socializing girls and boys (or members of different social classes or cultures) into specific cognitive and emotional patterns of structuring reality and of expressing it: we have specifically pointed to two patterns, the analytic and the gestalt patterns; the first being "male" and the second, "female," the first meaning a very causal, temporal, object-oriented view of the world and the latter an expressive, evaluative, semantic structuring. We have also argued that the analytic mode is much more highly valued in western societies. Related to these patterns is the expression of emotions. The analytic pattern tends to reinforce the suppression of emotions, due to the logical structure imposed upon the material being processed. Gestalt (semantic) structuring both reinforces affectivity and is, in turn, reinforced by it. When mothers interact socially more with daughters than sons, thus fostering gestalt language development in girls (Nelson 1981 makes this point), and fathers are more demanding of their sons, thus favoring analytic language development in boys, they contribute to this sex-linked difference in analytic thinking.

Lynn (1979) points out similar correlations between field dependence and socialization. Field independence, the ability to perceive an object embedded in a patterned background, is highly valued in western cultures and occurs more often in males than in females. Field *dependent* children of both sexes are generally more sensitive to social cues from others, and Lynn argues that such such findings imply that socialization experiences are "important precursors of differences in cognitive style" (175) and cites the factors which contribute to field independence. They are, in fact, similar to those which foster analytic thinking: "encouragement of separation from parents, imparting of standards for internalization and regulation of impulses, and maternal characteristics that facilitate these processes" (176).

It is not surprising to note that expressive speech and field dependence are encouraged by social interaction (the activity valued for girls in our society) and that analytic speech develops in referential discourse. Nor is it surprising that one is valued more than the other. What is interesting, in light of these findings, is the pressure exerted upon children to conform to the stereotypes according to which girls develop social skills and boys, referential ones. And it is ironic that, to the degree that mothers reinforce these traits differentially in the speech of their children, they may be assuring that their sons will better match the ideal of our society than their daughters.

## NOTES

1) Caretaker Talk apparently develops only in societies where older people try to engage infants in communicative interaction (conversations). Ochs (1980) found shared caretaking but no caretaker talk in the Samoan culture she studied, and Ward (1971) found that the nurturant and pedagogic features associated with middle-class Caretaker Talk were not characteristic of adult-child interactions in a Black community in the southern United States.

2) Researchers have only recently begun to explore the cognitive function of affective features of Caretaker Talk (Lewis and Rosenblum 1980). We will discuss this more fully below.

3) At a Mother-Daughter Workshop held in Los Angeles in September, 1981, the most frequently unresolved anger expressed by the daughters was fury at any maternal expression of symbiosis. Particularly infuriating were the mother's responding to disliked behavior with "How could you do this to *me*?" or her thanking the daughter for having produced a grandson or granddaughter.

4) Gleason is basing her judgment on the practices of middle-class mothers, of course. In a description of child-rearing practices in Rosepoint, a Black community near New Orléans, Ward talks of threats as being a major form of control used by the mothers studied. Their threats fell into two major classes: *1) substantive warnings* (which could realistically be fulfilled, such as "If you do that again, I'll whip you"), and *2) invectives or imprecations* (threats which sound dreadful but which have no possibility of being fulfilled, such as "I'll break your neck if you do that again"). Minton, Kagan and Levine (1971) found that less educated mothers issued twice as many prohibitions and mitigated them less than did mothers with more than a high school education (their children also disobeyed more often).

5) Rebelsky and Hanks (1971) estimated his average interaction time with the infant at 30 seconds per day at the time they made their study. That time has probably increased in the United States in keeping with the changing roles of parents.

6) In our in-depth interviews with mothers, we asked as one of the central questions, whether they found any similarities to their own mothers in their interactions with their children. Often enough the answer was "I've tried to do everything differently from her, but sometimes I hear myself and know that I do" — this often accompanied by hollow laughter.

7) The research cited by Krashen and Winterowd deals with language functions associated with the left brain (analytic, deductive, logical) and the right brain (gestalt, inductive, imagistic). Something of the relative value placed on these two modes of brain functioning is revealed by the terminology used to identify the hemispheres: the left brain has been labeled the *major* hemisphere, and the right, the *minor*. Males show more left-brain lateralization than females.

8) Only in the research of Lewis and Freedle (1972) is there a verbal measure favoring boys, but that study, too, showed mothers spending more time vocalizing with daughters than with sons. According to Lewis and Freedle (1972), mothers held their three-month-old babies more and responded more frequently to the vocalizations initiated by them if the baby was a boy. However, since the boys responded less often to their mother's vocalizations than did the girl babies, the mothers studied actually spent more total time vocalizing with their more responsive daughters.

9) These are, of course, exactly the arguments we put forward in our theory of Socio-Psychological Variation.

# 4. SAMPLE, METHODOLOGY, AND COLLECTION OF DATA

## 4.1. *Introduction*

In the following, we will outline the plan of our empirical research, which is designed to test the hypotheses and the theoretical framework outlined above. After a discussion of the methodology used in assembling and analyzing the data and of the explicit definition of categories, we will present, analyze, and interpret the data from Austria and the U.S. both individually and from a cross-cultural perspective.

## 4.2. *Methodological Considerations: Qualitative and Quantitative Methods in Sociolinguistics*

Before entering into a discussion of the specific methods used in our study and in order to legitimate our own approach, we must consider the historical background of the controversy which has existed between two methodological extremes in social science research: between *qualitative* and *quantitative* paradigms. In German this is known as the *Positivismusstreit*: the quarrel between logical positivism, on the one hand, and ethnomethodology and symbolic interactionism on the other (Adorno *et al* 1969; Cicourel 1970; Habermas 1970; Filstead 1971; Sudnow 1972).

The distrust of qualitative methods began in the late twenties, at a time when the "young" science of sociology was struggling for acceptance by the scientific community. Quantitative methods were developed to underscore the seriousnesss and respectability of sociology, since only data which could be reduced to numbers were considered to be scientifically precise. Sometimes, indeed, as they refined their methods and made them more explicit, researchers forgot the contents — the *meaning* — of the object under investigation (Filstead 1971). This occurred, as well, in behaviorist psychology and in other quantitative approaches to psychology which (especially in Europe) neglected psychoanalytic methodology and interpretive techniques (Habermas 1977).

Within the social sciences, the positivists rejected non-quantifiable data, directing their polemics eventually against the ethnographic method, as well as against the use of qualitative illustrative material, qualitative parameters, or qualitative analyses of case studies. They argued that unique observations should not be generalized, that interpretation of meaning is too subjective and value-laden to be incorporated into objective research, and that ethnomethodology is flawed by its failure to separate theory adequately from empirical research. One cannot separate these, however. No research can be done without the values and attitudes of the researcher entering into it, and the complexity of social interaction can never be entirely quantified. Categories like *role, conflict, code, network, variation,* and *affectivity* can never be completely and unequivocally operationalized. We believe, therefore, that more than one method has to be used to get a reliable picture of reality in socio- and psycholinguistic research. More than one data source is necessary, as well, including interviews — both standardized and in-depth — participant observation, questionnaires, texts, and so forth. Only this guarantees the possibility of confronting self- and other-assessment. We consider this desirable in light of the research by Blumer (1962), Deutscher (1971), and Wodak (1981d), who demonstrate that self- and other-assessment are very different and must, therefore, be confronted. We need to consider experience both within the social situation under investigation and outside of it to understand its meaning. Without an interpretation of that meaning, even the best analysis of structures and functions will fail to give insight into social behavior (Holenstein 1976).[1]

Naturally understanding, introspection, and hermeneutics are important in text and discourse analysis. However, it is difficult to generalize from small qualitative case studies consisting of only one or two conversations; these can best be used for illustrative purposes. In order to observe general principles, a large corpus of data, drawn from several different sources, is preferable. When analyzing such data, quantification (using qualitative parameters) is absolutely necessary if we are to be able to draw conclusions about the material (Wodak 1981a). As a consequence, we have elected to use several different kinds of data, a variety of research tools, and both qualitative and quantitative analyses in our study of mother-daughter relationships.

### 4.2.1. *Analysis of Essay Content*

Content analysis has been a useful tool in the social sciences since the early twenties (Stone *et al* 1966 and Lasswell 1965 discuss its history). The reliability of the method has been questioned because of the subjectivity of the categories chosen and because of the complications involved in assigning an utterance to one and only one category. Although restriction to quantifiable linguistic data (such as text length or the count of given lexical items) overcomes the charge of unreliability, it is difficult to relate such indicators to the meaning of utterances and texts. The problem becomes even more complex when researchers try to assign meanings to non-linguistic units based on sociological and psychological categories. Kracauer (1959, 639) criticizes content analysis based upon isolated quantifiable units, arguing that categories should be defined in a way considering "the structure of the text as a whole, i.e., the linkage, manifest or latent, which makes the atomist units a gestalt" (cf. also Ritsert 1972, 20-1). As long as a structural or generative-transformational paradigm reigned in linguistics, according to which semantic and pragmatic elements were ignored, linguistics could not provide content analysis with non-syntactic objective criteria for classifying language behavior.

Qualitative categories derived from an interpretation of the text are self-evidently related to its meaning. However, they are difficult to verify. Since all researchers bring specific interests and some common-sense opinions to the investigation of data, we think that they are obliged to make such opinions and interests explicit. Because "meaning" derives from context as well as from content (Wittgenstein 1967), meaning cannot reliably be assigned to items isolated from context, and assignment is consequently somewhat ad hoc. A *purely* qualitative approach generates additional problems, however. Wunderlich (1979), for example, discusses problems of separation, identification, and classification, which make the assignment of speech act categories to utterances extremely difficult (see also discussions in Soeffner 1979).

Does this leave us with only the opposite extreme proposed by Oevermann *et al* (1979): an *objective hermeneutics* which rejects any classification at all and relies only on interpretations gained in long discussions by a team of researchers and derives validity from "the explicitness of the claim of the criteria used" (387)? A difficulty remains unresolved, since "pure hermeneutics" cannot be generalized. Even psychoanalysis, the science which has used hermeneutics in both theory and practice, has a verification related only to the case at hand, in that the patient either is healed or is not (Habermas 1977 207-9).

Recently psychologists and psychoanalysts have used qualitative content analysis of letters (Paige 1966; Weisz 1980; Mack and Hickler 1982), suicide notes (Ogilvie, Stone and Shneidman 1966), therapeutic interviews (Psathas and Arp 1966), and literature (Ellis and Favat 1966), but without integrating psycholinguistic notions, as well. The study of psychotic language behavior by Maher, McKean and McLaughlin (1966, 488-90) considers just one linguistic unit (the word), but does not consider context. Leodolter (1975b), in a study of schizophrenic language behavior, incorporated psycholinguistic theory and demonstrated that important characteristics of psychotic language and communication can be isolated linguistically at the text level. But none of these studies quite succeeded in incorporating psychological, linguistic and sociological theories into a framework for analyzing both qualitative and quantitative measures in language.

Wodak (1981a) resolved the dilemma by using an interdisciplinary framework (selecting categories from linguistics, psychology and sociology) and by combining both qualitative and quantitative methods in analyzing narrative units in therapeutic discourse. A quantitative content analysis of a large set of narrative units using qualitative categories was supplemented by an in-depth qualitative analysis of several texts in order to reveal explicitly how category assignment had been made. In addition, the qualitative analysis overcame the limitations of a purely quantitative approach, showing the relevance of isolated units in an interpretation of the complexity and levels of meaning in therapeutic discourse. The linguistic, psychoanalytic and sociological categories used were explicitly defined and founded in a theoretical framework. She used multiple raters to confirm the categorization, and illustrated each category by at least one example, thus making it possible for the reader to verify the reliability of the classifications made.

This is the method we have used in our study, as well. It satisfies the seven requisites for developing a measuring instrument, suggested by Stone *et al* (1966, 225-7). These include:

1.    the definition of data and research interests;
2.    the definition of the language community being studied;
3.    the definition of the theoretical framework in terms of categories containing symbols of the defined language community and the rules for applying these to verbal data;
4.    the use of several raters to evaluate the category consistency and content validity;
5.    the assessment of the degree of category stability by applying the instrument to different sets of documents obtained from the same sources in various situations and over a time interval (made possible in our study through the replication of the research in the U.S.);

6.   demonstration of the correspondance of the objects of measure-
ment to properties of the source and to the proposed theoretical
constructs (done through the detailed qualitative analysis and
through the use of several data sources);

7.   validation (checking the coherence of the theory and of various
implications of the theory).

### 4.3. The Design of the Empirical Study

### 4.3.1. The Cross-Cultural Comparison

In electing to conduct the same empirical research in two cities, we do
not wish to suggest that our findings illustrate differences which hold, in a
general way, between Austria and the U.S. A much richer sample from each
country would be necessary to justify such generalizations. We are, rather,
interested in consequences of specific differences between the two cities.

One of the initial considerations is the strong conservatism of Vienna,
as opposed to the lack of established traditions in Los Angeles. Vienna was
the center of the Austro-Hungarian Empire, which disintegrated after World
War I. Before the war, Vienna was a vital and splendid city, the center of
the government, culture, arts, and sciences for a large and influential segment
of Europe. After World War I, it remained merely the capital of a small,
impoverished country, whose power had been completely destroyed. The
effects are still evident in a national nostalgia for the great days of the empire
and a national pride in the very real artistic and intellectual achievements of
the nineteenth and early twentieth century. Despite this nostalgia, following
World War I significant social changes occurred in Vienna, including
advances in social reform, school reform, equality for women, liberalized
educational opportunities, and Austro-Marxism. This forward thrust into
the twentieth century was ruptured by the economic and political upheavels
of the twenties and thirties, and it dissipated, largely, in the thirties and
forties. Under the domination of Austro-Fascism and Hitler, and with the
assistance of some Catholic clergy, a new ideology appeared, one which
neutralized the progressive gains of the twenties. Of interest to our study is
the ideology which affected women's ideals: the slogan *Kinder, Kirche, und
Küche*, according to which women were made the custodians of children,
morals, and the home.

After World War II, Austria was slow to recover its autonomy (remain-
ing partitioned by the allies until 1955). Its intellectual and artistic elite had
fled (a loss still felt). Vienna had been transformed from a cultural center

into a border town between East and West. And the war had left it with a very homogeneous population (only 5000 Jews remained, and it was no longer open to immigration from Eastern Countries, other than to refugees, who were granted asylum).[2] The country is 95% Catholic, with religion being taught in all schools. Only since 1969, when the Socialist Party gained nation-wide control, have progressive reforms in social welfare, employment, schools, health, and women's issues begun to appear. Compared with the U.S., interest in feminism is new, and its effects are only beginning to reach a large segment of the population. Social class is still conferred through family and education, and since education correlates with class (see our results), there is less social mobility than in the U.S. Loyalty to social class and the traditions associated with one's class are stronger than in the U.S. (where definition of class is far more fluid and class-related traditions have not become firmly established).

We have discussed Vienna at some length because its situation is less familiar to English and American readers than is that of Los Angeles, and because its greater conservatism bears directly upon our findings. The family structure and values of contemporary Viennese society are closer to those on which Freudian and post-Freudian theories of mother-daughter relation-ship were developed than are those of Los Angeles. Whereas Vienna has well-established traditions, Los Angeles has been too recently established to have created traditions. It was a minor city, smaller than San Francisco, until the 1920s, when its population began to increase as a result of migration from the U.S. South and Midwest, and — eventually — from all over the world. In 1931, half its population had resided in Los Angeles less than five years (Weaver 1980).[3] By 1950 seven-eighths of the buildings in the city were less than thirty years old. And in the ensuing years, immigration has accelerated, especially from Mexico, China, Japan, Cuba, South America, Indochina, Samoa, the Phillipines, and — most recently — Viet-nam. In contrast with the cultural homogeneity of Vienna, Los Angeles is polycultural: in fact, it has school systems in which students speak 44 different languages. In 1982 white Angelenos of European descent became a minority of the population of the city — the next two sizable populations being, in order of numbers, Mexican and Black Americans.

There is also a contrast between reverence for the past in Vienna and the orientation toward the future in Los Angeles. As early as 1927 Bruce Bliven called the city "a melting pot in which the civilization of the future may be seen bubbling darkly up in a foreshadowing brew" (quoted in Weaver

1980), and Los Angeles continues to be called "the city of tomorrow."

### 4.3.1.1. *The Austrian Design*

The empirical investigation includes the collection of data from five sources.

1. Written essays were collected from schools chosen because of the social class of their student population. The students averaged twelve years of age, the year in which the children reach puberty. The topic of the essay, "My Mother and I," was chosen because it assured that the students would have material on which to write and because it encouraged the production of expressive writing dealing with the subject matter of interest to us. Students were assured that the essays would be confidential and that they would not be graded, but other than that they were allowed free rein in choosing what to say and how to say it. The essays were used to check our hypotheses concerning sex-specific differences in the verbal expression of emotions and in the nature of the relationship between mother and child, as well as ethnic- and class-specific differences in language and in the subjective view children have of their own and their mother's roles. The essays were subjected to both qualitative and quantitative analyses.

2. Interviews conducted with the girls provided additional self-assessment and social information from the children about the family structure. We think — and we will elaborate on this point later — that it is very important to have several sources of data gained by different methods.

3. The background data for the boys were obtained by interviewing the teachers, since Austrian school officials did not allow time for interviewing them. The data gathered enabled us to classify the boys socially and to obtain information about their family structures, information necessary for comparing the essays of the boys with those of the girls from a socio- and psycholinguistic perspective. Since we were concentrating on mothers and daughters, not on the analysis of whole families or of other family dyads, further inquiries of the boys were thought unnecessary.

4. Ten mothers of daughters from each school were selected at random and were interviewed at length. These sessions provided us with the self-assessment of the mothers, their evaluation of the mother/daughter relationship, and their evaluation of their relationships with their own mothers. We also inquired about the structure of the family, the satisfaction they felt with their roles as women, and their hopes for their daughters.

5. At the end of the interview, the mothers took a brief psychological test designed to give us insight into their personality characteristics. This

provided another source of data to supplement our picture of the mother/daughter relationship and to facilitate our cross-cultural comparison.

### 4.3.1.2. *The U.S. Design*

Since the U.S. data collection occurred a year later than the Austrian one, it was possible to change some elements of the study in order to do small pilot studies of how other factors might influence our findings.

1. The essay collection was identical, but a larger sample was taken in order to test the effects of a wider age spread upon our findings. One classroom of 10-year-olds, one of 13-year-olds, and four of 11-12-year-olds were included in the U.S. sample. Schools were chosen to provide an ethnic sample, as well. One school outside the Los Angeles metropolitan district was included (to enable us to look at urban-rural effects). We included two classrooms from one school, to which students had been randomly assigned, in order to be able to check teacher effect.

2. Identical interviews were conducted with the U.S. girls insofar as possible.

3. Boys were interviewed in the U.S. study, in order to test some of the family structure variables examined in the data from the girls and to explore new issues.

4. Only 15 mothers were interviewed in the U.S. The Austrian mother sample was so small that only a much larger sample from the U.S. could have been used to test its results, and we were less interested in developing a statistically-based theory about mother-types (a project for a much larger study) than in finding a basis for matching Austrian and American mother-daughter pairs for our Case Studies. These studies provide a qualitative test of the effects of the personality characteristics we examine.

5. The personality test was translated into English and administered to U.S. Mothers (see Appendix III for translation).[4]

### 4.3.2. *Collection of the Data*

The fieldwork was begun in Vienna and replicated in Los Angeles. We assumed that certain features of the mother/daughter relationship would be the same in both cultures, due to general structural pressures involved in female development under the tutelage of the mother. On the other hand, we expected some differences to evolve as a result of specific cultural differences, such as ethnicity (which could contribute factors not found in a class-society) or criminality in the U.S. culture (which might contribute stresses not found in the more conservative Austrian society).

### 4.3.3. *The Ethical Dilemma and the Observer Paradox*

In our methodological considerations, we have emphasized the importance of participant observation in socio- and psycholinguistic fieldwork. Therefore, the question naturally arises: why did we not, in the scope of this study, undertake observations of natural interactions between mothers and daughters?

In the study of institutionalized speech situations like courtroom interaction or doctor-patient consultations, the observation of spontaneous discourse is possible once permission has been granted.[5] We are dealing here with the intimate sphere of people's lives, however, and our topic is one which has long been surrounded with taboos (Rich 1977; Lynn 1979). Although recent interest in the topic has been accompanied by a relaxing of those taboos, an investigation of the mother-daughter relationship in natural speech situations in their own homes is practically impossible. To undertake the observation and report on family interactions without the knowledge of the participants would, of course, be unethical. If the study were undertaken openly with families of friends, an unbiased study would not be easy on two counts: 1) it would be difficult to maintain the necessary observer distance to permit an objective analysis and 2) concern about jeopardizing the friendship might well interfere with a frank exposure of conflicts and behavioral problems observed among the family members. Manipulation of the case studies so that participants could not recognize themselves would inevitably bias the data presented.

The observation of family interaction by strangers is just as problematical. Although we might have succeeded in intruding upon middle-class families, it would have been difficult — if not impossible — to gain access to families of other social classes or ethnicities than our own, families who might fear or resent intrusions by outsiders, or people made uncomfortable (through prejudice or awe) by being made the subject of a scientific investigation. In any event, the observer would have been at once a stranger and a guest: normal, everyday behavior would have been directed toward her instead of toward family members.

An experimental arrangement would not have provided natural data. One might create a natural setting and tell mother and daughter pairs to role-play their conflicts or conversational routines. But very few persons would be prepared to do this, and it would have been impossible to establish whether or not the interactions reflected spontaneous family interaction. Subjects are self-selected for such studies; they may volunteer because they are aware that they have problems, or because they are exhibitionistic. In such a case, the sample is not random.

We might have attempted to tape record ourselves in everyday interactions with our own mothers and daughters. But again, our data would have been biased by our own goals, theories, and interests. While it is possible to control for bias in interpreting data (by using a number of raters and a variety of sources), it is much more difficult to overcome bias in *creating* the data to be studied.

All of these considerations prompted us to attempt a large, empirical investigation, using school children selected by chance. The schools used in the study were chosen by school administrators, both in Austria and in California, as were the classrooms visited. The mothers to be interviewed were selected at random. We telephoned them at their homes, and they were free to accept or refuse (only one Austrian mother refused). All participants (children and mothers) were assured that their responses would be confidential and that their anonymity would be preserved. This made it possible for us to acquire a self-assessment from the mothers and daughters independent of each other. Our data, of course, tell us only about the self- and other-assessment of those involved. The degree to which mothers and daughters gave honest answers to our questions is also vital. In order to be able to estimate this, we asked both of them some of the same questions and compared their answers. In addition, we placed information given by the daughter in her essay beside that secured by interview, and we compared the mother's self-assessment with the personality profile obtained from the Giessen Test.

The interview with the girls was probably our most biased and standardized method of acquiring data. Certain kinds of socio-economic and psychologically revealing questions were forbidden by school regulations. The students were often intimidated by the tape recorder, or were hostile to the interview situation. And the interview had to be short (a fifteen minute maximum), so that the information acquired was limited and chances of putting the child at ease were reduced. Consequently, these interviews served chiefly to compare certain information in the essays with answers given by the mother and to estimate the frankness (by comparison with information given in the essay) of the child in the interview. The interviews also provided data about the social background and family structure of the child.

The discussions with the mothers were much less formal, less standardized, and more in-depth (following suggestions of Friedrichs 1973). Because of their agreement to participate, the mothers were relatively frank and honest in their answers.

### 4.3.4. *Analysis of the Data*

The data are analyzed in several ways. A quantitative analysis of the essays and interviews, on the one hand, allows us to generalize cross-culturally about the relationship between the mothers and daughters in our sample. A qualitative analysis, on the other hand, drawing together the material from essays, interviews, and tests, both supplements and differentiates the quantitative results, more clearly illustrating our findings than do mere numbers. In addition, we include sixteen case studies, which provide insight into the mother/daughter relationship across two generations. Table 1 summarizes the sequential states of our fieldwork and analysis of the data.

## 4.4. *The Empirical Investigation*

### 4.4.1. *Description of the Austrian Sample*

#### 4.4.1.1. *Sociological Factors in Austria*

The attribution of social class was based upon information gained in the interviews (for the girls) and on conversations with their teachers (for the boys). Profession, school, and salary of both parents were used and weighted to estimate social class, using the scale developed by Oeverman (1972) and refined by Leodolter (1975a, 208). Since the mothers were especially important in our study, close attention was given to establishing their social class independently of that of their husbands. Non-working women were not automatically assigned the social class of their husbands; rather their own background and schooling were considered (Nichols 1981).

All Austrian children begin school at age 6 and continue for at least 8 years. First they go to a *Volkschule* for 4 years. Then their parents and teachers together decide how to stream the child during the next 4 years. Some go to the *Gymnasium* (which prepares them for the university) until they are 18. Some go into either the A-stream or the B-stream of a *Hauptschule* until they are 14. A-stream students may, if their grades are adequate, move to the Gymnasium when they are 14; B-stream students leave school and go to work at that age. Streaming decisions are made on the basis of the child's academic record and the finances of the parents (schooling is free in Austria, but not all parents are able to continue supporting the child to the age of 18). When they leave the Hauptschule, children have been trained for trades and expect to get jobs immediately. Many will move out of the house and begin supporting themselves at 14 (an important fact to remember in comparing the maturity of the Austrian and U.S. students).

### 4.4.1.2. *The Austrian Schools Chosen*

In the autumn and winter of 1980-81, 104 essays on the topic "My Mother and I" were collected in three Viennese schools from four classrooms of 12 and 13 year-old girls and boys. The schools were selected by school administrators, to whom a proposal had been sent asking for schools in class-specific neighborhoods.

*School A* is a Hauptschule. Most of the children are from working-class families who cannot afford to support them beyond the age of 14 or are students who have been identified (by criteria never made fully explicit) as being unable to succeed in the Gymnasium and university. Since these schools contain A-stream and B-stream classes for each grade, one classroom from each stream participated in our study.

*Schools B* and *C* were Gymnasiums, comprehensive schools which end with the *Matura*, a final exam which students must pass in order to be admitted to the university. Two Gymnasiums were included in the study, one from a middle-class suburb of Vienna and one from an affluent suburb. School B is a huge school (1400 pupils) in a middle-class neighborhood, very modern and progressive. School C, in an upper-middle-class neighborhood, has more social prestige, is smaller (300 pupils) and is more conservative. Although less modern and progressive than school B, it is very personal (pupils are well-known by the teachers and principal), and both parents and teachers are very proud of the school.

### 4.4.1.3. *The Nature of the Austrian Sample*

The total sample of Austrian children consisted of 104 students, 62 girls and 42 boys. Tables 2A, C and 3A show the distribution of children according to school and social class (a chi-square analysis demonstrated that class-distribution is significant in these schools). Table 4A shows the class distribution of the 30 mothers who participated in the study. Table 5 gives further information about the mother sample: included are her marital status, her profession (if any), the number of children in the family, the position of the child studied (whether youngest, middle or oldest), and the caretaker in the afternoon. The latter category is especially important in the Austrian study. Since schools still generally meet for only half a day, children come home at one or two o'clock and, if no parents or other caretakers are there, are completely on their own for several hours of the day. Although the possibility of paid after-school care exists in some areas, such care is not widely available, especially to middle- and lower-middle-class families. We were interested in this feature because children left on their own sometimes develop feelings of loneliness, boredom, or neglect — negative feelings that may be important to our study. Or if there is another caretaker than the mother in the afternoon, that person may absorb some of the positive or negative affectivity usually directed toward the mother.

### 4.4.2. Description of the U.S. Sample

### 4.4.2.1. Sociological Factors in the U.S.

Although Austria is a stable socially-stratified society, in which it is possible to identify four social classes with some reliability, the situation in the U.S. is quite different. There is greater fluidity because there is more potential for vertical social movement and because of a large number of factors that must be considered in assessing social class in a heterogeneous society (Nichols 1980, 1981). Thus, it would have been impossible to find a population sample matching the four classes identified in Vienna. Los Angeles does have identifiable ethnic populations, however, and these were chosen to provide related sub-cultural variables for our study. Four ethnic groups are well represented in the school system and all of them share a long tradition in Los Angeles of cultural leveling (reducing idiosyncracies of origin in favor of a local cultural norm) and yet all continue to hold to common values, traits, and customs that differentiate them one from the other.[7] They are Mexican-Americans, African-Americans, and — separated for our study because of a specific school population — two groups of European Americans: Jewish and Non-Jewish. In trying to provide terms to designate these four groups, we became aware of how complex ethnicity is. Any labeling is inevitably arbitrary, suggesting shared and excluded traits that may or may not exist, and, in fact, some of our students belong to more than one group. However, terms are necessary if social sub-groups are to be discussed, so we have selected *Chicano* (children of Mexican descent), *Black* (children of African descent), *Anglo* (children of European descent), *Jewish*, and *Other*.

We will, occasionally, refer to the social class of members of these groups, but always within limited contexts. Administrators, when asked to characterize their schools, usually include an estimate of the social class range of their community and, hence, of their student body. Thus, the principal of a school in a community generally referred to as an "Upper Middle Class Suburb" refers to its students as "Upper Middle Class." And, in fact, the community visibly contains a considerable proportion of well-to-do families living on large estates behind secured gates. The principal of another school, in a community of refinery and dock workers, where most of the houses are small two-bedroom, one-bathroom boxes on tiny plots of land, calls its student body "Lower Middle Class." Clearly the terms have some meaning and validity. However, no Los Angeles school is homogeneous — nor even approaches homogeneity; so, as a matter of curiosity, we asked teachers to ascribe social class to each of their students (only one refused), the ascription being recorded for each member in our sample. (We did not use their guesses in our statistics, but we will discuss them below.) Generally, students in the U.S. sample are identified by ethnicity and sex, with no ascription of social class. When class *is* mentioned for the U.S. sample, we refer to the class attributed to the school population generally (see tables 2B, D, 3B, 4B).

### 4.4.2.2. *The U.S. Schools Chosen*

In the winter of 1981-82, the Viennese study was replicated in California, with the alterations noted above. Essays on the topic "My Mother and I" were collected from 182 students in five schools in the Los Angeles area. The schools, as in Austria, were chosen by the administration, this time on the basis of socio-economic and ethnic factors. An attempt was made to secure a sample representing, insofar as possible, a socio-economic cross section of students from Black, Chicano, Anglo, and Anglo-Jewish families.

*School A* (most like the A-stream in Austria) was in a lower-middle class community near the Los Angeles harbor. The school population was estimated by the principal to be composed of 75% Spanish surnamed (the majority of the Chicano students in our study came from this school), 2% Black, 16% Anglo, and 7% other Americans (largely Asians). Many of the fathers were employed as dock workers or as laborers in the nearby oil refineries. Mothers who worked generally held clerical positions. The school saw part of its function as being to motivate the students to aspire to higher educational goals than their parents had achieved. Mothers of students in School A assume that their daughters will go on to college.

*School B* (most like the B-stream in Austria) is as nearly rural as a school is likely to be in the Los Angeles area. It is sixty miles from the city center, in a community that is largely self-contained (residents live, work, and find their entertainment within the community). The population is largely Anglo, and frequently both parents work at low-paying service or clerical jobs. Though they lack higher education themselves, many of the parents hope their children will go on at least to junior college.

*School C* (most like School B in Austria) has a long and proud tradition as one of the best schools in the Los Angeles system. It is in a neighborhood which has changed in the last fifteen years, during which time the school population has changed from being chiefly Jewish to roughly 40% Jewish, 40% Black, and 20% other (Oriental and Anglo). Parents are often professionals (doctors, nurses, lawyers, academics) or merchants. The houses are large (two baths, three or four bedrooms), with immaculately kept yards and gardens. Mothers tend to be highly involved with the teachers, appearing readily for conferences and school affairs. Two classes participated in this school, contributing two sizable ethnicities: Black and Jewish.

*School D* (most like School C in Austria) is in an affluent beach community near Los Angeles. Students here belong to tennis clubs, own horses, fly to Aspen or Sun Valley for skiing vacations, and — generally — live out of doors. From early spring until late fall they spend their free time at the beach and have little interest in reading or television as a means of amusement. Their modern, elegant school buildings and small classes would satisfy parents paying for a private school education.

*School E* (no Austrian equivalent) is a "Magnet School," one of the schools in the Los Angeles system designed to provide special educational opportunities for any students whose parents choose to send them there (some children have a two-hour bus ride from home to school). Originally intended to offer special educational facilities to ghetto students, these schools, in fact, tend to draw at least half of their population from middle and upper-middle-class families. The school population is roughly 60% Anglo, 20% Black, and 20% other). Because of the self-selection operating in the magnet schools, students tend to be highly motivated and to value the educational facilities available. They are granted a great deal of autonomy (open classrooms, freedom to come and go to the library to work on research projects, and so forth). Their parents generally hold high educational values and, themselves, have had some higher education.

### 4.4.2.3. *The Nature of the U.S. Sample*

Table 6 lists the sociological parameters secured from interviews and essays and used in correlation with other categories for analyzing the data. Included, since the results are remarkable, is information on the social class attributed by the teachers. No Jewish students were ascribed lower- or lower-middle class status by their teachers; no Anglos were ascribed lower-class status; and no Chicano students and only one Black were ascribed upper-middle class status. Teacher comments upon ethnic students about whom they were uncertain ("There is money there, but . . ." or "She has nice clothes, the best of everything, but . . .") demonstrate in their thinking the kind of two-valued responses revealed in the matched guise tests developed by Lambert and his colleagues at McGill university.[8] What we are seeing here is evidence that stereotypes held by the teachers serve as the sort of "anchor points" Williams (1973) identified through his use of matched guise tests. Apparently some teachers begin with a subjective definition of social class which includes conformity to ethnically defined behavioral patterns.

### 4.4.2.4. *Collection of the Essays*

In order to remove pressure from the students and to create an atypical writing context for the production of the essays, we wrote the topic on the board, told the students (without further explanation) to write whatever they chose, and promised them that spelling, neatness, and accuracy would not concern us. The teacher was present, but did not give any further information and did not look at the written texts.[9] Their presence was required by the schools and was important for maintaining discipline. The writing of the essay was voluntary (written permissions by the parents was required in Austria, although the topic was not revealed in advance). The students were guaranteed anonymity and confidentiality and were assured that the essays would not be used for any sort of school evaluation. If a student asked, "What shall I write?" or "Is this supposed to be a story or a description?" the answer was, "Write anything that comes into your mind" (a directive similar to one of the constitutive rules in therapeutic sessions).[10] Thus an open situation was created, quite different from the normal school situation. Two symptoms of its unusual nature were evident: as soon as the usual norms were removed in the Austrian classrooms, the boys became naughtier and in both samples, the students discussed their lives more frankly in writing than they did in the interview.

### 4.4.3. *The Selection of Categories for Analysis*

Although some studies exist which attempt to isolate sex-specific differences in the written language of school children (Bodkin 1975; Graves 1975; Conrad 1979), we found it necessary to develop our own categories in analyzing the essays written for our study. We were not interested in sex-specific language behavior in general, but rather in differences of expression growing out of the situation under investigation. We assumed that significant differences exist between the mother-daughter relationship and the mother-son relationship and, hence, that we would find related differences in the quality of emotions evoked by the topic "My Mother and I." We are studying not only differences between the sexes, but, even more important, specific style-ranges of variation *within one sex*, through a comparison of the essays and interviews provided by the girls. Sex is only one of the variables important to our study. Variation in language behavior is always dependent upon a complex of sociological and psychological factors which interact with and, in fact, may neutralize the effects of any single variable, such as sex. We have, consequently, included such variables as the educational style of the home (whether strict or liberal), the ethnicity or social class of the child, and the nature of the mother-child relationship as inter-dependent variables influencing the form and content of the essays. We call this approach a study of *Socio-Psychological Variation* (SPV) in discourse (Wodak 1981a; Dressler and Wodak 1982) and discuss it more fully in Chapter 5.

## NOTES

1) Holenstein provides a good criticism of "pure" system-analysis and system theory. People using both approaches have often neglected the many and divergent meanings of utterances and functions of interactions.

2) Large numbers of refugees came to Austria from Hungary in 1956; from Czechoslovakia in 1968; and from Poland in 1981. Russian Jews have also immigrated to Vienna. However, the immigration leaves unaffected the percentage of the population which is Catholic (95%) (Wodak 1981c).

3) Information on Los Angeles is based upon a study by Weaver (1980).

4) Our Case Studies provide contrasting evidence to that reported by Ervin-Tripp (1966) who found that tests given in different languages evoked shifts in personality variables.

5) The fact that institutionalized situations are easier to gain access to than private conversation explains the strong interest of sociolinguists in such transactions. There are other advantages, as well. Since institutionalized interactions have great social significance to the participants, the presence of an observer may be forgotten during the course of the interaction. Furthermore, such situations are standardized, which means that many factors can be held constant during the process of an extended investigation (Leodolter 1975a, 201-2; Labov and Fanshel 1977, 359-60; Wodak-Leodolter 1980).

6) When asked for their phone numbers, so that the researcher could contact their mothers, the Austrian girls were terrified and needed repeated assurances that nothing they said would be revealed to their mothers.

7) Although there is now a substantial Asian population in Los Angeles, no single ethnicity approaches the numbers of the four groups studied here.

8) In the matched guise study, tape recorded segments of speech are presented to a subject for rating; among the samples are passages in which the same speakers are heard using different dialects or languages. A comparison is made of the hearer's response to the speaker in each guise (Tucker and Lambert 1969).

9) In one U.S. school, the teacher preferred to administer the writing assignment herself.

10) This manner of writing the topic on the blackboard without further comments created a very open situation. In psychotherapy, the constitutive rule (*Grundregel*), "Say anything which comes into your mind" provokes the process of free association, the most important data base for the psychodynamic process. We may have evoked a similar situation through our statement of topic. One source of evidence for this speculation is, for example, the extremely high degree of transference which occurred in the Austrian sample (see definition of categories).

## 5. DEFINITION OF THE CATEGORIES

### 5.1. *Introduction*

The coding of the following categories was based on the interpretation of the content of the essays by a variety of raters (including sociologists, psychologists, writing teachers — and the authors). In each case, the entire essay was considered and the *dominant* characteristic was coded.

### 5.2. *The Schema of the "School Essay"*

The three rhetorical text forms taught to elementary school children are *description, narration,* and *exposition. Descriptive essays* present sensory details organized so as to present a person or scene vividly, as though the reader were there to see it. *Narrative essays* describe specific past experiences; the sequence of clauses have a fixed temporal relationship to each other, the order in which they present the material matching the order in which events originally occurred (Labov and Waletzky 1967). *Expository essays* are designed to inform or to make something understandable to the reader: to clarify an idea, to explain something, to analyze a situation, or to define a concept.

A significant difference between these three essay types is the degree to which the form focuses upon the writer's thesis. In description and narration, the evaluation is embedded within the details presented; although the writer's attitude or idea about the subject governs what details will be chosen and how they will be arranged, the evaluation may remain implicit. Exposition requires the writer to convey an understanding of the subject to the reader, and the author's evaluation is the central focus of the essay. We assigned the topic "My Mother and I" in order to elicit expository writing from our students; we wanted informative essays dealing with the mother-child relationship. Had we wished to obtain descriptive essays, we might have presented a topic focusing on one person ("My mother," for instance). Narratives could have been elicited by giving a topic naming an activity shared by mother and child (such as "Going places with my mother"). But our two-pronged topic focuses on both the mother and the child, suggesting that the writer comment in some way upon that specific dyad, thus encouraging an expository development.

Students differed in the degree to which they commented on their relationships with their mothers. Not all of them wrote expository themes, choosing instead narratives or descriptions which lacked any evaluative comment about the relationship required by the topic as stated. Others used the expository form but wrote on a neutral topic ("My mother and I do lots of things together"). Since the student's choice of an expository form failed to correlate with attitude or willingness to address the topic, we were unable to use it as an analytical category for our study. What we noticed, instead, was that irrespective of the expository form chosen, our writers produced essays which fell into two groups, or *text types*, clearly differentiated on the basis of whether or not the essay included evidence of the author's own reflection upon or attitude toward the material presented.

## 5.3. *Text Categories*

### 5.3.1. *The Category of TEXT TYPE*

We call the two text types we have identified *reflective* and *unreflective*,[1] distinguished according to whether or not the essay included the student's evaluation of the mother-child relationship, rather than by formal characteristics of the text. The distinction we are making is very similar to that originated by John Dewey (1933), who differentiates reflective from unreflective as follows: "Reflection thus implies that something is believed in (or disbelieved in), not on its own direct account, but through something else which stands as witness, evidence, proof, voucher, warrant; that is, as *ground of belief*" (8). We assume, as elaborated above, that these text types are themselves schemas (in which the evaluation represents a causal ordering of the material), and that the choice of schema can be predicted on the basis of socio-psychological factors such as age, sex, class, or ethnicity of the writer.

Cognitive factors are also involved in the choice. The two types correlate with the two principles of storing and retrieving experience introduced by Tulving (1972): *episodic* and *semantic*. Episodic knowledge is autobiographical, involving episodes or events that share temporal or spatial relationships, or other accidentally *shared* attributes that provide the context making them accessible to memory. This kind of memory preserves a fairly faithful record of what has happened to the person in the past. Semantic knowledge is organized in terms of meaningful concepts and cognitive referents. It includes information other than that gained through experience (derived by inference, association, induction, reading, and so forth). Since semantic knowledge can be stored with multiple interpretations or as instances of more than one generalization, subjective interpretation may distort it, rendering it inaccurate. Tulving argues that some information is stored *episodically*, passing into storage without being interpreted. Such material may be retrieved later associatively, according to accidentally shared traits, or may be forgotten. A second kind of experience is inspected and assigned some meaning before being stored away *semantically* as part of a larger pattern of experiences with similar meaning(s). Its semantic storage requires that it be compared with generalizations about and abstractions from many similar episodes (Kintsch 1974). Interpreted experiences feed into one's developing view of the world and are, in turn, organized and shaped according to that world view before being stored away in memory (this is the way prejudices color our interpretation of experience).

People differ in the kinds of experiences which they notice and interpret and in the subjects about which they form attitudes. Thus, the same act may be stored episodically by one participant and semantically by another. A topic like "My Mother and I" can tap either kind of experience. The child who reports episodic experience produces information unexamined for meaning. The result is an *unreflective text type*: an essay which reveals no evaluation of the subject by the child. If semantic experience is reported, the child is recalling information which has been interpreted and categorized. The result is a *reflective text type*, an essay which reveals the child's assessment of the experience reported.

### 5.3.1.1. *Reflective Texts*

Essays of this type evaluate the child's relationship with the mother. She is characterized in some way, and the qualities presented are always related to the child's subjective, personal response to her. It is the child's impression of the mother or a view of their life together which informs the selection of details presented for the reader. In reflective essays, the writing process often becomes for the child a means of exploring that impression, rather than of communicating information to the reader (what Flower 1979 calls *writer-based prose*). Since involvement with the material, or with the exploration of an idea, taxes the writer's cognitive resources, so that the immature writer may lose control of the compositional elements of the essay, reflective essays often lack cohesion or lapse into incoherence.

### 5.3.1.2. *Unreflective Texts*

Considered as unreflective texts are essays which provide no evaluation of the information presented. The content of such essays is episodic and only incidentally related, often taking the form of a list of uninterpreted experiences. Details are usually neutral and impersonal, taken from everyday life at home. If the essay form is expository, the thematic sentence of an unreflective essay is likely to consist of a cliché that has not really involved the writer in an evaluation of the material. These essays are seldom incoherent, either. Coherence suggests a temporal sequence or a causal connection not found in many unreflective essays, in which related details and experiences are simply strung together. (Examples of reflective and unreflective texts are discussed in the "Analysis of the Essays" section, below.)

### 5.3.2. *The Category of COHERENCE*

Within the scope of this category, we are interested in the treatment of the topic, "My Mother and I." Is the relationship described coherently and logically, or do ruptures and contradictions occur? Incoherence has multiple causes and takes several forms.

One major source of trouble arises as a result of cognitive strain. If a child — or writer of any age, for that matter — is struggling to formulate a vaguely thought-through idea, attention is fractured and the written discourse may get out from under the writer's control. As a result, it may show ruptures, illogicalities, inconsistencies, elipses, and even smears (Shaughnessy 1977). However, the child writing about simple and familiar material can monitor the writing process. Thus a writer spinning out episodic experiences can retrieve them from memory and convert them to writing with relative ease, since they need only be examined for the content "mother and I." Writers using such materials can write at whatever level of competence they have achieved, devoting their attention to control of the special syntax of writing, the problems of handwriting, and the questions of form.

If, on the other hand, the child is drawing on semantically coded knowledge, writing becomes more difficult. The material to be retrieved is more complexly indexed, being marked not only for content, but also for meaning — or meanings (such as affect, attitude, or any number of related responses to the experience remembered). Children using semantically coded material must search for experiences having *two* attributes in common: the content ("mother and I") and some generalized idea about the nature of their relationship. That idea may be triggered by the topic, itself. Or the child may pull out a random experience, find it semantically coded with an evaluation, and then seek another to match it, repeating the process until the material is complete. But once the central idea is chosen, all other experiences retrieved from memory should relate both to it *and* to the mother-child dyad, if the essay is to be logically consistent.

The controlling idea selected by the child may be only one of a number of competing possibilities suggested by the topic, and experiences retrieved during the memory search may not always agree with the idea on which the child has focused. Thus not only does the retrieval from semantic memory require a more complex search, each detail must be examined for consistency, as well. Quite a bit is going on simultaneously for immature writers, even with a topic as simple and familiar as "My Mother and I," *if* the child writes a reflective, expository theme. The ability to produce neatly written, competent prose may very well deteriorate under these circumstances.

A second factor which contributes to incoherence in our writing sample is the sensitivity of the topic. In the act of writing the essay, the child frequently encounters problems of ambivalence and taboo. She may retrieve from memory not only the material sought (things liked about the relationship, for example), but also associatively stored material (things *not* liked). If this occurs, she is, in a sense, working with two texts: the explicit one cited in the abstract, and an *implicit* one consisting of antithetical, taboo material — a sort of "shadow text[2]," which reflects a larger psychological conflict. Often evidence of the existence of a shadow text is revealed by qualifiers (adjectives, adverbs, and particles) which carry an implicit message contrary to the expressed one. Such an essay will strike the reader as coherent, but vaguely unsettling. (This is discussed more fully under "Particles" below.) Sometimes the writer develops both texts into a single essay (comparison and contrast are expository techniques used for developing two antithetical texts simultaneously by ordering them identically and playing one off against the other).

Our students rarely attempted to use comparison and contrast in developing their essays. It is a difficult form to manage, even for experienced writers, since it requires two memory searches, the sorting of two sets of data into identical patterns, and then the arrangement of these ordered sets into a hierarchical design (in ascending order of importance, for instance). If incoherence results, it is, again, likely to result from cognitive overload.

Often, of course, writers are able neither to suppress shadow texts nor to incorporate them skillfully. Bits and pieces slip into an essay, yielding inconsistencies and contradictions. We have coded incoherence because we believe that it reveals ambivalence on the part of the writer. As a matter of interest, in comparing essays on socio-psychological parameters we have divided coherence into three subcategories: *consistency*, *illogicality* and *contradictions*.

### 5.3.2.1. *Consistency*

In essays classified as consistent, sentences have a logical sequential connection with one another (signalled, for example, by appropriate connectors such as *and* or *so*). Subordinate clauses do not contradict the assertion of the main clause, and examples illustrate the main assertion of the essay (if, in fact, there is any). Unreflective essays are generally consistent, since a simple list of events may be coherent if they share a related theme, even though the author makes no unifying generalization about them:

> Me and my mother always go places and do a lot of things. On Fridays my mother takes me to a Pizza Parlor and we order a large pizza with cheese and sausage. On Saturdays we go to the movie. The last movie we saw was Star Wars. On Sundays we go to church after breakfast. Me and my mom have fun together when she is not working. (Boy, Black, U.S.)

### 5.3.2.2. *Illogicality*

Significant for this category is a sequence of assertions lacking any elaboration or explanation. This often occurs because one incident suggests another as the child is in the process of writing and both find their way onto the page without the child making explicit the logical connection between them. The effect of such lapses is to rupture the logical flow of the discussion, forcing the reader to attempt to tease out the associations which provide the unifying contexts for a sequence of ideas. In the following essay, for example, the girl connects alternating negative and positive statements incorrectly. The connector *also*, in the fifth sentence, signals that material similar to that in the preceding sentence will follow, but it does not. This appears to result from the writer's difficulty in handling the cohesive devices required by a complicated pattern of development:

> When she sees a spot she goes completely crazy. But when I get a bad mark in a test she is very sympathetic. I wanted a dog for three years. In the fourth I got one. She can also be really furious when she is annoyed about something and she doesn't cool down again so quickly . . . . (Girl, LMC, Austrian)

More than a cognitive problem is involved here, however. In part, the difficulty arises because the girl is working with two antithetical texts — a positive one and a negative one.

### 5.3.2.3. *Contradictions*

Essays containing contradictory or inconsistent assertions and examples were put into this category. This kind of incoherence obviously comes from ambivalence. While the child is struggling to get the desired text down onto paper, parts of the shadow text materialize. In the following example, the ambivalence is quite transparent: contradictions both qualify positive statements and mitigate negative ones.

> My mother and I are very close, and we should be able to tell each other everything, but sometimes we cannot. We love each other very much and forgive each other no matter what happens. She doesn't always have time for me, but I know she loves me. (Girl, Anglo, U.S.)

Most immature writers have not yet mastered the technique of suppressing contradictions in writing. As a result, their writing is more likely to reveal their ambivalence than is their speech (where they have had far more experience in using guile to conceal their thoughts).

### 5.3.3. *The Category of CLICHÉS*

This category is used to register the presence of stereotypical remarks, such as "I love my mother very much," or "My mother and I are like best friends," or "Mine is the best mother in the world." Clichés usually occur at the beginning and/or end of the essay and are very strongly influenced by social and cultural norms which define an ideal mother-child relationship. Interestingly enough, ambivalent or contradictory content often follows such clichés, underscoring their superficial, stereotypical nature.

In the scope of our theoretical framework, we assume that there will be cultural differences in the definition of the parent/child relationship and that these will be reflected in the use of different clichés. It is also possible that clichés denoting the ideal relationship will differ according to sex of the child or to other sociological parameters. We are curious, as well, about the function of clichés. Do they result from the expository imperative to begin and end the essay with a generalization? Do they accompany (and mitigate) essays with ambivalent content? And does their use occur independently of the quality of the relationship with the mother?

### 5.3.4. *The Category of LENGTH*

This is the only category which is defined quantitatively: we distinguish between *short* (up to 25 clauses in the Austrian sample or 90 words in the

U.S. sample), *average* (between 25 and 40 clauses or 90 and 165 words), and *long* (more than 40 clauses or more than 166 words). Classifications were established so that 64% of the essays constituted the average, with 18% classified as short and 18% as long. We considered length because of previous sociolinguistic studies which have argued that quantity of verbal production correlates with social class (Bernstein 1970; Oevermann 1972) or sex (Swacker 1976). We hypothesize that any single sociological or psychological variable is insufficient as an explanation of differences in length. For instance, in our study the *topic* must be expected to interact with sex as a variable. Attitude or affect provides yet another dimension. The questions we phrase include the following. Do girls write more than boys on the topic "My Mother and I"? If so, is this because their relationships are more complex? If not, why not? Do girls with deeply troubled relationships write longer or shorter essays than the average? Longer or shorter essays than girls with good relationships? Although length is the simplest category to quantify, it is the least understood of those we have elected to code.

### 5.3.5.  *The Category of SEMIOTICS*

This category enables us to investigate possible differences in modes of expressiveness. Since language incorporates nonverbal as well as verbal behavior, we assume that semiotics can be used to express opinions, ideas, and feelings about a topic when a child cannot (or will not) express them verbally.

Under this category we have coded *any* visible manipulation of the graphic code: drawings, underlining, extra-large letters, arrangement of the lines on the page, extra-textual words or expressions, or even squiggles. A great variety occurred. Some children wrote poems. Some arranged prose sentences to look like poems. Some created acrostics. Some used hearts for the "O" in "LOVE." There were drawings of animals, flowers, valentines, and — in the U.S. — Pacman eating up tiny circles. Some children, feeling the need to signal the end of the essay but unable to compose a coda, wrote "The End" — indenting it to the far right of the page; or "THE END"; or "THE END!" or "THE END?"

Here again we are interested in determining whether semiotics are predictable on the basis of any socio-psychological variable. We assume that the *quality* of the relationship will determine the nature of the embellishment and that parameters like educational style or affect will determine whether or not expression will be verbal or nonverbal. We hypothesize, for example, that anxious children who draw their feelings rather than write about them may have been socialized in a repressive way. Or that boys, for whom an expression of love for their mothers may be taboo, will feel freer to express that feeling nonverbally. Or that ambivalent writers may use drawings to mitigate the negative content of an essay — or to contradict its positive statement.

### 5.3.6. *The Category of PARTICLES*

By *particles* we mean those uninflected words which qualify, mitigate, or restrict a statement in some way (German words like *eigentlich, doch, mal, eben*; English *sometimes, somewhat, actually, mostly*).[3] We are interested specifically in particles used to qualify assertions about the mother. Since revealing family secrets to strangers is taboo, some children use particles to compensate for negative essay content. The following, for example, only hints at the real chaos of the child's home — which involves a disintegrating marriage and a disorganized homelife (we have italicized the qualifications):

> On weekends she goes *somewhere*, but not *all* the time and *maybe* she will get into a fight with my dad, but she *still* loves him. (Girl, Anglo, U.S.)

Particles also betray underlying negativity, as in the following:

> My mother and I get along *pretty* good. We can share problems and she understands me *most* of the time. *In fact*, I am *very* close to my mother. I *really* like my mom a lot. We agree on things and we *hardly* ever argue. (Girl, Anglo, U.S.)

Particles used in this way demonstrate an underlying ambivalence and, thus, relate to the contradictions discussed under "Coherence" above. They are evidence of a shadow text with content quite different from that being inscribed on the paper, a text the writer is only partially suppressing.

Not all particles express ambivalence, of course. In fact, detailed studies of a variety of particles in German (Weydt 1979) have shown that *many* different pragmatic considerations govern their use. Lakoff (1975) argued that particles were a feature of female speech which indicated uncertainty and hesitancy, especially hedges (*sort of*) and intensifiers (*really*). Subsequent researchers have insisted that feelings of powerlessness constitute the independent variable accounting for their use, and since women feel powerless more often than men, women use them more often — but only in powerless situations (Kramarae 1981). Since both girls and boys in our study use qualifiers, we expect particles to be significant for our theory of Socio-Psychological Variation: their presence must be explained by factors other than sex of writer.

We hypothesize that the more unrepressed children are, and the more liberal their educational style, the more open and clear their statements will be. That means simply that the presence of mitigating particles can indicate either fear of direct expression or unresolved problems with ambivalent feelings. An essay free of particles reveals nothing about the genuine feelings of the writer. In the heat of the moment, either an angry or a loving child can write a sincere though one-sided essay about the mother, free of any ambivalence whatsoever (we have such essays). Clever writers may choose to misrepresent the situation. Mature writers are trained to delete contradictory or ambiguous material routinely from their essays. And, of course, some writers may be completely unaware of ambivalent feelings and, hence, find no need for mitigation. Because of the complexity of possible interpretations, we decided to code only the presence or absence of particles with mitigating or qualifying functions and to test their correlation with all parameters.

### 5.4. Sociological Categories

### 5.4.1. The Category of SELF-IMAGE

This category codes the image or picture of self that the child has expressed in the essay. The self-image reveals something of the relationship with the parents and of the family structure. It also tells something of the dependence or independence felt by the child. We identified three categories:

1. *Daughter or Son*: the child still sees self as dependent. Possibly strict parents, who do not allow the child much freedom, will prolong such dependency.
2. *Girl or Boy*: the child still sees self as immature, but is separated from (free of) close dependence on the parents.
3. *Adult*: the child represents self as grown-up, equal to the parents.

### 5.4.2. The Category of MOTHER ROLES

We chose subcategories naming the different roles which mothers play vis à vis their children. We assume that it is important to identify how children view their mothers — which role seems most salient to them. We expect cultural and class differences to emerge, because the roles of women are valued and estimated differently by different cultures and by different groups within a culture. We assume, also, that the quality of the mother-child relationship will influence the role foregrounded by the child.

We distinguished six major categories for the Austrian sample, with a seventh added for the American study. For statistical purposes these were combined into HOUSEWIFE (*housewife* and *wife*); MOTHER (*mother, daughter, lover*); WORKING WOMAN — and FRIEND, the latter added for the U.S. sample.

1. *Mother*: a person who supplies emotional or material nurturance to the child (love, care, gifts, emotional support), who controls the child's behavior, or who serves as teacher or model for the girl.
2. *Housewife*: woman performing household chores, providing such services as meals and clean clothing.
3. *Wife*: chosen if the child describes the parents' marriage.
4. *Daughter*: chosen if the child shows the mother interacting as a daughter with the grandmother.
5. *Lover*: chosen if the child presents the mother chiefly as a love object.
6. *Working woman*: chosen if the dominant characteristic of the description is the job of the mother.
7. *Friend*: someone who interacts with the child on an equal footing; seen as sharing in tastes, pleasures, and activities.

## 5.4.3. *The Category of SELF-ASSESSMENT*

This category supplements the category of "Self-image" and identifies the child's responses to sanctions. Three categories are identified:

1. *Obedient*: Such children do not question any obligations or sanctions from the parents. They present themselves as good children. Often such essays include rationalizations: "even if some of the restrictions are not to my taste, my parents know what is good for me." At a deep-psychological level, of course, there may be suppressed emotions beneath such utterances.
2. *Naughty*: Such children describe themselves as being naughty or disobedient, sometimes full of pity for the parents.
3. *Defiant*: Such children are angry at the restrictions imposed. Their essays describe some strategies used in fighting against those restrictions. Sometimes the stance taken by the writers involves distance and irony, as though they were confiding in a good friend, laughing about silly, unnecessary conflicts and reactions on both sides.

### 5.4.4. *The Category of EDUCATIONAL STYLE*

This category is very important from several points of view. First, we wanted to examine the relationship between educational style and ethnicity or social class (Bernstein 1970 and others have suggested that lower class homes are more repressive and that sanctions are more nonverbal than in middle class homes). Second, we wanted to test for sex-specific differences. And third, we assumed that the quality of the relationship with the mother would be influenced by the educational style, for both girls and boys.

We identified three categories:

1. *Strict*: The child mentions many sanctions and prohibitions, often unexplained.
2. *Liberal*: The child seems happy and understands the few restrictions which the parents impose. Often such children believe themselves to have a lot of freedom and the trust of their parents, and they are proud of this.
3. *Neglect*: The child complains of loneliness. Such children often feel too free and unprotected and are unhappy because nobody seems to care what they do.

### 5.4.4. *The Category of QUALITY OF SANCTIONS*

This category supplements EDUCATIONAL STYLE. We assume a repressive socialization of the child does not necessarily imply nonverbal sanctions. Often, in fact, guilt is transferred through very subtle communicative strategies. Therefore, we hypothesized that sex- or class-specific differences may occur in the quality of sanctions, and that these might influence the relationship with the mother.

1. *Verbally Explained*: The mother justifies and explains her restrictions and prohibitions. The child is able to understand and predict the intentions of the mother.
2. *Verbally Unexplained*: The mother does not explain restrictions, and the child may not understand the rationale underlying them. In such cases, the child often attempts to supply a rationalization ("We know mothers have a hard time of it, after all").
3. *Inconsistent*: This category includes examples where children describe capricious behavior from their mothers: although they are sometimes allowed to do a given thing, if the mother happens to be in a bad mood they are not.

## 5.5. Psychological Categories

### 5.5.1. The Category of MOTHER RELATIONSHIP

This is, of course, a very important category for our research, not only in itself but also as a contributor to textual categories (*particles, coherence, etc.*). We are interested in whether the relationship with the mother correlates with marital status or employment of the mother, with educational style and social sanctions, and whether negativity toward the mother shows any correlation with sex, class, or ethnicity.

Initially we distinguished seven subcategories of the relationship. In order to do a statistical analysis, these were combined into three sets: SOLIDARY (*affection, solidarity, admiration*); SEPARATE (*conflict, distance*); and ENMESHED (*rivalry*). The latter was left as a separate category because of its special importance in the development of the relationship between mothers and daughters (as one of the necessary steps toward separation).

1. *Affection*: The child writes an essay explicitly expressing affection for the mother and describing the relationship as a good one.
2. *Solidarity*: This category was assigned if the overriding impression was of a very equal relationship. The child understands whatever difficulties the mother has.
3. *Admiration*: The child admires the mother very much, without any apparent ambivalence.
4. *Rivalry*: The child admires the mother but is jealous of her and wants to outshine her.
5. *Conflict* (ambivalence): The child is full of hatred and describes a bad relationship. Although we didn't expect it, some children wrote quite openly about such relationships.
6. *Confidence*: The child confides in his/her mother. Generally an impression of solidarity with the mother is given.
7. *Distance*: The child has gone beyond anger to contempt. Such writers seem rather mature and already separated from the mother.

### 5.5.2. The Category of AFFECTIVITY

Here we coded the overall impression given by the essay of the affect and emotions of the child toward the mother.[4] We think that such an interpretation is valid since the context in which the essays were written was quite open ("Write whatever comes to mind"). Within this category we are particularly interested in exploring correlations with the quality of the mother-child relationship and the sex, class, or ethnicity of the child. The linguistic correlates interest us as well: how emotions are expressed and what textual markers correlate with what different emotional states. Although we coded five separate categories of affectivity, for the statistical analysis these were combined into two sets: one positive and one negative.

The original categories were:

1. *Hate*: The essay is full of anger and hatred toward the mother.
2. *Love*: The essay contains many expressions of affection.
3. *Guilt*: The essay is full of justifications and self-reproach. Sometimes such essays talk about the mother's problems, which are so enormous that the child does not dare approach her with her own.
4. *Jealousy*: The child is jealous of the looks or job or other qualities of the mother and may sometimes feel neglected.
5. *Fear*: The essay is full of implicit ambivalence which the child does not dare express openly. Repressive parents may produce children who are afraid to speak frankly.

### 5.5.3. *The Category of RELATIONSHIP TO THE RESEARCHER*

As the essays were written for others to read, the children knew there would be an audience. In this category we estimate what transference the child has made to the reader. Six subcategories were possible:

1. *Positive*: The child seems to confide in the researcher, writing about everything which comes to mind, with very little evidence of defense.
2. *Rationalization*: Defense mechanisms are explicit (rationalizations occur, for example), and the real feelings are hidden or mitigated.
3. *Regression*: The child writes in a very immature style, perhaps choosing only impersonal qualities of the mother. The real relationship is not discussed.
4. *Projection*: The child projects anger upon the researcher ending with questions like, *Why do you put your nose into affairs which are of no concern of yours?*
5. *Denial*: Statements are always mitigated or contradicted.
6. *Negative*: Rejection of the topic; the student writes three or four sentences, complaining that the study is "stupid."

## NOTES

1) Phelps (1980) has used "reflective prose" in a somewhat similar way.

2) This term has been borrowed from Phelps (1980), who speaks of *any* text in the writer's mind (including the one being inscribed) as a "shadow text." For clarity, we are using it here to identify only those texts that are being suppressed.

3) The word *particle* has different referents in English and in German. In English, the word currently refers to affixes or to those "preposition-like" words that combine to form separable or phrasal verbs (for example, *up*, in "Look the word up" or "Look up the word"). In German it refers to uninflected qualifiers (van Dijk 1977).

4) In Wodak 1981a,f two levels of affectivity were distinguished: emotions which were expected to occur because of the content and emotions which were actually expressed. In speech, suprasegmentals are good indicators of emotional state. In writing, it was necessary to consider the entire essay.

# 6. SOCIO-PSYCHOLOGICAL PARAMETERS OF THE
# MOTHER-DAUGHTER RELATIONSHIP. THE SPV

## 6.1. *Introduction*

We hypothesized in Chapter 2 that the mother-daughter relationship would differ significantly according to certain sociological and psychological variables within the family constellation. We assume, as well, that different qualities of the mother-child relationship will manifest themselves in language variation, yielding style ranges which can be statistically measured and will correlate with specific types of relationships. We speak of this interaction between sociological and psychological parameters and language style as SOCIO-PSYCHOLOGICAL VARIATION (SPV). Before discussing cultural SPV, we will draw together findings of our research dealing with the nature of the mother-daughter relationship, showing how these differ from those of mothers and sons.

## 6.2. *Sex-Related Socio-Psychological Variation*

As we pointed out in defining the categories to be tested, we began with two sets of parameters, one comprising sociological and one psychological variables. We give the results of our analysis below, following the same order. However, at this analytic level, we will no longer divide them into two separate categories. Since social and psychological factors interact with *all* relevant parameters and with each other, we have in each case a complex set of *Socio-Psychological Variables* (SPV).

As we began to compare the results of our research in Austria and the U.S., we were surprised at how much the two cultures differed in the degree to which sex of child influenced our findings. To underscore the significance of these differences, we will discuss the analysis of our data in two sections: first the Austrian and then the U.S. findings. Then we will point out what contributions are made by psychological, cognitive, and sociological variables.

### 6.2.1. *The SPV MOTHER ROLE*[1]

Austrian girls and boys appear to differ in the ways in which they perceive their mothers (results significant with $\alpha = 0.0001$). The roles dominating in the essays written by girls were either *mother* or *working woman*; in the boys' essays, the dominant role was *housewife* (someone performing domestic chores). If the portrait of the mother indicates the salience of the role for the child (and it should, unless the child is repressing the most important perception of the mother), the selection of a mother role reflects some of the experiences of the mother which have been most impressive to the child. Interpretation of the psychological salience of the two mother roles selected by girls is not difficult. Girls have received more nurturance, over a longer period of time than the boys, and as they approach adolescence girls are subject to more supervision and a greater number of restrictions. Thus, both aspects of the maternal role (nurturance and authority) are more relevant to the mother-child relationship for girls. What accounts for the importance of the role of the working woman? Occasionally it occurs for psychological reasons: the girl feels neglected and, therefore, is jealous of the mother's employment. But both roles also occur as a result of sociological factors. On the one hand, girls are strongly socialized to become mothers (an imperative still felt by young women in their twenties and thirties);[2] on the other, the new opportunities available to them as professional women make girls deeply conscious of the alternative roles available to them and, consequently, conscious of how their own mothers manage the professional side of their lives.

Interesting here is the traditional role of "housewife" produced by the Austrian boys, one often denigrated even by the women who fulfill it (who apologetically explain that they are "just" housewives). Like the girls, the boys are producing models related to their future expectations. Interviews with the boys in the U.S. sample revealed that they generally expect — at this point in their lives — to marry women who will stay home and keep house for them, and that is a female role that they are internalizing. Thus, our interview data show that adolescents tend to perceive their mothers in light of their future expectations for themselves or their wives. Girls see themselves as mothers and/or career women; boys see their wives as homemakers; and both notice how their own mothers perform these roles.

The difference between the perceptions of the mother-role evident in the writing of U.S. girls and boys was less significant (0.0047). There was, however, a striking difference between the Austrian and U.S. responses in general. The U.S. results required that we establish a category not used in

Vienna: "friend." In fact, "friend" was second to "mother" in the essays of both boys and girls, "housewife" and "working woman" accounting for only 4% of the mother roles in the essays.

### 6.2.2. The SPV SELF-IMAGE

Very closely related to the mother roles presented in the essays were the self-images of the girls and boys (sex-related differences were significant at the 99% level in Austria). Austrian girls perceived themselves most often as *adolescents* creating an identity for themselves outside of the home. Boys, however, presented themselves vis à vis the mother, either as *son* (thoughtlessly and passively receiving domestic services) or as *man-of-the-house* (an image appearing in essays from boys living in single parent homes, where the child has stepped into the role of the absent father). There are various possible interpretations of this difference. Their tendency to structure reality analytically may mean that boys fail to consider the mother-child relationship as a totality. Or taboos on a libidinous perception of the mother may cause the boy to maintain an objective, uninvolved public stance toward the relationship with her. The *content* of the American essays presents some support for this latter interpretation. One or two essays revealed quite clearly the working out of libidinous feelings for the mother, and several (only from the boys) expressed anxious wishes that the mother would not die[3](from a psychoanalytic perspective the latter can, of course, represent a death wish — a desire that the mother *might* die, thus ending for them the libidinal conflict). We must keep in mind, as well, that all psychoanalytical studies of adolescence (such as Blos 1962) have shown that girls mature more rapidly than boys, and that the latency period is longer for males than for females.

### 6.2.3. The SPV EDUCATIONAL STYLE AND RULES

Children in Austria and in the U.S. perceived themselves to be subject to the same types of rules and punishment, with no differences emerging on either parameter.

### 6.2.4. The SPV SELF-ASSESSMENT

In self-assessment, Austrian girls were more frequently *defiant* than the boys (0.0134). Since neither educational style nor rules showed any correlation with sex, the greater conflict and anger experienced by the girls has origins other than in these two factors. The origin is, in fact, best revealed by a *qualitative* analysis of the content of the essays. Boys complain about punishment, about school work (especially maternal responses to grades) and about their own behavior that is characterized as "naughty." In each instance, the boys have provoked the sanctions they dislike. Girls, however, complain about over-protection (especially restrictions against going to parties or having boy friends), about having to help out at home, and about not being allowed to stay up late. Their complaints are against rules imposed categorically, rules having no relationship to their behavior. Boys can, presumably, see the justice of sanctions, and can even control their enforcement by behaving well, studying hard, and so forth. Girls are helpless to manipulate the situation. If they believe the restrictions to be unnecessary, if they have brothers or older sisters who have more freedom, if they see their own mothers doing some of the things forbidden to them — all of these may exacerbate their angry belief that they are being treated unjustly. But the heightened feelings of defiance and conflict also result from the separation process which the girls are beginning to undergo at this age. They are opposing their own values to the model presented by the mother, rebelling against her hold on them, creating a new model in reaction to hers. The mother-daughter interactions, thus, are constantly complicated by the critical mind-set of the daughter at this point in her life.

Sex-linked differences did not occur in the U.S. data, another example of the tendency for American boys and girls to exhibit less marked sex-linked differences in behavior.

### 6.2.5. The SPV RELATIONSHIP WITH THE MOTHER

In the Austrian sample only boys described non-problematical relations of pure affection with their mothers, and only girls discussed the problems disturbing their relationship with her (0.0001). The rivalry and conflict between mother and daughter represent for girls a sort of mid-point between symbiosis (enmeshment) and separation (individuation), the latter being a point only few of the girls have begun to reach.

In the U.S. data, the boys expressed more ambivalence and the girls less than in the Austrian sample, so that both approached the mean. As a result, the differences between them were less, although the tendencies were in the same direction (0.0082) (see tables 8A, B).

### 6.2.6. The SPV AFFECTIVITY

The correlation between affectivity and sex of writer supports our theoretical assumptions that girls express their emotions more explicitly than boys (0.0001 in Austria; 0.0059 in the U.S.), but there is a qualitative difference, as well: boys and girls express *different* emotions. As we discuss elsewhere, girls use more linguistic forms associated with emotional response, and they use these to discuss a wider range of emotions (love, fear, guilt, hate, and jealousy). Austrian boys rarely expressed their feelings at all, and then they mentioned only positive ones (love or admiration). There are two possible reasons for their less explicit expression of feelings about their mothers: the relationship may be less problematical than it is for girls, or it may be *too* problematical (that is, tabooed). We believe the second interpretation to be highly likely in light of the seriousness for the boy of the Oedipal conflict (Freud 1931).

The pattern in the U.S. was not so intense. American girls reveal less negativity, perhaps because they experience less repression at home and school, or because of the "happy family" ideal of the American culture (we discuss this more fully in the cross-cultural comparison below).

## 6.2.7. *The SPV RELATIONSHIP TO THE RESEARCHER*

In Austria, on the measure of transference toward the researcher (as either a *confidant* or an *enemy*), boys viewed the female researcher more positively than did the girls (0.0016). Perhaps a mother-transference accounted for some of the greater negativity of the Austrian girls.

No significant difference in transference occurred in the American sample. The children are accustomed to psychological tests and inquiries (in one of the classrooms, the first American girl interviewed greeted the interviewer rather proudly with, "I'm usually picked first for these things"). American children may feel less need to confide in strangers (an open relationship with one's parents is a feature of the ideal American family). And they may feel stress less because they are more immature. Lynn (1979), citing Kagan and Moss's study of maturation, reports that "Relative independence from parents, such as seeking advice from people outside the family, is a sign that the tie to the parents is being severed" (1962). Failure to confide may reveal the opposite: a close, continuing parental bond. For whatever reason, American children revealed less ambivalence than did Austrians.

As for the strategies being used, Austrian girls tended to regress or rationalize and boys, to project, or identify with the aggressor (0.0016; no difference in the U.S.). The degree of rationalization found here, correlating so strongly with the females, may result from taboos surrounding the ideologies involved in motherhood. The girl who writes, "I hate it when my mother makes me clean my room, *although* I know it is for my own good" is indirectly expressing guilt at her anger. The girl who writes "I sometimes get really mad at my mother, but I *still* love her" is assuring the reader that she stops short of the absolute taboo: hatred.

### 6.3. *Cultural Differences in Socio-Psychological Variation*

We have, to this point, related our findings solely to sex and gender, since this is the data important to our study. However, we will list below some of the findings related to two other cultural parameters tested in the course of our research: social class and ethnicity.

### 6.3.1. *Social Class and Ethnicity*

The *class* and *ethnicity* variables correlated with little in our study. This is, in part, to be expected given the topic investigated. We have hypothesized that the mother-daughter relationship evokes conflicts, irrespective of class or culture, because of inherent psychological factors involved in the relationship. Neither psychological factors of the mother-child relationship (such as affectivity or self-assessment) nor sociological factors of the home environment (such as educational style) correlated with social class in the Austrian sample. Variables in the specific family situation (mother personality, position among siblings, relationship between parents, etc.) proved to be more influential than social class. In fact, the only variable showing a strong correlation with social class was "Relationship to the Researcher." Austrian working class children had a more positive attitude toward her than did middle class children (0.0004).

In analyzing school populations in the U.S., we realized that socio-psychological variables complicated the isolation of influences resulting from ethnicity. In one school, which has a sizable Chicano population, the affectivity of boys was significantly more positive than in any other school. In fact, no boys at all in that school wrote negatively about their mothers, whether their ethnicity was Chicano or not. Since ethnicity is the sociological parameter on which this school differs from all others in our study, we assume that ethnicity is an important factor accounting for the difference. In this school, Mexican-American family values appear to have become the norm to which the school population conforms (or claims to conform).

## 6.4. *A Socio-Psychological Theory of Text Planning (SPTT)*

### 6.4.1. *Sex and the SPTT - Macrotextual Level*

#### 6.4.1.1. *The Textual Variable TEXT TYPE*

Sex of writer clearly affected the text types produced by the children in our sample. The Austrian girls wrote *reflective* essays exclusively, while the boys tended to write *unreflective* ones (0.0001). U.S. girls produced more essays of the *reflective* category than boys (significant with $\alpha = 0.0002$), but both kinds of essays were written by both sexes (see tables 9A, B).

Three kinds of factors — psychological, sociological, and cognitive — account for the differences in the type of text of the essays produced by girls and boys. First, the topic ("My Mother and I") clearly triggered different psychological responses from the two sexes, resulting in different material content from each. Boys and girls experience their mothers differently, as we pointed out in Chapter 2, and these differences are reflected in the degree of involvement with the topic our children demonstrated and in the kinds of feelings it evoked. The relationship between text type and affect in the U.S. data is significant at the 99% level, and with the relationship to the mother also at the 99% level (*negativity* on either parameter corresponding to the production of *reflective* texts). Since boys achieve individuation with less conflict, they tend to write at a more superficial level, with more emotional distance, listing events occurring during a typical day without having searched those events for any particular meaning (see discussion of episodic and semantic knowledge above). Girls have not achieved such an easy separation; they are still deeply involved with their mothers emotionally and are concerned with the problems that frustrate their desire for a combination of individuation from and solidarity with the mother. Their emotional responses are more complex. In addition to simple feelings of love or hatred, they express conflicting emotions of admiration, fear, guilt, jealousy and hatred. Their essays explore these feelings and relate them one to another, yielding generally a reflective text type organized around an evaluation of the mother-daughter relationship.

Sociological factors also contribute to the differences found. In the U.S. sample, choice of text type related to factors evolving within the family interaction. Children who presented themselves as naughty or defiant tended to write reflective essays (self-characterization was significant with $\alpha = 0.0011$ in the U.S.). Self-image was also related to Text Type (0.0001). Writers who pictured themselves as either children or adults (rather than as sons or daughters) wrote reflective essays, suggesting that those who were struggling for separation were led to focus upon the relationship at this point in their lives. The quality of the sanctions used in the home were focal in reflective texts (with $\alpha = 0.0003$). An additional factor — one difficult to measure — probably influenced the tendency of Austrian boys to avoid reflective essays: taboos surrounding the open expression of feelings by boys. Boys more than girls are constrained to suppress any display of such emotions as love, fear, and grief. Because it lacks a thematic statement about the topic (mother and self), the unreflective essay provides boys with an objective form in which to produce their essays.

Another factor accounting for sex-linked differences in the essays is the cognitive response of the child. It is clear from the content that the mother-child relationship is a subject about which the girls — especially the Austrian girls — have already thought a great deal. They have developed a perception of their interactions with their mothers, one that has helped them to organize the experiences occurring in their daily lives. None of them produced unreflective essays, though most of the Austrian boys did. This reflects different cognitive strategies used in responding to social interaction and, in this case specifically, to mother-child interaction. The essays demonstrate that girls, more than boys, examine such experiences and evaluate them before storing them in memory. Or, to use Tulving's terminology, girls tend to store social interaction events in memory as *semantic* knowledge and boys, as *episodic* knowledge. Semantic storage is, of course, a circular process. Once an experience has been coded with meaning, that semantic category exists in memory and new experiences are searched for evidence of it (this is the way prejudices shape our interpretation of new experiences).

It is precisely here that we begin to see the cognitive effects and the linguistic consequences of the different kinds of socialization observed in Chapter 3. The mother's early, intense social interaction with the daughter assures that certain qualities of that interaction will have great salience for the girl, thus contributing to the development in the girl of evaluative, semantically stored knowledge of social experiences. For boys, social interaction is not so important; other aspects of their experience with the mother presumably have more significance for them (our discussion of clichés will demonstrate what some of these aspects may be). Related to the different cognitive responses to experience of the mother are the different cognitive strategies evolved by girls and boys: the *gestalt* (female) and the *analytic* (male) approaches to processing reality. Gestalt patterns are expressive and evaluative; analytic are causal and temporal. Gestalt patterns are subjective; analytic are objective. Again, our essays give evidence of just such types of response to a topic — even to a very subjective one: Girls wrote subjective, expressive, evaluative essays; boys wrote analytical, objective ones.

### 6.4.2. *Sex and the SPTT - Microtextual Level*

Several elements at a micro-linguistic level of the text correlate with the sex of the writer. We were curious to identify them and to discover what additional socio-psychological factors predict their presence. We have elected to analyze *coherence, clichés, length, semiotics,* and *particles* in terms of the SPTT (our Socio-Psychological Theory of Text Planning).

### 6.4.2.1. *The Textual Variable COHERENCE*

The essays written by Austrian girls exhibited more ruptures of logic and more contradictions than did those written by the boys (0.00001). As we pointed out in the definition of the category "Coherence," this does not reflect a greater logicality in the writing of boys. (There was no sex-linked difference in coherence in the essays from U.S. boys and girls.) Several other factors contributed to the findings. The first is text type (significant with $\alpha = 0.0001$ in the U.S. sample). Questions of logic do not arise in the unreflective presentation of episodic experience. Events are sometimes presented in chronological order (a recital of events occurring during a typical day) or are linked by chance associations of time, place, or participants. But since no interpretation is forced upon them from the outside and no hierarchical or causal organizational pattern is superimposed upon them, they require no manipulation by the writer. They are neither coherent nor incoherent. They are simply reproduced with their associative links.

In reflective essays, on the other hand, events are generally selected with an eye to illustrating or justifying a central thesis being explored and supported by the writer. In such a case, experiences which are reported must, in addition to their natural connection of time, place, or participants, also share a common meaning. Thus, the writer is manipulating two dimensions instead of one: selecting experiences with a common experiential content and arranging them so that they convey to the reader the same generalized meaning they have for the writer. Since we hypothesize that girls are dealing with richer and more problematical shadow texts than boys — that the nucleus of antithetical experience evoked by the retrieval of emotion-laden material is greater for girls — cognitive and psychological factors explain much of the correlation between coherence and sex found in our study.

Psychological factors influenced coherence, as well. Affect was significant at the 99% level in the U.S. (negative affect correlating with incoherence). School was also significant at the 99% level in the U.S., a finding which suggests that the cognitive problems of writing are being solved with different degrees of success in different classrooms.

### 6.4.2.2. *The Textual Variable CLICHÉS*

We identify as "cliché" any sentiment repeatedly expressed in the essay sample. To an extent, the expository text form invites the use of clichés, since its three-part schema requires an opening and closing generalization. For convenience of reference, we have labeled the three parts of the expository schema as follows:[4]

1. THE ABSTRACT--one or two sentences which orient the reader to the material to follow (U.S. teachers speak of the *topic sentence*, which serves to focus the reader's attention both on the topic to be explored and on the writer's point of view toward the topic). In our essays, the abstract was generally a statement about the child's relationship with the mother.

2. THE DEVELOPMENT--the exposition itself, which explicitly develops the writer's attitude, belief or claim about the topic.

3. THE CODA--one or two sentences which signal that the essay is at an end (also called *the conclusion*).

It is to be expected that immature writers, faced with the need to write an abstract and a coda, will produce clichés. The topic ("mother"), too, elicits clichés. In both cultures, it is laden with prescriptions, proscriptions, ideology and sentiment that have found their way into clichés about *mother, mother love, motherhood,* etc. When we established the category, we expected to find a rich abundance of clichés in the essay content, and we did. What we were not prepared to find was the high degree of cultural specificity in the pattern of their use *and* in their content which unfolded in our data.

Austrian girls used more clichés than boys (0.0008), a sex-linked difference resulting in part from the reflective essay format. The decision to write a poem also led children into cliché use — so much so, in fact, that we eliminated poems from our quantitative analysis (there were two in the Austrian and twelve in the U.S. sample). But there are sociological and psychological factors influencing their use, as well, since the essays by American boys, too, tended to be unreflective, but their cliché use was similar to that of the girls. Since cliché use correlated with incoherence in our essays (0.0141), and incoherence was one of the textual markers of suppressed negative feelings, positive clichés may well have occurred in some essays to mitigate negative content. This was transparent in the Austrian essays, where girls who wrote negatively or ambivalently about their mothers often began and/or ended their essays with highly positive clichés. Cliches also provide a satisfactory alternative to honestly discussing the topic, providing refuge to children who felt uncomfortable making private information public (several Austrian children ended their essays with sentences like "These are family affairs" or "Why are you poking your nose into private matters?").

No sex-linked differences in the number or type of clichés occurred in the U.S. essays. In part this occurred because the boys wrote a larger percentage of reflective essays than did Austrian boys, and in the U.S. data, reflective text type tended to correlate with the use of clichés (0.0018).

It is impossible to convey, on the basis of our statistics, the nature or magnitude of the difference in use of clichés by the Austrian and the American students, since we counted only the presence or absence of clichés, and not the number of them per essay. It was in this latter quantity that the U.S. sample far exceeded the Austrian one. Clichés accounted for the majority of the abstracts and codas in the U.S. essays, as expected, but they accounted for a substantial portion of the content of the exposition, as well. Some essays consisted almost entirely of clichés (see Essay C at the end of this chapter).

This was not the case in the Austrian essays. The opening and closing clichés were often only vaguely related to the expository content, which was generally a thoughtful rendering of the student's own experience for which the clichés served a cosmetic function — to mask ambivalent content.

The kinds of clichés used in the two cultures also differed. Austrian girls usually favored clichés stressing trust, understanding, and companionship, and they phrased them in personal terms ("I love my mother very much and am glad to have such a nice mother"). Boys more than girls focus either on the mother ("My mother is very nice") or on an abstraction ("The relationship between me and my mother is very good").

The sex-linked differences in quality were less in the U.S. study (as is true on most of the parameters of our study). Both boys and girls used clichés laden with affect ("My mother and I are very close" or "Me and my mom are very good friends"). They cited different kinds of nurturance, however. Girls frequently mention physical or psychological nurturance ("She takes care of me when I am sick" or "I can tell my mom everything and she will understand"). Boys are more likely to stress material nurturance ("My mom is nice to me because she always buys me what I want" or "She gives me money whenever I need it").

A profound contrast between the cultures occurred in one large cluster of clichés found in the U.S. but not the Austrian essays: "My mom is my best friend" or "Me and my mom are very good friends"). Both boys and girls in the American sample produced this cliché (although more girls did than boys), and it reflects an ideology present in the American but not the Austrian culture: *Be a pal to your kid*. Related clichés of shared pleasures ("We play games together" or "We go to the movies and make each other laugh") stress the equality of the relationship between mother and child, an equality especially valued by the girls, who say "We like to clean the house together" (versus "I try to help her around the house" from the boys) and "We have the same tastes" or "We tell each other everything" (said by the girls, but not the boys).

### 6.4.2.3. *The Textual Variable LENGTH*

We elected to compare length of essay with sex of writer because of the interest feminist linguistic studies have demonstrated in sex-related quantitative differences of verbosity. Women, according to folklore, are more verbose than men; empirical research, however, has failed to find evidence that this is actually the case. Consequently, we decided to consider length as one of the variables that might be determined by sex of writer.

Our findings surprised us. We rather expected, given the topic, that girls would write more than boys, but this was not precisely the case. In Austria, although girls tended to write both the longest and the shortest essays, no significant correlation with sex was found. The correlation of sex with length was 0.0001 in the U.S. sample, but it is difficult to determine how directly the U.S. finding derives from the sex of the writer. The factors influencing length are complex, extending beyond our parameters. The topic certainly is a factor, since girls are more involved with their mothers than boys. This alone might account for the longer essays being written by the girls. Affect was also a factor (significant at the 99% level in the U.S., longer essays correlating with negative affect). Girls in Austria tended to write short essays when there was a serious, unresolved problem with the mother, but this did not occur in the U.S. sample. And a large number of the short essays from Austrian boys came from a single school, where the boys were undisciplined and knew they could get away with misbehavior. Their essays were shorter, in general, and some boys wrote jokes or essays so silly or incomprehensible that they had to be excluded from the study.

### 6.4.2.4. *The Textual Variable SEMIOTICS*

We expected boys to use semiotics as an outlet for expressivity more than girls, since boys are socialized to suppress the verbalization of affect (see discussion in Chapter 3). This did occur in the Austrian sample (significand with $\alpha = 0.0149$), but there was no significant difference in the U.S. (another instance of less sex-linked differentiation in the U.S. sample). There *was*, however, a tendency (with $\alpha = 0.0944$) for ethnicity to correlate with use of semiotics, one which supports our hypothesis that semiotics substitute for verbal expressiveness. In our study Chicano males, as well as females, tended to express positive affect for the mother openly. On the other hand, only one Chicano in our study used semiotics. The more significant variable in the U.S. was school (0.0075), with more than one-third of the U.S. essays containing semiotics coming from a single classroom (in the Magnet School, where independence and originality are encouraged).

### 6.4.2.5. *The Textual Variable PARTICLES*

As we have said, in their essays the girls confront the problems they experience with their mothers more frankly than do the boys. It might be expected, therefore, that their essays — which are chiefly reflective in text type — would show other signs of the tension felt between what society suggests that a "good" daughter should feel toward her mother and what the writer actually does feel, and that this tension would be reflected within the text by linguistic markers.

This is, in fact, the case. In the essays one finds both positive remarks which are qualified or limited in some way by negative particles ("My mother and I *sometimes* get along very well"), as well as negative remarks immediately followed by positive disclaimers ("*Nevertheless*, my mother and I are good friends"). Since the content of the girls' essays is expected to be more ambivalent than that of the boys, and particles signify ambivalence, we expected a correlation between the use of particles and the sex of the writer; that is, in fact, what we found (at the 99% level). The correlation was significant in Austria, but in the U.S. it was only a tendency (significant with $\alpha = 0.0311$), whereas affect was a much stronger influence (0.0001). We had expected that particles would correlate with text type, as well, and they did in the Austrian data (0.0001). Again, in the U.S. sample there was only a tendency (0.0144).

### 6.5. *Conclusions about Gender and the SPTT*

The sex of the child has been our most important variable, since it is precisely because mother and daughter are of the same sex that their relationship acquires specific characteristics, differentiating it from others. Although we have shown that sex of writer relates to characteristics of the text produced, we do not believe that it is possible to hypothesize that girls will, as a general rule, write more reflective texts, use more particles or adjectives, or write more clichés than boys. Quite the contrary. We argue that the presence of these indicators results from a highly complex constellation of factors: sex of writer, topic, societal norms, cognitive approach to the material, and so forth — social and psychological factors that interact to produce the variations found in text types and in language behavior. Our findings demonstrate that sex, as a variable, depends strongly upon both psychological and sociological variables for its effect. The appropriate label for that constellation of sex with socio-biological factors is, of course, *gender* (Thorne 1981). We have discovered quite different gender-role patterns in Austria and the U.S. In the U.S., there is less differentiation evident than in Austria, where traditional patterns of sex-linked behavior remain strong. Girls and boys tend to be more alike on almost all parameters. Many factors contribute to the lower gender-role distinctions in the U.S.: the impact of feminism; equal opportunity legislation, which includes laws against differentiated treatment of children, depending upon their sex; and the general movement in the U.S. toward unisex clothing, patterns of behavior and mores, a movement felt especially strongly in a large urban center like Los Angeles.

### 6.6. *Essay Analysis*

The singularity of our essays disappears in a quantitative analysis. Unfortunately, one is obliged in a quantitative study to settle upon a single predominant feature in coding the essay, and as a result its actual complexity is considerably reduced. We provide the following qualitative analyses of typical texts in order to demonstrate the types of texts produced and to provide illustrations of the categories analyzed.

### 6.6.1. *Essay A - Austrian Girl*

This essay was written by an Austrian girl, LMC, 13 years old; no siblings; mother divorced, at work all day; daughter goes to day care center after school; has career ambitions; does not feel at a disadvantage because of her sex.

### My Mother and I

Unfortunately my mother is an unbearable Virgo by the zodiac. When she sees a spot she goes completely crazy. But when I get a bad mark in a test she is very sympathetic. I wanted a dog for three years. In the fourth year I got one. She can also be really furious when she is annoyed about something and she doesn't cool down again so quickly.

When she does the weekly cleaning on Saturday she curses because of a little work. Then if I ask her something she shouts at me 'HELP ME INSTEAD!' I really like helping my mother with the housework, but only when I feel like it. On TV I can watch almost anything I like and my mother is also very generous with pocket money. I get 100 shillings as pocket money. If I had a boyfriend she would fly into a rage. But otherwise we get on very well.
STOP! (The rest is a family matter.)

Essay A is a reflective essay, in which several characteristics of the mother are described and evaluated. It consists of a loose sequence of brief examples of everyday life and behavior. There are two mother roles in the foreground: the housewife and the authoritarian mother. As a result of the mother's strictness, her daughter is afraid to rebel. She would like to have a boyfriend, but then the mother would really fly into a rage. The effect of this kind of up-bringing and of the quality of the restraints used is quite obvious in the mother-daughter relationship described here. With many single mothers, a good mother-daughter relationship develops out of solidarity — as a result of the girl's feeling that she is necessary to the mother (see discussion of Essay C, below). In this example, however, the mother is too restrictive and the restraints are not sufficiently explained for the relationship and the conflict of separation to be assimilated and developed positively. As a result, the child's relationship with the mother is marred by conflicts and ambivalence, the predominant emotions being anger, fear, and even disappointment (expressed in the example of the dog for which the child longed). Only two of the mother's traits are positively evaluated (she does not criticize the daughter's exam results and she provides lots of pocket money). Otherwise, the impression evoked is that of a very impatient, explosive, overtaxed woman whose daughter is afraid of her.

The opening is especially interesting. Originally, the text began with the characterization of the mother as an unbearable "*Jungfrau*" (*Jungfrau* is used in German for both "virgin" and "Virgo"). The words "by the zodiac" were added afterwards, eliminating the ambiguity. This indicates a particularly repressive attitude on the mother's part; it is certainly connected with the sentence, "If I had a boyfriend . . . "; and it contrasts sharply with the end of the text ("But otherwise we got on very well").

The coherence is correspondingly characterized by ambiguity and contradiction: no theme is dealt with in detail, the good characteristics appear suddenly in the overall context; the child's ambivalence can be strongly felt. The mother's "thing" about cleaning seems to be focal to the daughter (other restrictions are only indicated). The final sentence, "But otherwise we get on very well together," provides a very good example of the use of a stereotypical cliché designed to mitigate the content of the essay. But even this is retracted by the last expression in parentheses ("The rest is a family matter"). The attitude toward the researcher is, similarly, contradictory. On the one hand, the writer regards the researcher as a confidant (the essay discusses the mother-daughter relationship with astonishing frankness), and on the other the relationship is marked by fear ("STOP!"), and the researcher is regarded as meddling in the child's private life. The interview with this girl was characterized by much stronger resistance than is the essay: the girl did not dare describe her relationship with the mother as frankly in speech as in writing.

The essay is short as a result of the writer's failure to go into detail, but it is extremely expressive. The evaluation is made principally by the use of adjectives and emotionally charged verbs *unbearable, crazy, annoyed, curses*). The girl used crayons to write, beginning each paragraph with a different color. In the margin she drew a flower, which appears to mitigate the negative content of the essay. Even the use of block capitals has its own expressive function. "HELP ME INSTEAD!" can be construed as an appeal to the interviewer, as can "STOP!" This makes clear to the reader that she could write a great deal more, but she has elected to stop (the rest being a family matter).

### 6.6.2. *Essay B - Austrian Boy*

This essay was written by an Austrian boy, LMC, 13 years old, youngest child; mother married, homemaker.

#### My Mother and I

> I get up at about 7 o'clock and my mother makes me my breakfast. Afterwards she makes my bed and I get washed and then go to school. In the meantime, my mother goes shopping and makes lunch. At 1 o'clock I come home and eat (lunch). Then I do my homework and afterwards I help my mother in the kitchen. After that I go to the park with a friend. My mother reads or sews something. Then when I come home from the park I

play with my mother, and afterwards there's dinner. After dinner I study with my mother, then I watch TV, and after TV I go to bed. After that my mother washes the dishes and then she also goes to bed.

In this essay the text type is quite obvious. It is unreflective, an episodic description of everyday life. The text describes the course of a day which, as it were, is taken as representative of the relationship to the child's mother. However, the relationship is not mentioned at all, and there are no evaluations of the mother in the essay.

The text is short and is coherently presented, chronologically organized from the moment of getting up in the morning to that of going to bed at night. It is lacking in clichés or semiotic expressivity, and feelings are avoided completely. There are neither adjectives nor particles which might indicate an underlying evaluation or a metacommunicative intention. The mother appears solely in the role of a housewife: she cooks, goes shopping, sews, and is there for the children when they need her. It is precisely such descriptions that convey, on the one hand, an impression of unproblematical attachment to the mother and, on the other, one of a total repression of feeling or inability to regard the mother as anything other than a housewife.

The boy's self-evaluation and self-image project the impression of a good son (he helps in the kitchen) in a household without conflicts or quarrels. The type of up-bringing and the restrictions imposed are rather more liberal than those mentioned in essay A: the child is allowed to go to the park and play and to watch TV. There is apparently nothing which matters much to him which he is forbidden to do.

### 6.6.2.1. *Comparison of Austrian Essays A and B*

Although both texts appear to be extremely different, they can be regarded as typical of the general differences occurring in the writing of Austrian boys and girls. Not one girl wrote a neutral essay of the type in Essay B, and only a few boys wrote reflective essays. Also clear are differences in the relationship to the mother (which was unproblematical — or suppressed — for most of the boys) and in the expression of emotions (girls revealed more awareness of and ability to verbalize their emotions).

The greater maturity of girls at this age was also evident in our essays. Boys were able to reflect upon their relationships with their mothers only if they had had traumatic experiences to deal with (such as the divorce of the parents or the death of one parent). Otherwise, their essays revealed an unexamined acceptance of the nurturance of the mother as something to be taken as a matter of course.

### 6.6.3.  *Essay C – U.S. Girl*

This essay was written by an American girl, Jewish, 12 years old; one younger brother; mother, divorced, works as school teacher; cared for by a housekeeper after school; wants to be an actress; does not want to marry, but wants children (perhaps by adoption).

> My mother and I have a very good relationship. We talk together and share our feelings together. We help each other out with criticism and with compliments. We are very close. We are closer than my dad "is" to me or my brother. My mother and I act as "one." We have a serious relationship, but we joke about "life" (for example, divorce, money, time). But don't think that we are perfect, because we are not. We have fights. Fear raising fights. But we always make up. I think we make up because, not for the reason that we are mother and daughter, but for the reason that we are friends — best friends. She is my best friend. Someone I can trust. Someone that understands. Someone that is fun to be with, someone that I can "spill my guts" with, and someone that I can love and know that she loves me as a best friend and a daughter. I truly believe that my mom and I will remain friends forever and ever and ever. Just like a fairytale — one that has a very good ending.

There is a sharp contrast, here, between the quality of the writing and the quality of the content. The writer has some difficulty with cohesive devices (she uses *but* repeatly, for instance, and has trouble with the sequence "I think we make up because, not for the reason that . . . ." But she handles parallel constructions with ease — the sequence of phrases beginning with *Someone*, for instance, and the even more difficult construction "not for the reason . . . but for the reason." By exploring possibilities provided by the conventions of written prose, this girl produces an essay with some individuality (including her attempts to use quotation marks for emphasis).

On the other hand, she does not explore the thesis idea with any originality at all. Her essay illustrates the clichéd content prevalent in the U.S. sample. The only sentences bearing exclusively upon the writer's own situation are the contrast of her relationship with her mother, her father, and her brother; the insistence that she and her mother have a serious relationship; the mention of the things they joke about; and the reference to "fear raising fights." Otherwise, the essay comprises generalizations that occur repeatedly in the texts written by U.S. children (by both boys and girls): the relationship is good; mother and daughter share their feelings; they help each other; they are very close; they are best friends; there is trust and understanding between them; they have fun together; and they will remain friends forever. All of these generalizations recur throughout the U.S. sample, often being phrased in identical words. In several ways the girl acknowledges (or hints at) her awareness that all of this is too good to be true. First, she warns the reader, "But don't think that we are perfect, because we are not." She exaggerates "my mom and I will remain friends forever" into "my mom and I will remain friends forever and ever and ever." She puts quotation marks around such clichés as "My mother and I act as 'one'" and "someone I can 'spill my guts' with" (a method immature writers often use to acknowledge that they are quoting clichés). And she concludes with an admission that all of this is "Just like a fairytale — one that has a very good ending."

Also typical of the essays written by girls in the U.S. is the symbiosis still evident in the relationship between this writer and her mother. The essay focuses almost solely on the closeness of the mother-daughter dyad; neither the mother nor the daughter is described separately, and the only reference to other people occurs in the comparison with father and brother. On the other hand, a symbiotic dependency is not acknowledged at all. Quite the contrary occurs. The girl emphasizes throughout the equality felt by mother and daughter. They joke together about adult topics (divorce, money, and time); they share feelings; they help each other; the girl enjoys a reciprocal right to criticize or compliment her mother; and at one point the girl explicitly attributes their closeness to the fact that they are friends, not that they are mother and daughter. In fact, she protests too much: five times in this short essay she asserts that she and her mother are "friends," "best friends," or "friends forever and ever." But she has, in fact, written a fairytale for the reader.

One consequence of the superficial content is that no clear picture of the mother emerges. In Essay A, written by the Austrian girl, we see a mother refusing something the daughter wants, giving in later, losing her temper — in short, interacting with her daughter. The daughter's fear of her mother is, at least, well motivated. In Essay C, the mother remains a shadowy figure of near-perfection, and the only clue that the girl has ambivalent feelings occurs in the sequence "We have fights. Fear raising fights." By setting off "Fear raising fights" as a fragment, the girl supplies it with rhetorical emphasis that seems intuitively appropriate: it stands out, but it also stands alone. There is no context supplied which accounts for the fear. Ambivalence remains an unexplored emotion in the essay, just as it may in this girl's life. (U.S. girls contrasted strikingly with Austrian in the lesser extent to which they explicitly acknowledge negative affect in the mother-daughter relationship.)

### 6.6.4. *Essay D - U.S. Boy*

This essay was written by a boy, U.S., Chicano, 12 years old, oldest child; mother married, homemaker.

> My mother is a very nice person to me, because she always buys me all kinds of things. Like last year in baseball season, I really wanted a baseball glove. Then about a week later, she came home from shopping with a white bag. Then I opened it and there it was — a brand new glove. And whenever she goes to the grocery store, she takes me with her and she gives me money whenever I need it, like when my friends are going to the show, I just tell my mother to give me some money and she gladly does. She also cares about me, because every time I take my math book home, she tells me to do my homework, and when it is report card time, she asks me if I got any F, and whatever that F is on, she tells me that by next report card, if it gets better, up to a C or a B, she tells me she will give me a surprise. And she is also a very good cook, especially when she makes enchiladas for dinner. I love her enchiladas because she makes them so good. And for Christmas she gets me the things she thinks I would like the most. For example, the year before this one, I used to see the racetracks, and when it came to opening my presents, I saw a big box, and it was mine, so I opened it, and there was a racetrack. And she helped me build it right away, and I still have that racetrack. I always play with it. And she takes us to restaurants, and on our vacation she even sent us to Mexico with our grandmother, because we wanted to see her so much, and we were over there for about a month-and-a-half, and when we came back, I brought her a beautiful sweater that I bought over there.

This essay is longer than the average, but it is typical in other ways of the style and content of essays written by American boys. Although it lacks a coda (rather typical of the U.S. essays), it is reflective: it comments upon the mother and provides illustrative support of the opening generalization. But it is strongly narrative, as well, consisting of a sequence of minimal narratives used to illustrate the nice things his mother does for him.

The abstract ("My mother is a very nice person to me") contains an evaluation of the mother typical of the essays written by boys in the U.S.: the mother is judged not in terms of her interaction with him, but in terms of what she does to please him. The role presented here is of the nurturant mother, and what is interesting is the series of details he has selected. The activities he values include her buying him things he really wants, giving him money when he wants it, supervising his homework, cooking his favorite foods, helping him build a toy racetrack, taking him to restaurants, and sending him on vacations. At no time does the boy mention the reciprocal feelings which are part of their relationship. In the one activity which they share (the building of the racetrack) he does not make clear whether it was the assistance she gave or the fact that they enjoyed the track together that had salience for him. Nor does he reveal his feelings for her; they are only implied. In the final sentence he reveals only indirectly something of his feelings for his mother ("when we came back, I brought her a beautiful sweater that I bought over there").

### 6.6.4.1. *Comparison of U.S. Essays C and D*

As we have said, sex-linked differences were not as evident in the U.S. data as they were in the Austrian. Nevertheless, distinctions were evident. These two texts typify the kinds of similarities and differences that occurred in the writing of American girls and boys. Both tended to write reflective essays (unlike the Austrian children); however girls tended to focus more directly on the relationship than did boys, who rather rated the mother in terms of her approach to an abstract model of motherhood (one went so far as to give her a numerical rating: "eight-and-a-half or nine out of a possible ten").

### 6.6.5. *Comparison of Austrian and U.S. Texts*

The essays written by the two girls exemplify the differences in maturity evident in the data obtained from the two cultures. Although both girls have written reflective texts, the American girl does not examine the topic as honestly as does the Austrian girl. In fact, her essay contains some evidence that she may be repressing ambivalence about her mother (fights are to be feared and to be made up; mother and daughter are to remain friends "forever and ever and ever"). Austrian girls focus upon their struggles with their mothers; American girls attempt to make them peripheral, focusing instead on their solidarity with the mother. (We will discuss the possible consequences of this finding in our Concluding Remarks.) Boys in both cultures expressed fewer emotions and wrote with more objectivity and distance than girls (the boys in Essays B and D hardly appear at all, for instance, except as recipients of nurturance from their mothers).

Another strong cultural difference between the essays of Austrian and U.S. children is illustrated by Essay D. There is an astonishing focus upon automobiles and upon material values in the American data. Typical shared activities cited in essays written in Los Angeles include driving to the market, driving to a shopping mall, driving to a restaurant, going for a drive in order to have a heart-to-heart talk, driving to visit relatives, and being driven to the houses of friends — it is clear from the essays that Los Angeles families spend a lot of time together in their automobiles. Even more striking is the number of references to the mother spending money on things for the child (treats, restaurant meals, clothing, toys, tickets to amusement parks and movies, and money for arcade games). American children often expressed guilt at receiving things from their mothers that they didn't deserve. Nevertheless, one boy's blunt statement rather frankly displays a covert evaluation appearing in various guises throughout the U.S. essays: "My mom is a very nice lady. She gives me everything I want" (CNR1218). Essay A demonstrates that Austrian children, too, evaluate their mothers in material terms (the girl resents being denied a dog and cites as positive the amount of pocket money she is given). But a comparison of Essay A and Essay D illustrates the difference in *degree* that was evident to us as we read the two sets of essays. If Austrian children value material nurturance from their mothers, American girls and boys revel in it, and some of the American boys cited nothing else as being of value in their mother's behavior.

### 6.7. *Influence of the Schools - Vienna and Los Angeles*

The schools in both cities exert strong influences upon the attitudes and beliefs of their students, despite what seem to be profound external differences. In Vienna, schools are authoritarian and conservative. The progressive impulses in education which died out in the thirties and forties have not yet returned to any significant degree (although resurgence is under way), and strong links remain between the schools and the Catholic Church. For a variety of reasons, the schools tend to perpetuate the class system, although they have been dedicated to the ideal of providing an equal opportunity for everyone since the late sixties. Linguistic variety continues to identify and to reinforce class differences. In addition to the financial situation of the parents and the impressionistic assumption of the teacher, language is one of the indicators used in streaming children. Furthermore, those who enter the universities do not join a vital intellectual and artistic world upon graduation. If they remain in Austria, they join a culture which sustains and is sustained by the achievements of the past.

Schools in the U.S. are more relaxed (extending to the freedom of the open classrooms in the magnet school). The social system is — in theory — an open one. People do overcome limitations imposed by race, language, or social origins to a degree unimaginable in Vienna (although thousands are as securely fixed within the stratification of the U.S. system as are the Viennese). A substantial number of Americans believe that they can create a place for themselves within the system. Generally, Viennese expect to *find* a place already defined for them and to slip into it (albeit with much more security and greater social welfare benefits than are available to most workers in the U.S.).

The effects of the two school systems differ accordingly. The Viennese schools perpetuate a well-established tradition and provide the means whereby students can find a place within it. The U.S. schools respond to a greater degree of diversity in student population and they tend to level to a common value system generated by the local cultural majority, rather than by the social or educational traditions of the country at large. Given the diversity of the American population, especially in cities like Los Angeles which are still receiving large numbers of immigrants annually and where a school can have a yearly transient rate of 25%, schools cannot hope to generate a national norm.

We are not surprised to find that schools correlated with many of our psycho-sociological variables in Vienna. In that city neighborhoods are stable; schools are socially stratified; and, consequently, schools, neighborhoods and families form a sort of stable, homogeneous pattern which perpetuates specific kinds of values and achievements (see Tables 2a, c, 3a showing correlation between school type, sex and class in Vienna). We *were* surprised to find the same kind of correlation in Los Angeles. One of our schools comprises roughly 75% Chicano, 15% Anglo, and 10% other. One school is roughly 40% Black and 40% Jewish. One is a new school, opened within the last few years, drawing students from neighborhoods as far as two hours away. Nevertheless, the same sort of correlation between school and socio-psychological variables occurs in Los Angeles as is found in Vienna. This occurs, we believe, because the schools have — to some extent — replaced the functions which used to be fulfilled by family networks, identifying for students and parents alike community values and attitudes. U.S. parents frequently choose neighborhoods, when they are house hunting, on the basis of the quality of local schools. Often they seek deliberately to acculturate their children to the values of those schools which they have selected. A clear example of how this occurs and how it affects the parents as well as the students, was revealed in the course of our study of one Los Angeles community. School C in the U.S. sample was, until ten years ago, made up largely of children of UMC Jewish parents who had strong intellectual interests. As Black families moved into the neighborhood, their parents occasionally approached teachers to ask how best they could see that their children were integrated smoothly into the school community. One teacher reports having urged them to do as the other parents in the school were doing: to take their children to museums and libraries, to expose them to music, art, and the theater — in short to provide them with the kind of intellectual stimulation the Jewish parents were giving their children.

## 6.8. *Sex and Gender - The Effects of Feminism*

### 6.8.1. *Feminism and Sex Specific Differences in Writing*

We began with the hypothesis that girls and boys are socialized differently and that, consequently, their cognitive and emotional worlds are shaped by different experiences. We assumed that these differences would be evident in their language behavior as certainly as in any other kind of behavior that we might have observed and recorded.

This was, in fact, the case, and we review the matter fully in our discussion of the SPTT (Socio-Psychological Theory of Text Planning). We were surprised, however, that the Viennese data produced quite different results than the U.S. data. The essays of Austrian girls and boys were clearly differentiated in form *and* content. The Austrian girls wrote reflective essays laden with positive and negative affect, openly discussing their problems with their mothers. The boys wrote unreflectively, generally avoiding affective expression of any kind.

In the U.S., the essays by girls and boys were much more alike, often making it difficult for us to guess whether an essay was written by a boy or girl. Both wrote reflectively and unreflectively, and both expressed affect or avoided it. We assume that this represents a decrease of gender-role distinctions in the U.S., perhaps attributable to the greater impact feminism is having in Los Angeles than in Vienna.

## 6.9. *Concluding Remarks: The Socio-Psychological Theory of Text Planning*

We began with the assumption that language variety occurs in response to a number of cognitive, sociological, and psychological factors and that it is impossible to account for linguistic characteristics on the basis of any one of them. We outlined a Socio- Psychological Theory of Text Planning (SPTT) which enabled us to identify in a written text manifestations of cognitive strategies and of social or psychological attitudes and beliefs. Our study has convinced us that language variety must be studied using combinations of Sociological and Psychological Variables (SPV) because the effect of any one is influenced by the presence or absence of a number of others.

Our study reveals sex-specific differences related to the generation of written texts (such as choice of text types, use of particles, use of affective language, etc.) which have not previously been exposed in the literature. At the same time, we have stressed that the picture evolving is not a dichotomous one, definable in terms of sex, but that it depends upon a whole group of psychological parameters.

One of the variables we investigated in the course of our research was the influence of the mother upon the language of the daughter both directly (by her own model) and indirectly (by the nature of their relationship). Linguistic markers in the text provide a diagnostic tool for researchers wishing to infer socio-psychological factors on the basis of what a subject says or writes. Our comparison of the same linguistic indicators in interviews and essays provided interesting information about sociological and psychological differences between written and spoken discourse.

Thus, our theories of the SPTT and the SPV provide the link between the differential socialization of children, the differential development of the mother-child relationship (in different cultures, classes, family structures), and, finally, its manifestation in language behavior.

## NOTES

1)The numbers in brackets are the results of the Chi-Square-Tests ($\chi^2$). All results on the 95% and 99% level are taken as significant, everything less than 95% is a tendency. "(Significant with $\alpha = 0,0001$" f. ex. or "0,0001" or "$\alpha = 0.0001$") means that the probability of error is less than 1%." "Significant on the level of 99%" means the same- the probability of error is again exactly 1% or less. "$\chi^2$" means the result of the Chi-Square-Test; "$\alpha$" means the probability of error "df" means "degrees of freedom" (see Sachs 1969, 141).

2) Professional women, participating in a mother-daughter workshop in Los Angeles in September, 1981, voiced this imperative as the most threatening they had to deal with in their relationships with their mothers.

3) Frankest was the American boy who wrote "Sometimes before I go to bed, I just want to hug her and kiss her. And then I don't ever want to let her go" (CNR 5216). Only American boys expressed anxiety about the mother's death: "Me and my mom do so many good things together then sometimes I do not want her to die" (CNR 1222), "And what scares me is like thinking when your mom is going to die" (CNR 3321), and "I really hope my mom lives a long time, because if she is not around, I honestly don't know what I would do" (CNR 4228).

4) The terms *abstract* and *coda* are based upon the terminology Labov and Waletzky (1967) used in describing narrative structure.

# SELF AND OTHER ASSESSMENT

## 7.1. *The Administration and Analysis of the Interviews and the Giessen Tests*

### 7.1.1. *Introduction*

In this chapter we will present the results of the interviews with 30 mothers in Austria and 15 mothers in Los Angeles. The Austrian sample was drawn by chance, ten mothers of daughters in each school type being chosen and interviewed in depth. As discussed in Chapter 4, the U.S. mothers were also chosen by chance; however, interviewing continued only until we had eight Giessen profiles that matched those of the Austrian mothers chosen for Case Studies. Our primary interest was to keep constant as many variables in the family structure as possible in order to determine whether the same mother personality type has the same effect on the daughter's development in both cultures.

In analyzing the interviews of mothers and daughters, we use both quantitative and qualitative data to answer the following questions:

1.  What is the impact of the different sources of data? Are daughters more honest and open in the interviews or the essays, and what are the methodological restrictions of the interview as an instrument of fieldwork for purposes such as ours?

2.  What do mothers say about their relationships with their husbands, mothers, and daughters, and about the methods they use in educating their daughters?

3.  In what ways do the mother types found in the Giessen Test correlate with the development of the daughters? What influences do the personality variables of mothers have on the relationship with the daughters?

4.  How do the answers of the mothers correlate with the opinions of their daughters? (This is the confrontation of self- and other-assessment.)

5.  Do cultural and social differences exist in the way mothers handle the interview situation? In the way mothers and daughters perceive

their lives and their relationships with each other?

6. What linguistic variables are identifiable in the interviews with mothers? What similarities occur in the mother-daughter speech samples?

In Appendix I, Case Studies drawing upon all data sources from mothers and daughters in both cultures will illustrate the complexity of the mother-daughter relationship as delineated within the scope of our interdisciplinary framework.

### 7.1.2. *Methodological Remarks*

We are aware that interviews present only the self-assessment of the interviewee. Since it is impossible to record natural situations in which mothers communicate with their daughters, we elected simply to confront self- and other-assessment by comparing similar issues covered in the mother and daughter interviews, and in the daughter's essays. In-depth interviews were used with the mothers, since they allow for more open and honest conversation than does a standardized question-and-answer format (Lazarsfeld 1944; Friedrichs 1973). The interviews were structured with the recommendations of Lazarsfeld in mind. He recommends that important considerations in conducting and analyzing in-depth interviews include:

1. explaining the meaning(s) of answers received;
2. exploring one important complex of opinions held by the interviewee;
3. studying complex attitudes expressed;
4. interpreting possible motivations prompting the responses received;
5. interpreting and differentiating statistical relationships, especially of rare or deviant cases.

One disadvantage of the in-depth interview is that only a small part of the data is standardized (and therefore, quantifiable). An additional disadvantage for us is that the sample is small. That is why the focus of this chapter is on the *qualitative* analysis of the materials. We are working with descriptive tendencies in discussing the mother interviews, while only occasionally referring to significant results.

The interviews with the daughters differed in kind from those with the mothers. The situation was more formal, the time shorter, and the answers apparently less valid than information obtained through other sources.

Because of the differences in format, the comparison of the daughter inter-views with those of the mothers has to be viewed with care.[1] In analyzing the interviews, we are interested in both the form and content of the answers, in the self-assessment of the mothers and daughters, and in the confrontation of the interview data with the essays and with the personality features of the mothers gained from the Giessen Test.[2] Again, we decided to use both qual-itative and quantitative methods of analysis in the hope that a rich source of data would supply various but important perspectives on the meaning of the material collected.[3] The Giessen Test — a psychological test covering person-ality traits with antipode answers to questions on a scale with 7 degrees of differentiation — was generally completed by the mothers without difficulty or questions (in Austria, only two mothers had no time left to complete it). The resulting profile was analyzed qualitatively (in the case studies) as well as quantitatively, using a cluster analysis, which defined 8 mother-types (dis-cussed below). The cluster types were developed to see what impact certain personality traits have upon the daughters and to establish a basis for cross-cultural comparison of mother-daughter pairs.[4] Thus, the application of a variety of field techniques and methods of analysis allows the modeling of a differentiated picture of the mother-daughter relationship. Our Case Studies will illustrate in a qualitative way the different types of mothers, and by comparing Austrian and U.S. mother-daughter pairs of the same cluster-type, we will be able to discuss cultural differences and their influence upon the mother-daughter relationship.

## 7.2. Interviews

### 7.2.1. Procedures

#### 7.2.1.1. Interviews with Daughters - Procedures

The interviews with the daughters took place during regular school hours, the girls leaving the classroom one-by-one to talk to the researcher. The sessions with each girl had to be brief (roughly fifteen minutes) so that the interviewing could be completed in one visit. This involved a minimum of disruption of the classroom, and it assured that the girls would not get together and talk over the questions before all had been seen.

Since the time allowed for the interview was short, the questions had to be standardized and, generally, the answers were quite brief. However, if the child wished to pursue a topic, the interviewer permitted it, responding to any subject that interested the girl or that helped to put her at ease. Most of the girls remained shy, however, giving answers which they might have thought the researchers expected (answers frequently differed from information contained in their essays).[5]

### 7.2.1.2. *Interviews with Sons - Procedures*

The interviews with the boys in the U.S. study followed the same format. These had to be scheduled for a different day, since the interviews with the girls required an entire morning. However, the boys did not know in advance that they would be interviewed. At the beginning of our project we had said — and believed — that we would interview only the girls. When both teachers and their male students were disappointed in this, we saw an opportunity to test in Los Angeles whether or not important information had been missed in Austria. Thus, we returned to the schools three or four weeks after the initial visit and interviewed the boys. We discuss some of our findings below.

### 7.2.1.3. *Interviews with the Mothers - Procedures*

The mother interviews were quite different from those with their children. Neither mothers nor children were told the precise purpose of our study; we explained only that it was a cross-cultural comparison of language and social development of girls in Los Angeles and Vienna. We had formulated a number of standardized questions for the mothers, which we embedded within natural conversation during the course of the interview. Although we wished to test certain of our hypotheses using the results of the interviews, we were interested as well in letting unforseen patterns emerge.

The setting of the mother interviews was less formal, as well. In Austria, the researcher went to the mother's home, had tea or coffee with her, and spent an hour or more interviewing her in a setting familiar to her. In America, since school administrators discouraged home visits, interviews were conducted wherever it was agreeable to the mother to meet: sometimes at home, sometimes in the school building, and sometimes over coffee. In both countries, the interviewer dressed conservatively but correctly, attempting neither to impress nor discomfort the interviewee, and a minimum of an hour was generally agreed upon for the interview. Surprisingly, all the mothers seemed very much at ease during the interviews. The difference in formality of setting between Vienna and Los Angeles was somewhat neutralized by the greater cultural informality in the U.S., where the university association of the interviewer confers less status than it does in Vienna.

In itself, it was interesting to speak with the mothers and to let them talk about their lives as women, as well as about their relationships with their daughters, husbands, and mothers. Mothers from all socio-economic levels and ethnicities were extremely pleased to have an interested auditor, gratified that someone was inquiring about concerns very important to them. They were, as a rule, interested in our study and asked to be informed about the results.

### 7.2.2. *Interviews - Contents*

### 7.2.2.1. *Interviews with Daughters and Sons - Content*

The information sought in the interview with the children is listed below.

1. Name, age, and social class (Austria) or ethnicity (U.S.).
2. Employment of father; employment of mother (not permitted in U.S. interviews).
3. Number, sex, and age of siblings.
4. How child relates to brothers and sisters.
5. Who cares for the child after school.
6. How much personal freedom the child has.
7. Whether there is a best friend. If so, whether in the same classroom, or school, or neighborhood.
8. What the child talks to the friend about.
9. How freely the child talks to the mother or father.
10. What the child likes to do during free time.
11. What happens if the child does something the parents disapprove of.
12. Whether there is anything the child wishes to do but is not allowed to do.
13. Whether the child likes to read. If so, what kinds of things. What authors.
14. Whether the child has career goals.
15. Whether the child wishes to marry, have children.
16. What the child likes to do on weekends or during summer vacations.
17. Whether the girl ever feels discriminated against or wishes she were a boy.
18. Whether the child is punished often. If so, what sort of punishment is used.
19. Whether or not the child found it difficult to write the essay. If so, why.

Items 1-5 provide sociological information; 7-9 provide information about the ease with which the child makes social contacts, but also provide insight into how close the parental relationship is; 6, 11, 12, and 18 deal with the educational style of the home; and the rest are general matters which reveal the creativity, the activity or passivity of the child, and so forth (see Table 10).

### 7.2.2.2. Interviews with Mothers - Content

Listed below are the data sought in the interview with the mothers.

1. Age of mother and employment, if any.
2. Schools attended; employment of parents or mother.
3. Marital status.
4. Number, sex, and age of children.
5. How children get along together.
6. How mother and daughter get along.
7. Any difficulties with the daughter.
8. Kind and frequency of punishment used in the home.
9. Whether daughter likes other children.
10. How daughter spends free time.
11. Whether daughter talks about her interests at home.
12. Whether the mother's relationship with her own mother has changed over the years. If so when this happened and how or why.
13. Whether the mother is like her own mother.
14. Whether the mother replicates any of her mother's behavior that she thought she would *not* do.
15. Any professional or educational wishes she has for her daughter.
16. Kind of life she would like for her daughter.
17. Kind of son-in-law she would like to have.
18. Whether the mother is content to be a woman.
19. Whether the mother has enough time for the daughter.
20. Whether the daughter has learned the facts of life from her or elsewhere. If so, from whom.
21. The relationship between the mother and father.
22. The relationship between father and daughter.
23. Whether the daughter enjoys school.

Questions 1-4 provide additional data for the sociological parameters; 5, 8, and 11 replicate questions asked of the daughter; 6-8 explore the mother-daughter relationship, as well as the educational style of the home; 13-15 explore the mother's relationship with her own mother, but also provide insight into the mother's satisfaction with her own life (as does 19) (see Table 11 for the coded categories).

### 7.3. The Giessen Test
### 7.3.1. The Test

After the interview mothers completed a Giessen Test (Beckmann and Richter 1975), a deep-psychological personality test (only two mothers were unable to complete the test because no time remained). The test comprises forty questions in which the mothers assess themselves on certain topics, using a scale weighted positively and negatively [3 2 1 0 1 2 3] (see Appendix III). Certain questions relate to each of the six dimensions investigated by the test:

1. *Social Resonance.* The self-assessment of attractiveness, and popularity.
2. *Dominance.* Behavior toward others ranging from dominant to submissive.
3. *Control.* Records how vivacious, controlled, or compulsive the mother believes herself to be.
4. *Mood.* Extremes of mood range from hypomania to depression.
5. *Self-Disclosure* (Permeability). Registers whether the subject reveals much or little about self to others.
6. *Social Potential.* Measure of readiness to socialize, ranging from sociability to isolation.

The results of the Giessen Test provide several possibilities for analysis. On the one hand, it is interesting, qualitatively, to compare profiles of subjects as a way of establishing comparable mothers in the two cultures — as we attempt to do in our Case Studies (see Appendix I for examples of mother-profiles and Table 12 for the coded categories).

Furthermore, each personality feature can be correlated with linguistic markers and with such issues, raised in the interviews and essays, as how dominance correlates with the relationship to the daughter, to the profession of the mother, or to her contentment with life. For the descriptive and explanatory statistical analysis, we considered only two poles on each dimension, positive or negative (the profiles show whether answers placed mothers on the extremes or near the mean on any one quality). Finally, with the use of a cluster analysis (in which similar profiles are put together by a computer program to establish a type), we were able to isolate specific types of mothers.

*7.4. Summary of the Most Important Results of the Analysis of Combined Data from Interviews, Essays, and Giessen Tests*

In addition to providing the self- and other-assessment which we were interested in comparing, the sociological, psychological, and linguistic indicators chosen provided a complex picture of the mother-daughter relationship. In this summary we will focus on the most important results, showing the influence and impact of "socio-psychological variation" upon the relationship. Again we will divide the results, considering first the contents of the data and then a few linguistic markers in the essays and interviews.[6] As only 30 Austrian mother-daughter pairs were studied in depth, we are discussing relative tendencies, not valid generalizations. Thus, correlations with the essay variables will (with few exceptions) remain on a descriptive level. On the other hand, we think that even this sample is representative of many of the mother-daughter relationships existing in the Austrian culture, thus allowing us to draw tentative conclusions and to compare these with the information obtained in the American sample.

In considering the interviews with the daughters, we are specifically interested in the perceptions of the mother as it corresponds with or differs from those contained in the essay. The interviews with the mothers provide insight into the entire family network and structure (including relationships between family members), as well as into her own development as a woman (her relationship with her own mother, her satisfaction as a woman). We assume that the comparison of some of the linguistic indicators used by daughters in written and spoken discourse with those of the mothers (in the interview) give evidence for the impact of sex-specific language socialization for the influence of certain of the characteristics of Motherese and of an emotional and cognitive education which results in different modes of structuring reality for boys and girls.

*7.4.1. Comparison of Data Sources*

As we have mentioned, the combination of data sources used has provided us with an opportunity to test the validity of various kinds of collection techniques. We have examined the nature of the discrepancies that turned up in the information received from various sources to discover 1) where greater honesty was to be expected and 2) where the privacy, taboo, or ideology surrounding a topic prevented our subjects from responding honestly. Consistent differences in the information contained in the girls' essays and interviews demonstrated that they felt freer to write honestly than to speak honestly about their relationships with their mothers. Differences between information supplied by mothers and daughters suggested areas to us where one, or the other, or *both* felt uncomfortable about revealing private family matters.

The information obtained on *educational style in the home* provides a good example of the impact of the various techniques, as well as of the ideologies and taboos influencing mother-daughter responses. The daughters responded more frankly in their essays than in their interviews. Although 46.7% of the Austrian girls complained in writing that the educational style of their homes was strict (Essay A, in Chapter 6, discusses this in detail), only 23.3% of them were frank enough to say the same thing in the face-to-face interview situation. Similarly, the method of punishment used is clearly a subject surrounded by taboo. When asked what kinds of sanctions they used, 100% of the mothers said that they used only verbal punishment with their daughters, whereas only 86% of the daughters agreed that this was the case (there is a fuller consideration of this question below in the discussion of privacy and taboo).

Our study has convinced us that multiple sources do help the researcher interpret the meaning of responses to questions, tests, and topics, but that all data must be examined with care, using all the resources available, including — of course — some not used here (see discussion of methodology, Chapter 4).

### 7.4.2. *The 30 Austrian Mothers - Data Analysis*

The sample of 30 mothers and daughters used in the following analysis represents a fairly homogeneous grouping. In 21 families, the daughter in our study was the only daughter or the oldest daughter; in 9 she was the youngest or second youngest. Using these 30 mothers, we did a quantitative analysis of the correlation between socio-psychological parameters of the mother and those of the daughter to provide a sort of general overview of attitudes and actions of the mother that appear to have specific consequences for the attitudes of the daughter. Then we collected the results of the Giessen Tests for these mothers and sorted them (using the computer) into eight groups (or clusters) of profiles showing systematic similarities. These clusters provided the basis for our Case Study comparisons between the two cultures, but they also enabled us to form a typology of mother types in our Austrian data and to compare personality traits of the mothers with behavior and attitudes of their daughters.

7.4.2.1. *The Austrian Mother Interviews - Tendencies and Significant Results**

The relationship of the mother to her own mother shows an interesting correlation with the relationship of the mother to her daughter: a woman who has a difficult relationship with her own mother tends to create a better one with her daughter. Furthermore, the mother's assessment of the relationship with the daughter is verified by the perception the daughters have of the relationship (0.04), as revealed in their essays. Possibly the good relationship of an adult woman with her own mother implies a lack of separation; this may explain why it often co-occurs with jealousy on the daughter's part and a bad relationship with the husband. Ambivalent mothers tend to perceive themselves as different from their own mothers; they have achieved separation and are attempting to pattern their own mothering in contrast to that which they experienced.

We find confirmed in our data the generalizations in Chapter 2 that the relationship to the husband has an important impact upon the family structure and, thus, on the mother-daughter relationship. A good relationship with the husband correlates with a good father-daughter relationship (0.03), with fewer difficulties between mother and daughter, and with a liberal style of education in the home. The mother's satisfaction with being a woman also correlates with a good relationship to the husband (0.07) and with daughters who perceive themselves as good and obedient (0.03). Finally, the father-daughter relationship is generally better in UMC and MC homes, as are the husband-wife relationships (0.03). These families are less stressed by financial pressures and crowded housing conditions, and the father in such families has more time for his children.

The impact of the mother's employment is complex. Occasionally, employed mothers express feelings of ambivalence toward their husbands, resulting from role-conflicts and time-pressures. Employed mothers wish their daughters to find satisfying employment as adults and want them to be independent (0.064). Although maternal employment does not influence the mother-daughter relationship, it does tend to correlate with a negative father-daughter relationship.

Related to employment of the mother is the question of afterschool care for the children, something of a problem in Austria, since schools are in session only half the day, and children regularly come home at 1:00 or 2:00 p.m. Working mothers may have a relative available to care for the child;

---

* See note 1, Chapter 6, 111 for the explanation of quantitative results in brackets.

they may hire someone to do so; or they may leave the child to care for herself during those hours. The argument of some Austrian political parties against all-day school or against day-care for school-aged children is that the mother-child relationship will suffer if the mother does not provide the primary after-school care. Our findings do not support their thesis. The arrangements made — or even the fact that the mother is not the caretaker in the afternoon — showed no correlation with the relationship between the mother and child. The *quality* of the time spent is more important than the quantity (see also the Essay Analysis).

Affectivity does show a correlation. One might predict that alternative child care in the afternoon would distance the child somewhat from the mother, with some affection or anger flowing toward the afternoon caretaker rather than toward her. Such a transfer does not appear to have occurred among the boys and girls in our sample. More intense feelings of both kinds, positive and negative, were expressed for the mother by children receiving alternative day care (0.0061).

Personality factors of parents and children also influence the contentment of all family members within the home,[7] but it is not always easy to pinpoint the source of the problem. If a masochistic mother marries a difficult man, and if a disruptive home situation results, it is fruitless to try to assign blame. What is obvious is that when one family member is *perceived* as particularly difficult to get along with, it is likely to disrupt the entire family. When both parents get along easily with other members of the family, they tend to be perceived as the stabilizing force.

These results demonstrate the influence of the family network and of the generational conflict on the mother-daughter relationship. Only by considering all aspects mentioned are we able to arrive at a realistic picture of the feelings and perceptions of the participants, as well as their attitudes toward this most important of female relationships.

### 7.4.2.2. *Correlation of Giessen Traits with Mother-Daughter Relationships*

For the cross-tabulations, all of the Giessen scales for each trait were pulled together into two poles, a positive or negative one. Otherwise, the sample would have been too small to allow for generalizations.

1.  SOCIAL RESONANCE: Positive social resonance correlates with a positive relationship with the daughter and the husband (0.0104). These mothers are generally liberal in educational style, are employed outside the home, and are content with their lives as women (0.047). Their daughters, too, have positive feelings

toward their femininity (0.048). Their answers are expressive, with a relatively high incidence of adjectives.[8]

2.     DOMINANCE: Dominant mothers have a good relationship with their daughters, encountering few difficulties, and they are content with their lives, are generally employed outside the home, use few adjectives in their logically consistent answers. They know what they want and are able to express wants explicitly and directly. Their daughters, who do not yet have boy friends, are similarly frank and articulate (0.08). Again, the mother's satisfaction with being a woman passes on to the daughter.

3.     CONTROL: Relaxed mothers (with little control) give relatively short answers, have a good relationship to their husband, as well as to their own mothers. Their educational style is liberal, and they have few difficulties with their daughters. Again, the results do not surprise us. Liberal mothers who are not overly controlling have better family relationships and happier daughters. Their daughters, who use stereotypes and particles in their essays (0.023), are jealous of and ambivalent in their relationship with their mothers (0.0184).

4.     MOOD: A positive mood correlates both with a good relationship to the husband (0.028) — although it is difficult to decide which is the source of which — and also with a positive relationship between the father and daughter (a happy family life). Such women also have positive relationships to their own mothers, are content with their lives (0.0634), and have positive attitudes toward the school and the values of the daughter. Their answers, which proceed logically, have a relatively high incidence of adjectives. Their daughters are content to be women (this correlates nicely with our theoretical assumption that depressed mothers will handle their daughters in a restrictive way, that their depression will be reflected in their daughters' development).

5.     SELF-DISCLOSURE: Open mothers have good relationships with their daughters and husbands, but they often express ambivalence toward their own mothers. They are content with their lives; they are often the caretakers of their children in the afternoon; and their daughters do not feel discriminated against.

6.     SOCIAL POTENTIAL: Sociable mothers express less ambivalence about their own mothers (perhaps they are easy-going and

have more distance). They practice a liberal educational style and have few difficulties with their daughters (0.076). Although their answers are short, these mothers like to talk and their answers are descriptive. *Un*sociable mothers (who are generally ambivalent) give reflective answers.

Clearly, social resonance, dominance, control, and mood are the Giessen variables which are most significant to the daughter. Ideally, a popular, dominant, boisterous, confident, open, and sociable mother will educate her daughter in a liberated, emancipated way and lead a happy and contented life as a woman, a mother, and a professional.

## 7.5. *The Giessen Clusters: A Typology of Mothers*

The cluster analysis systematizes division of profiles according to shared similarities. Eight clusters seemed adequate for categorizing the thirty mothers in the Austrian sample.

1. *Passive Mothers* (the traditional mother). These mothers were PATIENT, RELAXED, TRUSTING and DISSATISFIED.
2. *Active Mothers* (lacking self-confidence). These mothers see themselves as UNATTRACTIVE, TRUSTING and IMPATIENT.
3. *Introverted Mothers*. These mothers see themselves as IMPATIENT, UNATTRACTIVE, DISSATISFIED and only RARELY SOCIABLE.
4. *Positive Mothers*. This is the largest group (lacking extremes on any scale). They are DOMINANT, OPEN, SATISFIED and ATTRACTIVE, with NEGATIVE SOCIAL RESONANCE.
5. *Hysterical Mothers*. These mothers feel themselves to be POPULAR, SLIGHTLY SOCIABLE, IMPATIENT, TRUSTING, and HYPOMANIACAL.
6. *Negative Mothers*. These mothers are the negative ones: ISOLATED, UNATTRACTIVE, DISSATISFIED, OVERLY PATIENT, CLOSED and RELAXED.
7. *Modern Mothers*. This mother is the prototype of the liberated, modern mother. VERY SOCIABLE, TRUSTING, POPULAR, CHEERFUL, DOMINANT and VIVACIOUS (a consistent characterization, without contradictory qualities).
8. *Masochistic Mothers*. These mothers have contradictory traits that are extreme on all scores. OVERLY PATIENT, UNATTRAC-

TIVE, SOCIABLE, VIVACIOUS and RETICENT. They share traits with manic-depressives or even masochists.

### 7.5.1. *The Correlation of Mother-Types with Daughter Variables*

A quantitative analysis of the 8 clusters yielded the following tendencies.

1. *Passive mothers* have difficult relationships with their daughters. Their liberal educational style results from their passivity: they are unable to exercise active, consistent control. Although their daughters do not feel discriminated against as females, they are in opposition to their mothers. Passive mothers seem to provoke in the daughter a confrontation between traditional and modern values.

2. *Non-confident, active mothers* are content with their lives. Although their daughters perceive the educational style of the home as liberal, they are very ambivalent and have negative feelings towards their mothers. The tension between the mother's small degree of self-confidence and her vitality must lead to conflict with the daughter, since the model is inconsistent, full of explainable ruptures.

3. *Introverted mothers* have good relationships with their husbands. Although their daughters perceive themselves to be very open towards their mothers (this may be a bias of the daughter interviews), there are difficulties between the mothers and daughters.

4. *Positive mothers* are ambivalent towards their own mothers; consequently, they attempt better relationships with their own daughters. They are content with their lives. Their daughters are open and define the educational style of the home as liberal. Although they are positive toward the researcher (positive mother-transference), they feel jealous of their mothers. It can be concluded that positive mothers are sometimes difficult for their daughters to compete with.

5. *Hysterical mothers* are content with their lives, are very expressive (using many adjectives), and are generally employed outside the home. Their daughters are open, define the educational style of the home as liberal, and do not feel discriminated against as females. A high incidence of stereotypes occurs in their essays. The mothers, who are extremely positive in their mood (hypomaniacal), influence the feelings of their daughters and con-

vey positive perspectives and opinions to them.

6.    *Negative mothers* have bad relationships with their daughters and are ambivalent about their own mothers. Their children use negative adjectives, are in opposition to them, and express negative feelings toward them.

7.    *Modern mothers* present the ideal case described above. They are content with their lives, are liberal and are employed outside the home. Their daughters are in competition with them, using negative adjectives in discussing the relationship. Daughters of such mothers are jealous and have a relationship of rivalry.

8.    *Masochistic mothers* have very bad relationships with their daughters, who feel ambivalent toward them and are opposed to them, rejecting the model presented by the mother. A high incidence of negative adjectives occurs in their essays.

In the examples used to illustrate our findings, we will in each case indicate the cluster to which the mother belongs, and in Appendix I we will present Case Studies, with one Austrian and one American mother-daughter pair representing each of the mother types, to illustrate certain typical relationships developing within each type.

### 7.6. *Cross-Cultural Comparison of Mother and Daughter Responses*

### 7.6.1. *Satisfaction with Being a Woman*

A topic somewhat related to class and ethnicity — but not categorically — was satisfaction with being a girl or woman. Austrian mothers were eager to talk about the question and were honest and open about whether or not they were satisfied with their lives. It appeared that all of them had thought about the subject with a consciousness of the specific problems women have today. The examples chosen illustrate an important issue: employment does not necessarily make a woman happy or satisfied with her life. The important factors are the sort of work the woman does, how the family life is organized (whether, for instance, she can draw upon a family network for assistance, or whether the husband shares in the care of the house and children), and what possibilities the mother has had to fulfill her own goals.

> *CNR4, Case Study 3, Cluster 1*
> I:    But you continue to work as a teacher. Uh, are you satisfied with your life as a woman on the whole?
> M:    (Laughs). I think, well, it's like this. It's a question if I'm satisfied

with my general life as a woman? I think I am *not* content in general with my life as a woman. But I've partly solved it for myself.

This mother expresses ambivalence about her job and her life as a woman, an ambivalence shared by her daughter, as well. The daughter rejects the mother's model, expressing hatred and defiance (see Case Study discussion); she rejects the opposite sex (does not wish to marry); and she complains about feeling discriminated against as a girl and about the chores she is expected to do in the home.

In the following example, the mother has made a number of compromises for the sake of her family, but she seems to be content with her life:

> *CNR 42, Case Study 6, Cluster 4:*
> M:  Well, actually, I'm very satisfied. I have found a way that makes me happy. . . Of course, I've tried several things. For instance, when the children were small, I had a parttime job for two years, which was really good, since I only worked for two hours a day. . . . Uh, I found out that maybe I could do more than just housework. I felt a little closed in, and I really couldn't do what I wanted or follow my own interest. And I thought, actually, I should stay with what I could do. "You have chosen. You are a housewife and mother. Stay with the children." I do it that way, that — in the mornings, when my children are in school . . . this is for me. In the afternoons, I'm there for the kids, and the evening is the time for my husband.

Mothers who are content with their lives (in the Austrian sample) wish their daughters happiness, have good relationships with their husbands, and have good relationships with their daughters (all at the 99% level). The interdependence of personality traits and mother satisfaction will be elaborated upon in the Case Studies. Daughters of mothers who are content to be women generally do not feel discriminated against as girls and perceive the educational style of the home as liberal.

Satisfaction with being a woman was related to a complex of socioeconomic factors, and Austrian girls showed more class-specific responses to the question of satisfaction with being female than did their mothers. The only group which consistently tended to express dissatisfaction was the set of working class daughters (0.018). This can be interpreted as the falling together of two negative roles in one: that of being a woman and that of being a member of the working class. Working class mothers have less satisfactory relationships with their husbands in the Austrian sample, and life is harder for many of them, especially those who have to work at jobs which are not particularly interesting to them.

In the U.S., the situation was quite different. All mothers and most

daughters professed themselves to be content with their sex, to feel no disad-
vantages inherent in being women or girls. Only three girls (a Black, an
Anglo, and a Chicano girl) thought boys had advantages over girls, and five
(3 Anglo, 1 Chicano, and 1 Black) were ambivalent: wanting to be girls, but
wishing for some of the privileges of boys. It is difficult to say whether or
not the answers represent unexamined stereotypical responses. Several girls
evaded a direct answer by replying "I like being exactly who I am." Several
sneered (implying that it was a dumb question): "I dunno; I've never been
a boy." And some professed never to have thought about the question. In
view of the reduction of gender-role differences in the U.S., it is possible to
believe that dissatisfaction with being a female has decreased, as well.

It is also sometimes difficult to evaluate the mothers' responses. In the
following example, the mother said that she is content to be a woman. And
when asked, "Do you feel all right that your daughters are going to grow up
as women?" she responded enthusiastically:

> *CNR 1110, Case Study 5, Cluster 7*
> M: Yes, I do. The world's changing. I know I have changed drastically
> in the last three years since I've gone to work. I've gotten out in that
> business world and I see it. No, the world's changing. I don't feel that
> they would be better off if they were men. Not at all. Not at all. They
> may get their freedom from home a little sooner if they were men,
> but aside from that, no. I can't see that their being female will be
> holding them back.

Is this an honest answer, or is the mother voicing a current ideology? Her
daughter's essay indicates that this mother is far less content with her life
than her answer would suggest.

> *CNR 1110, Case Study 5, Cluster 7*
>
> D: When my mom gets mad at my little sister, I help her be calm, and I
> ask her to be nice. But when she gets mad, she usually is angry at
> someone (her sisters, her mother, or her boss), but she gets over it
> because I help her to try not to be mean to them. So I ask her to say
> sorry to whoever she is mad at. When my mom is sick, I feel sad for
> her. She gets sick a lot, too. Like yesterday she was sick, and she is
> still sick.

The same kind of unanimity of response also occurred in interview responses
to the question, "Have you thought about what you want to be when you
grow up?" Most of the girls in the U.S. (but few of the boys) had formulated
hypothetical career goals for themselves. Boys as a matter of course expect
to work during their adult years, and few of them at this age have begun to

think specifically about what they wish to do. Girls are clearly receiving pressure to begin considering the question at an early age. They apparently are being told — in some schools — to shoot high, as well. In one classroom, of the 14 girls who had career goals (only 2 did not), 10 wanted to become doctors, 1 hoped to be an architect, and 1 a lawyer. Obviously someone — perhaps their teacher — had urged these girls not to settle for being nurses or secretaries.

When it became clear that boys had not yet formulated career goals, we began asking them, instead, how they felt about wives working. This gave us insight into the degree to which feminism was touching their lives, and — in fact — it provided additional insight into the degree to which the school a child attends affects his social values. In the working class school, a typical response was, "I hope my wife will not have to work." In the magnet school, answers focused upon the girl ("If she wants to" or "Whatever makes her happy").

### 7.6.1.1. Father-Daughter Relationships

The interview answers of mothers and daughters to questions about the father-daughter relationship showed regular consistency, indicating that both shared the same perceptions of the relationship and that both felt free to answer frankly:

> *CNR 49, Cluster 4*
> I:    And what do you tell your father?
> D:    Exactly what I tell my mother. He wants to hear everything, too.
>
> I:    And how is the relationship between you and your husband?
> M:    Well, well, my husband sacrifices a lot of time for the children. He is really here for the whole family. He really doesn't particularly want to do anything without us. He likes climbing really high in the mountains. But he understands that the children can't go that high. So we all go together, the four of us, with a belt, and we all climb . . . . If he sees something beautiful, or if he wants to do something, the children are always included. He wants to experience things with them.
>
> *CNR 42, Case Study 6, Cluster 4*
> I:    And what do you tell your father?
> D:    Him, I don't tell so much. I only tell him about, well, my test grades, or about tests, but uh, problems or, so, I don't go to him with those.
>
> I:    How do your husband and daughter get along?
> M:    He has A VERY GOOD AND VERY LOVING RELATIONSHIP . . . He is not there very much for the children. We only see each other at breakfast. . . . And then, in the evening, but not, really,

regular. . . . but he has, I mean, he is, if there are any problems, let's
say in school, physics . . . .

*CNR 75, Case Study 7, Cluster 6*
I:    Do you tell your father as much as your mother?
D:    No.
I:    Why? Afraid?
D:    No, not afraid, but I don't have any real contact with him.

I:    How is the relationship between your husband and daughter?
M:    Theirs is a tense relationship . . . because, I think, well, that, uh, my
      husband doesn't really understand the girl, and her problems.

In CNR 49, both mother and daughter agree that the relationship is positive.
In CNR 42, the mother tries to depict a loving relationship, but gradually
contradicts herself, thus verifying the daughter's version of the relationship.
Again in CNR 75, both agree about the relationship (this time that it is
unsatisfactory). The Case Study of the mother-daughter pair in CNR 75 will
illustrate how this kind of relationship to the male sex (the father-model)
influences the daughter.

### 7.6.2. *Relationship Between Mother and Daughter*

We asked daughters, "What do you tell your mother?" or "What do
you talk to your mother about?" as a way of assessing their relationship with
the mother. Although the interview data from the daughters was generally
more biased than that of the essay, on this question some of the daughters
appear to have spoken quite frankly and openly, as judged by comparing
samples from both mothers and daughters:

*CNR 38, Cluster 5*
I:    What do you tell your mother?
D:    Well, I talk about school, and . . . and whatever there is to tell, new
      . . . new things, and, actually, I tell her everything. I have no secrets
      from her.

I:    What is your relationship with your daughter like?
M:    You mean generally? Well, let's see, I uh think we have a very good,
      uh — and I think also a very correct relationship to each other. So,
      uh, I am completely honest with her. I don't make up stories, which
      she would get to the bottom of when she is older anyway, uh, and I
      don't hide my feelings. My soul is spread out in front of her, and if
      she wants to talk to me about something, she can always do it . . . .

*CNR 4, Case Study 3, Cluster 1*
I:    What do you tell your mother?
D:    Things that concern her.

I:  And does everything concern her?
D:  Well, that depends. If they are important . . . except when there are things that she can't do anything about or that are none of her business, that I just don't tell her.

I:  What is your relationship with your daughter like?
M:  Well, pretty good, I suppose. (Both laugh)
I:  Any problems?
M:  Well, it's hard to say. Generally, no. Of course there are always little things.
I:  Do you have to scold, punish?
M:  Punish? Generally, no, not at all, only when scold- . . .

*CNR 101 (Cluster 8)*
I:  What do you tell your mother?
D:  Actually, nothing. I don't know.

I:  What is your relationship with your daughter like?
M:  Well, very good — how should I say it? She is still my baby.

These illustrate a variety of possible relationships and their expression in the responses in our Austrian interviews. The relationship of mother and daughter in CNR 38 is obviously a good one at the present. Both affirm it separately. In CNR 4, both mother and daughter equivocate. The answer of mother and daughter in CNR 101 illustrate the often contradictory nature of the material obtained in the interview, contrasting the differences that occur in the assessment of self and others. Is the mother deceiving herself or is she trying to mask the truth in order to present a good image of the relationship? Only a detailed case study enables us to answer such questions, thus validating the use of four techniques in gathering data.

## 7.7. *Interview Contents - Cross-Cultural Comparison*

Social class in Austria and ethnicity in the U.S. were factors of small importance in the attitudes and feelings expressed by mothers and daughters about their relationships. However, there were responses which clearly varied according to socio-economic differences. One was future expectations.

### 7.7.0.1. *Social Class, Ethnicity, and Future Expectations*

Women from lower socio-economic levels in both cultures expressed more anxiety about the future son-in-law than did other mothers. For them, the son-in-law's status loomed more important than his ability to make their daughters happy:

*CNR 7, Case Study 2, Cluster 2 (Austrian, LMC)*
I:    Do you ever think about what sort of son-in-law you would like to have?
M:    Maybe, I think I'm a little practical; I think about someone who will bring some craft or trade with him, because, you see, there is always something to do in the house, and if somebody is not able to do this by himself, he can't afford to have it done. Besides, we have both this house and my mother's. She [the daughter] wants to move there. We've already talked about it and fixed it up. So, I hope she gets a husband who has money and can take care of the house.

*CNR 1114, Case Study 1, Cluster 8 (American, Chicano, LMC school)*
I:    Do you ever think about what sort of son-in-law you would like to have?
M:    Responsible, you know. I don't want anybody who drinks a lot. I don't like alcoholics or dope addicts. You always look for that for your daughters. And just a good upstanding citizen.

Middle class mothers appeared to assume that their daughters would marry men who could take care of them; they worried only about their daughter's happiness:

*CNR 4, Case Study 3, Cluster 1 (Austrian, MC)*
I:    What do you wish for . . . ?
M:    Wish? I mean, that's hard to say. I wish that she goes her own way, really. It depends on her. Wish? I don't have any specific wishes along those lines. She has to fulfill her own wishes, really.

*CNR 3105, Case Study 6, Cluster 4 (American, Anglo, MC school)*
I:    Do you ever think about what sort of son-in-law you would like to have?
M:    No. That's really up to them. I just want them to be happy.

The career expectations of the girls differed significantly according to the school (0.0027 in Austria and 0.0077 in the U.S.), a finding that is not surprising given the correlation between school and socio-economic status. In Vienna, working class and lower middle class girls assumed that they would work, and they had clear notions of what they wished their futures to be. As a rule, they put a high priority on developing a career *before* considering marriage and children. This was true of all girls in the U.S. sample, except for girls in the UMC school (we discuss this more fully below). In the U.S., girls receive pressure both from the schools and from their mothers at least to consider the possibility of pursuing a career:

*CNR 3101, Case Study 8, Cluster 3 (American, Black)*
M:    The only thing I ever told her . . . about the kind of man to marry

... that I really didn't wish for her to get married young, really young, because there are a lot of things to do and a lot of places to go, and to see, and to get involved with a person at sixteen or seventeen and get married — she'd miss a lot.

In both Austria and the U.S., upper middle class girls differed from the norm, in having only vague notions of a fairytale future, in which they would marry and live as their parents have lived. They were the only girls in our study who lacked career plans, apparently assuming that they would marry well and keep house for the rest of their lives:

> CNR 6117 (American, UMC)
> S:   I'd want to quit working when I get married and just stay at home and be a housewife and everything, you know, my kids, and stuff.

Some realized that their not working would depend on the earning capacities of the men they married:

> CNR 6104 (American, UMC)
> I:   Would you continue working after you got married?
> D:   I dunno. That kind of depends on what my husband does.

But some of the UMC girls, in both cultures, were quite unrealistic, spinning out plans for a career requiring long years of preparation (dentistry, veterinary medicine, pharmacy), expecting to throw the career over when they had families, or — even more unrealistically — to shelve it and return to it sixteen years later, if they chose:

> CNR 47, Case Study 6, Cluster 4 (Austrian, UMC)
> I:   What would you like to be?
> D:   Pharmacist, at the moment.
> I:   And do you want to marry and have children?
> D:   Yes, yes. I would love to.
> I:   And would you continue working?
> D:   No, if I . . . if I, the chi- . . . if I have children, then I don't want to work anymore.
> I:   Well, why study for such a long time then, in the first place?
> D:   Well, you can, then, when the children are bigger, are finishing high school, if they are independent, then you can start again.

### 7.7.0.2. Austria - U.S. - Sex Instruction

In Austria, social class correlated with answers given by the mothers to questions about how their daughters learned about the facts of life. Generally, working class mothers had told their daughters themselves, a finding corresponding to other reports showing that sexuality may be more suppressed in the middle than in the lower class culture. Asked whether she had found it easy to talk to her daughter about the subject, one working class mother replied:

> CNR 71, Cluster 4 (Austrian, WC)
> M:  Yes, there was no problem. It came about very naturally, from the outside . . . uh, well, a newspaper article on an exhibitionist, or something . . . I don't know, or from a friend who got her period earlier, or something from outside. It led to a serious talk about everything. It was very early — with both girls, and the children took it and forgot about it again, parts of it anyway, because it did not seem so exciting at the time . . . so I don't think it bothered them much, or us.

Middle class Austrian mothers who saw themselves as liberal (not wishing to control the information given to their children) waited to be asked:

> CNR 4, Case Study 3, Cluster 1 (Austrian, MC)
> I:  Did you tell your daughter the facts of life?
> M:  Well, not really. That is, actually, it is automatic. Whenever something comes up, it is explained, you know?

None of the mothers actually answered "No" to our question. Rather they qualified their answers (someone else had told her — the father or a friend — before the mother had the opportunity). Or they were evasive:

> CNR 48, Case Study 5, Cluster 7 (Austrian, MC)
> I:  How did you tell your daughter the facts of life?
> M:  What? (Masking her understanding)
> I:  Did you tell your daughter the facts of life?
> M:  Well, actually, always when she came and asked, surely . . . .
> I:  And did she? Or did you do it? Or . . . ?
> M:  Well, I actually waited, and that is, she came with all the questions she had.

Of the 30 mothers interviewed in Austria, 22 (73%) told the daughters themselves, either freely, or in answer to the daughter's questions. The other eight reported that someone else told their daughters before they had an occasion to discuss the question together.

In the U.S., responses were more problematical. U.S. mothers are told that they should be the ones to discuss sex with their daughters, and in the interview all the mothers said that they had done so — or would. Since we were not permitted to ask the daughters how they had learned the facts of life, we were unable to test the validity of this unanimous response. However, the information contained in the interviews and essays suggests that talk about "the facts of life" can vary considerably in context. It may be detailed and explicit:

*CNR 1107, Case Study 2, Cluster 2 (American, Anglo)*
M:   When she came home from school, it all just hit. Both of us. My
husband and I both. He was sitting there. And they give her so many
words — right? So, I said, "Okay, Ann. We have a medical encyc-
lopedia. We'll sit down and go over it." Well, uh, she'd read the book
from front to back; so I explained to her and we talked, and my
husband did and he said, "No, I'm gonna take a shower. I need a cold
one." . . . You know, this was very difficult.

It may be vague and piecemeal:

*CNR 1110, Case Study 5, Cluster 7 (American, Anglo)*
M:   Whenever they work up . . . I figure, if they've worked up enough
courage to ask me that question, then I'll give them an honest answer.

Sometimes the conversation appears to have focused on potential consequences of having reached the menarche, without any clear notion of whether
the mother has discussed the specifics of reproduction with the daughter:

*CNR 1114, Case Study 1, Cluster 8 (American, Chicano)*
M:   Well, they really // it was kinda hard for me. But I let 'em know when
they, you know, when they started menstruating to be careful, they
could have children if they're growin' up.

Two Black girls were the only ones in the U.S. group who included in their
essays references to discussion with their mothers about sex. One praised
her mother saying "She could be a doctor, because she knows so much"
(CNR 4103), implying that their discussions had been clear and straight-for-
ward. Another appeared to have received the equivalent of the warnings
referred to by the mother in CNR 1114 above:

*CNR 4107 (American, Black)*
D:   She tells me things like don't go around with too many boys at the
same time or you will get VD. VD is something you get when you
have sex with too many boys. She also told me don't have sex while
I am still young because I will have a baby and will have to drop out
of school.

The advice given here may or may not have included explicit information
on what "having sex" entails, but the warning given by this mother and the
Chicano in CNR 1114 above is clearly functional. Both girls were characterized by their teachers as eager to have boyfriends; both came from families
which would find it financially difficult to rescue them if they became pregnant
(thus early pregnancy for both could mean the loss of an opportunity to
create a career for themselves); and both mothers appear to be dealing realistically with the expectation that their daughters will have premarital sex.

### 7.7.1. *Wish to Marry*

When asked whether or not they wanted to marry, 73% of the girls in Austria responded affirmatively. Most of them also wanted to have children (76.7%). In the U.S. sample, a surprising 50% of the Chicano girls responded negatively to both questions. The role of the mother remains a contradiction in values in the Mexican-American community. Because she is a woman in a male dominated society, the mother role has low value, and the husband has social and sexual freedom denied to her. But because the mother is the central figure in the home and because home ties are highly valued, the mother figure is accorded enormous love and gratitude. This was obvious in the quantitative analysis of our essays. Children wrote almost entirely in positive terms about their mothers, especially the boys, who voiced no ambivalence or anger at all. Girls, too, voiced love and respect for their mothers, but not for the maternal role she represents to them.

We also looked at the data supplied by girls who did not wish to marry, but who did hope to have children. There were only three in the entire sample (from both countries) — but there are traits in common in their family situations. One had a bad relationship with her mother (revealed in the essay) and with her father (revealed in the interview):

> CNR 1108 (American, Chicano)
> (ESSAY)
> My mother and me are not that close. We live together and everything, but we are still not close to each other.
>
> (INTERVIEW)
> I: You can talk [to your friend] about things that bother you. Can you talk to your mom and dad, too?
> D: Well, not so much my mom — nor my dad.

Two had a good relationship with the mother, but a bad one with the father:

> CNR 75 (Austrian, LMC, Case study 7, Cluster 6)
> (INTERVIEW)
> I: Do you tell your father as much as your mother?
> D: No.
> I: Why? Out of fear?
> D: No, not fear, but I don't have a real contact with him.
>
> CNR 4109 (American, Jewish)
> (ESSAY)
> [My mom and I] are very close. We are closer than my dad is to me or my brother.

(INTERVIEW)
D:  It's fun to grow up with my mom. And it's a little easier with us cause my father doesn't live with us, so . . . but . . . I have my mother right there.

- - - - - - - - - - - - - - - - - - - - - - - - - - - - - - - - - - - - - - - - - - - - - - - - -

I:  How are you punished?
D:  With my mom, she yells at me. With my dad, he like, okay, he yells, but . . . I have this little thing I call *pounding*. He pounds. Like that's even a worse punishment than going into your room and being grounded for a week. You're just sitting there for like an hour and they're pounding and pounding and pounding.

### 7.7.2. *Privacy and Taboo*

In the course of the interviews, it became obvious that some of our questions came too close to complex taboos. For example, both mothers and daughters in Austria were very uncomfortable with questions relating to the educational style in the home. They insisted that there is little need for punishment in their families, that they usually talk things over when problems arise, that sanctions are always fully explained (and, thus, that parental anger is never capricious or inexplicable to the child). Mothers never acknowledged that they hit their children or screamed at them. Interestingly enough, in this case the essays were probably the most honest source of data we collected. In their writing, girls often referred to hitting and screaming — behavior touching the taboo against revealing intimate details of family life. In the U.S. sample, girls responded more frankly in the interview than did the Austrian girls; but they spoke only of hitting — never of screaming (although both frequently were mentioned in essays). Thus, the correlation of the educational style as perceived in the interviews and in the essay was *not* significant (in the Austrian sample it was only 0.2 and in the U.S. sample, 0.7), illustrating the difference and bias resulting from the different techniques used.

In the U.S., girls showed a similar discomfort with questions about how they got along with their brothers and sisters. If questioned directly, they answered "Okay," or even more often they made no reply, until the interviewer rescued them by making a hand gesture signalling "Sometimes yes, sometimes no," to which they assented. Indirect questions were more likely to elicit clues to the relationship:

*CNR 2105 (American, Anglo)*
I:  So you're the youngest. Is that good or bad?

D: Bad.
I: Why?
D: Because they . . . they're mean to me, and they sometimes . . . I don't get along with them.

Related to this reluctance to discuss sibling relationships, mothers in both countries showed an interesting evasive tendency, a desire to lead the conversation *away* from a discussion of the daughter who was the subject of the interview, focusing instead on difficulties with some other child in the family. In the following example, the mother was responding to a question about difficulties with the daughter and how she goes about punishing her. After answering the question about difficulties negatively, she went on:

> *CNR 7, Case Study 2, Cluster 2 (Austrian, LMC)*
> M: I think one deals more with the first child. With the second one [the son is younger] there were no difficulties, but he is another character and also not as open and also prepared to putter and things like that. The boy is not so interested in psychic problems, more practically oriented.

After the mother went on for some time about the son, the interviewer succeeded in turning the conversation back to the daughter by asking, "But it was different with your daughter?" (Similar examples occurred in the U.S. data. For a discussion, see the case histories below.)

It is as though the mothers are more comfortable discussing their fury at a child unknown to the interviewer than one whom the interviewer has already met. Perhaps it is easier to talk frankly to others about people they don't know simply because there is more safety in doing so (less danger of remarks getting back to the person discussed). Or it may be that divulging intimate details about family members to outsiders who know them is a universal taboo.

### 7.7.3. Mother-Mother, Mother-Daughter Similarities

In Chapters 1-3 we pointed out that some behavior patterns — including linguistic ones — pass from mother to daughter. Among the questions we asked in the interview were whether the mother thought she was like her own mother and whether she had ever noticed herself repeating behavior patterns of her own mother that she had thought she would never do. Mothers answered these questions quite honestly and, sometimes, ruefully (even those who had positive feelings about their mothers seemed apologetic):

> *CNR 37 (Austrian, MC)*
> I: Do you find yourself doing similar things?

M:    Yes, constantly. I mean, not all the time, but it's funny. All those
      things that made me so angry at my mother — I find them now in
      myself. [This mother has a positive relationship with her mother.]

*CNR 18, Cluster 1 (Austrian, LMC)*
I:    You said once (turning to her husband who was occasionally present
      during the interview) that if I get nervous, I talk louder, exactly like
      my mother. I don't notice it myself, but it could be true. My mother,
      you see, has this tendency, if she is anxious, her voice gets shrill. And
      I must do the same thing, as my husband has already noticed.

Some mothers are absolutely certain that they are nothing like their own
mothers, and yet a comparison of interviews with essays, or even of differences between one bit with another obtained in the interview, reveals that
they are less different than they imagine:

*CNR 4103, Cluster 3 (American, Black)*
M:    As I got older, I told [my mother] about all the things that I really
      didn't like [laughs] . . . I don't know whether it did any good, but it
      made me feel better. And I think she understood me a lot, you know,
      a lot better. But she was just so strict and rigid, and there was no
      variation from anything she said. So when I got older, and two hundred
      miles . . . two *thousand* miles away, I could call her and tell her what
      I didn't like.

Later — in the same interview:

M:    [My daughter] says, "All my friends say you're really mean." I says
      [laughs], "I don't care." You know, at nine o'clock she has to get off
      the phone. And when she has not done her homework, she has not
      cleaned her room, then she can't even *talk* on the phone. She says,
      "All my friends think you're really mean." I told her, "Big deal." But
      I *still* think I'm a lot lenienter than my own mother!

Some mothers were able to see themselves in their daughter's behaviors, as
well:

*CNR 4, Case Study 3, Cluster 1*
I:    Are you like your own mother?
M:    Well, I can't actually say. I . . . I don't think so. Of course, you could
      say in some things: but with my daughter, I notice that she repeats
      some things . . . .
I:    What kinds?
M:    Hmmm? Well, not like . . . but certain phrases, certain things which
      you say often, which you say automatically.
I:    Like you?
M:    Yes. . . . But I really can't remember my mother. I must say [both
      laugh] it's so long ago.

We do not want to imply that all our mothers dreaded being like their own mothers. In fact, 16.6% expressed only positive feelings for their mothers. Nor do we want to suggest that mothers found it impossible to break the mold of mothering received from their mothers. Many have, in fact, succeeded in living lives quite opposite to those their mothers lived (see especially Case Studies 2 and 5). What becomes apparent in our data is that most mothers reject the models presented to them by their own home experiences and attempt to rectify those behaviors that angered them when they were children.

### 7.8. Form of the Verbal Data from Mothers and Daughters

### 7.8.1. Comparison of Text Types

The text types we used for discriminating essay categories occur in speech, as well as in writing, and with much the same apparent basis. As we noted in discussing the text types of the essays, girls who wrote thoughtfully about the mother-daughter relationship produced reflective text types. We related this in the writing of the boys and girls to the presentation of a topic to which the writer had already given some thought and of the use to material that had been either semantically or episodically stored in memory.

A related tendency occurred in the interview data with the mothers. Unproblematical answers tended to be brief or to be couched in narrative or descriptive forms; ambivalent material, on the other hand, tended to be longer and to take the reflective format found in the essays. This is illustrated below by two answers to the questions, "Did you tell your daughter the facts of life yourself?":

> CNR 38, Cluster 5 (Austrian, MC)
> M:   Yes, there was no problem. It came about very naturally, from the outside . . . uh, well, a newspaper article on an exhibitionist, or something . . . I don't know, or from a friend who got her period earlier, or something from outside. It led to a serious talk about everything. It was very early — with both girls, and they took it, and forgot about it again, parts of it anyway, because it did not seem so exciting at the time . . . so I don't think it bothered them much, or us.

The answer of the mother in CNR 38 is clearly a reflective text type: the mother evaluates the manner in which the information was given to the daughter and its impact upon her, using a minimal narrative to elaborate her point. Evaluation is stressed throughout ("no problem," "very naturally," "did not seem so exciting," and "I don't think it bothered them much"). In contrast, the answer is embedded within a narrative in the the response below:

> CNR 42, Case Study 6, Cluster 4 (Austrian, UMC)
> M: Well, it's funny — my husband told her.
> I: Ummm?
> M: That was while driving the car and she asked, "What happens between a man and a woman? What do they do?" And my husband was upset and thought, "Ah, well. So, it's a little early, but all right" — because she's sitting there in the car and we are driving to Salzburg and then St. Pölten.
> I: Mmmm.
> M: And once the big one drove with me — the small one with my husband and so . . . this was quite funny. As we came home, I said "So, now she knows the facts of life" . . . and now I talk openly about menstruation, about conceiving children, and I don't think we walk around naked much in front of the kids. I mean, it's not that we want to show ourselves. . . .
> I: Mmmm.
> M: but if I happen to come out of the bath, and the children are . . . and my husband . . . we don't go out of our way. We look [pause]
> I: Mmmm.
> M: Yes, naturally.

The mother in CNR 42 really tells a story without evaluation other than "It's funny," which is a cliché comment rather than an evaluation of the experience being described. Her narrative fulfills much of the schema of Labov and Waletzky (1967) — the orientation, the complication, a temporally ordered sequence of events, the brief coda — but it lacks the evaluative comment upon the content of the story that is part of their narrative schema.

Evaluative answers occur slightly more often in the speech of upper middle class and middle class mothers than in that of lower class mothers (and so these mothers produce more reflective spoken texts).

### 7.8.2. *Comparison of a Mother-Daughter Text*

We had not expected to be able to compare mother and daughter texts in detail, given the differences existing in the interview situation. However, on one occasion a leading question from the interviewer elicited two versions of the same story, giving us an opportunity to inspect the two texts for similarities and differences. We will begin by reproducing the two versions below in the order in which they were recorded:

> CNR 1107, Case Study 2, Cluster 2 (American, Anglo)
> DAUGHTER'S VERSION
> I:    Do you eat lunch at school?

D: Yes, I bring it every day. My mom . . . well my mom sometimes comes and brings my lunch if I forget it. Or she goes and buys me something.

I: That's nice, huh? Did you ever forget it on purpose?

D: Yeah. One time I did. I left it in the car and it was under the seat. So my mom . . . My mom went and . . . and I called my mom, and she went "Leslie?" I went "Mom, I left . . . I, I forgot my lunch" and she said "Where is it?" and I says "I don't know." And she looked under the car — er, under the seat cause my books were right there and they got pushed under and she goes "Okay, I'll bring you . . . I'll go and buy you something." And so she did and then she looked under the seat and my lunch was there. And so she gave me my lunch and she ate the other one [laughs]. She goes . . . "Oh, you went and did it on purpose."

MOTHER'S VERSION

I: Leslie told me a funny story about forgetting her lunch one time [laughs] on . . .

M: On purpose? I . . . I, oh yeah. I went down. She came out of the classroom; I just honked the horn and I was just sitting there. "You forgot your lunch, didn't you?" "Yeah." And I says "Well, it's set in the car. You can't eat your lunch. You know. It's just set in the car. Forget it. It's been in the heat." So I went to Taco Bell and I picked her up some stuff. And "Oh! Thank you Mother!" She was really grateful for it, but I says, "No more!" [Laughs] "Don't do it to me anymore!"

The similarities between the two versions are interesting, to begin with. We have here an example of the kind of shared anecdote that serves a binding function between family members. It seems clear that the mother has brought Leslie her lunch on more than one occasion (Leslie says, that she "sometimes brings my lunch if I forget it. Or she goes and buys me something"). But both mother and daughter focus more saliently upon the positive incident, in which they participated cooperatively than the one which represented a contest of wills. Although the interviewer's prompt elicited a less positive anecdote from the daughter, the mother appears to have forgotten that incident. She picks up the interviewer's hint (as her "On purpose?" makes clear), but she chooses to discuss a different incident than the one proposed. Although the mother used the situation in which she was tricked as an opportunity to teach Leslie a lesson, she seems not to have taken the lying seriously enough to remember it. The event she remembers is one in which she was a good mother (bringing lunch to her forgetful daughter) and Leslie was a good daughter (expressing proper gratitude).

Although the narratives produced by the mother and daughter are of two different incidents, their remarkable similarity shows the strong identification between this mother and daughter. They use the same text type (narrative), many of the same lexical items, and similar dialogue patterns to make the scenes between the two vivid to the listener. If we compare these in terms of the narrative sequence isolated by Labov and Waletzky (1967), we find the following similarities:

1. *Abstract*: Both use "Yeah" to acknowledge that they will produce an illustration of the idea set by the interviewer. Leslie adds an explicit confirmation ("One time I did").

2. *Complicating Action*: Both present three incidents in the same order: 1) the first confrontation (both use dialogue for this); 2) the trip to the fast food store; and 3) the second confrontation (in which, again, they both use dialogue). The placement of the fourth shared incident — the discovery of the lunch under the car seat — differs crucially in each version. Leslie becomes confused, presenting the finding of the lunch midway in their phone conversation, although it is clear from the mother's next remark ("Okay, I'll buy you something") that she found the lunch *after* their conversation. In the mother's version, she has found the lunch at some point before the narrative begins. Understanding that the daughter has forgotten it, she elects to buy another and take it to school.

3. *Result*: The result, in both versions, occurs in the second confrontation. In the daughter's version, the mother brings her the forgotten lunch and eats the purchased one; in the mother's version, she throws out the forgotten lunch and brings the daughter the purchased one.

4. *Evaluation*: In both versions, the evaluation is implied. Both tell the narratives happily, as evidence of the basically good relationship between the two. Leslie laughs a little sheepishly that her mother has caught her in a lie (and has handled it without becoming angry). And the mother adopts the same good-natured, scolding tone she probably used when she brought Leslie's lunch to her ("No more! Don't do it to me anymore!")

5. *Coda*: Both signal the end of the story in the same way — with a laugh, followed by a last word from the mother.

### 7.8.3. *Concluding Remarks about the Comparison*

The language of mothers and daughters will sometimes be similar simply because the same socio-psychological variables are influencing both. Thus, either of them will produce a reflective text type when they are discussing a topic thoughtfully and judiciously. And particles or incoherence are likely to co-occur with ambivalence or the expression of strong feelings in speaking as well as in writing. A second factor influencing the degree to which language of mother and daughter will match is identification: the daughter who identifies strongly with her mother may produce speech very much like hers.

However, a study by Wodak and Moosmüller (1981) demonstrated that the language of sons at adolescence was generally *more* similar to that of their mothers than the language of daughters. First, the relationship between sons and mothers is less problematical at this age. Second, the daughter's rejection of the mother is reflected by rejection of her speech model. Thus, troubled mother-daughter relationships tend to result in the adoption, by the daughter, of very different speech styles. Third, Wodak and Moosmüller found that peer attitudes toward language use influence the daughter's decision to imitate or reject the mother's language model. In Vienna, the use of dialect is tabooed among speakers of the older generation, but not among the young. Thus, daughters may reject the status-marked usage of the mother in order to affiliate with her peers (slang serves a similar function in the United States). It is impossible to generalize, then, about whether daughters at this age speak in ways similar to their mothers. They do, and they do not, depending upon linguistic, psychological and sociological factors.

### 7.9. *The Mother-Daughter Relationship*

### 7.9.1. *Sex-Related Differences in the Mother-Daughter Relationship*

We assumed, to begin with, that mother-daughter relationships are inevitably of a very specific and complex nature, quite different from mother-son relationships. The analysis of the essay content written by girls and boys in the two cultures clearly shows this to be the case. The essays provide evidence, for example, that girls have given the relationship considerably more thought than the boys, and that they find it much more complex and problematical. The analysis also provides evidence that the affectivity of boys and girls is significantly different as a result of the socialization processes they have undergone. The girls in our sample have experienced and identified a whole *range* of emotions within the mother-daughter relationship; the boys have registered just one (love) — and often they mention none at all. We have related this difference in expressivity to different cognitive strategies used in response to affective experiences. Boys tend to store such memories episodically; girls reflect upon them and interpret them in light of a developing world view of what relationships can or should be, before storing them in memory.

Comparison of mother-daughter interviews provided a new awareness of the deep interest both mothers and daughters take in the nature of this most special of female relationships, one that the daughter is experiencing for the first time, one that is partially structured by the mother's own experiences as a daughter. Seldom physically present in the homes we studied, the mother's mother remains a presence, repeatedly evoked in the course of the mother's interaction with her own daughter. This continuity reveals that the maternal bond, even when viewed negatively by the daughter, remains peculiarly strong.

### 7.9.2. *Cross-Cultural Similarities*

We assumed, as well, that although the mother-daughter relationship will always be complex and difficult in cultures where the mother is the chief caretaker and socializer of the daughter, the manner and quality of separation and identification can vary as a result of a number of sociological and psychological variables. Our study has demonstrated, in fact, that neither social class nor ethnicity has significant impact upon the kinds of difficulties mothers and daughters encounter in their unfolding relationship.

Nor do many of the major sociological differences we considered in Los Angeles have a significant impact. For example, Los Angeles girls and boys are very dependent upon their mothers for transportation. Because there is inadequate public transit, the parents (usually the mother) must drive the children wherever they want to go. Even in areas where children can go places by using public transportation, mothers often take them because of fear for their safety (see Case Study 5). However, in the two communities outside the metropolitan area, where children can get around on their own easily, and where the crime rate is significantly lower than in Los Angeles, very similar mother-child patterns emerged.

The marital status of the mother and her employment outside the home also proved to be minor factors in mother-daughter interaction. What *does* emerge as important in our study is the finding that the mother's satisfaction with her role as a woman is significant, as are her personality type and the educational style she adopts in dealing with her children.

## 7.10. *Cross-Cultural Differences in Mother-Daughter Relationships*

An unexpected difference that emerged is the absence of conflict revealed by American girls in their essays and the continued closeness of their ties to their mothers, either as companion or friend. Rebellion in adolescence signals that final separation is under way; its absence should not be welcomed uncritically (Lynn 1974) — nor, of course, should its absence from the essay contents be taken as proof that conflict is not present.

Whether or not they represent the child's true feelings, the essays reflect an underlying ideal "happy family" ideology urged upon U.S. parents by manuals, by counselors, and by the media. Slogans and clichés provide pat answers to questions from outsiders about the family relationship, answers which permit the writer/speaker to create a facade conforming to the current ideology. In fact, the stronger the ideology, the more tabooed is nonconformity and the more necessary are clichés. The ideology tells us what *should* be true. It leads us to demand that it *be* true, and it requires us to believe that it *is* true.

Thus, although it is clear that we are sometimes dealing with a myth in the U.S. sample (some children who claim to be "best friends" with their mothers clearly are not), it is difficult to determine what is myth and what is reality. As we pointed out in discussing the strategies used in writing, reality constitutes a sort of "shadow text" which tends to break through into the student's consciousness in the act of writing, leaving visible traces on the page (rationalizations, contradictions, and lapses in coherence which reveal the presence of an undercurrent that the writer is attempting to suppress).

On the other hand, there is a large measure of reality in the happy family being described by the U.S. students. Parents and children *do* spend more time together; they *do* attempt to enjoy each other's company; and they *do* tend to treat each other as equals. The situation has positive consequences as well as negative ones. They are summed up by the remark of a German exchange student in one of the Los Angeles schools (who wrote an essay and was interviewed, but who was excluded from the American data): "Everyone is nicer here to everyone else; people are happier. It's all so relaxed, and easy."

What are the implications of the ideology described in the U.S. culture? One is that separation is being delayed (for the majority of our girls — with age making no significant difference); there is little evidence that final separation is yet under way. We are concerned that if too high a value is set on untroubled relationships within the family, separation may become extremely difficult, if not impossible, for the daughter. It may, of course, simply occur later, with no appreciable consequences. However, our discussions with Viennese mothers demonstrated that a woman's failure to separate from her own mother may diminish her ability to create close relationships with her husband and her daughter (see also Cohler and Grunebaum 1981 for evidence that this is so).

### 7.10.1. *A New Ideology in the U.S.*

The theory of the development of the mother-child relationship outlined in Chapter 2, which is based upon psychological and sociological studies produced in Europe and the U.S. in the last thirty years, accounted well for the information about the mother-child interaction pattern collected in the Austrian data. However, it became apparent to us, as we began to read the American essays, that a somewhat different structure had evolved in the U.S. The educational style in the home was on the whole more liberal. The atmosphere both in school and at home was more relaxed. And adult-child relationships were generally freer than those observed in the Austrian sample.

Of course, Los Angeles is not a typical American city. It represents in many ways an exaggeration of trends under way throughout the country, trends which *are*, however, representative of U.S. life. For example, while it is true East of the Rockies that American family networks are still very strong, even in large cities, the majority of the families in our study are nuclear. Often the parents have migrated thousands of miles away from families in the South, East, or Midwest, and, as a result, have few — if any — relatives living nearby. Viennese families, on the other hand, generally live within a dense network of relatives (often residing in the same house with some of them). That network provides a strong support system to the Viennese mother, a valuable resource often missed by lonely Los Angeles parents dealing with their children's problems without the advice and strength available from family members sharing their beliefs and values. But the network that sustains the Viennese family also inhibits its change, resulting in a greater conservatism in family styles in Vienna. On the other hand, freedom from family scrutiny permits Californians to experiment and to innovate in their own lives, without submitting every deviation from the traditional pattern to the approval of the network of relatives and friends.

This means that some of the differences in the mother-daughter relationship that we have observed doubtless represent extremes of difference that would not appear so impressive in a comparison between Vienna and New York or Vienna and Chicago. Nevertheless, the implications of the comparison are interesting, because the Los Angeles family structure is, we think, simply an *enabling* factor, not a *causal* one. What is occurring in our Los Angeles sample is an acceleration of tendencies underway throughout the American culture. The liberal educational style of the L. A. homes and the equality of children and adults represent ideals promoted by widely-read manuals on child-rearing in the U.S. Their effect, in fact, has been the creation of a new ideology of motherhood.

In the American family structures depicted in our essays, there was more social interaction between parent and child than in Vienna. Los Angeles children enjoy spending their free time going places and doing things with their mothers more than Austrian children, and the U.S. students set a high value on these shared activities (as opposed to the Austrians, who valued the freedom to act autonomously). Parents and children alike expressed pleasure in "having fun" together, something mothers deliberately foster (Case Study 5). They take pride in having their children prefer to be with them (Case Study 2).

Slogans like "Be a Pal to Your Kid" and "Have You Hugged Your Kid Today" express an ideal that many of the families in our American sample are working out. The "Happy Family" syndrome is evident in the number and nature of clichés in the U.S. essays; in the satisfaction with their lives expressed by the mothers (none admitted being dissatisfied); in the relative lack of anger or conflict in the girls' essays; and in the prevalence of the mother-role of *friend* (not found in the Austrian essays).

## 7.11 *Suggestions for Further Study*

There are several topics which we have only briefly discussed or pointed to in the course of our study that might be worthy of further investigation.

1. A longitudinal study of the same girls and mothers after a period of two or three years might provide interesting information about how stable the responses really are that we are finding. Specifically, such a study would provide us with information on how different strategies of separation evolve and are resolved cross-culturally or within the same culture. It would, also, enable us to distinguish and weigh the impact of the variables found to be of relevance (like satisfaction, ideology, and personality).

2.  Samples which include different family structures (single parents, divorced parents, or families controlled for number of children and position of daughters) would also provide more information on the impact of the environment on the development of the mother-daughter relationship. Of specific interest would be a study comparing more traditional role-sharing with "progressive" role-sharing, thus enabling us to distinguish between ideologies and the model learned at home in the acquisition of gender-roles, as well as the strategies of conflict-solving used in the mother-daughter relationship.

3.  More in-depth interviews with the girls might have provided a clearer idea of how much we are getting stereotypical "happy family" responses and how much there *are* valid differences between the Austrian and the U.S. family picture. In other words, it would be interesting to test whether changing the nature of the family structure (as it appears to have changed in the U.S.) really does change anything in the structure of the mother-daughter relationship.

4.  The pilot study of the boys in the U.S. revealed that girls, at this age, are being urged to think about career choices, marriage alternatives, and future expectations in a way that boys are not. It would be interesting to test the implications of this early pressure on the girls longitudinally and to examine when and under what conditions the boys begin to develop their own career and marriage plans.

5.  The pilot study of the boys suggests, as well, that feminist ideas have not yet touched their lives to the extent that they are influencing the thinking of the girls (and that the school is an important factor in both cases). This finding may have important implications for educators.

6.  A study of fathers and sons might test structures and developments of the male roles in a way parallel to our study of mothers and daughters. If the essays gathered were entitled "My Father and I," would any sexual repression be visible in the essays by girls? Would more conflict be evident in the essays by boys? Or would the primary socialization of both children by the mother continue to account for differences, even when the topic of study is the father?

7.    A comparison of neurotic and deviant cases of mother-daughter relationships (using cases handled by institutions and therapists) with the whole range of so-called "normal" cases might provide criteria for defining "normal" and "difficult" female development, thus differentiating some of the conservative views of Freud (Wodak 1984). His distinction of three types of development (the girl separates and identifies with the mother; the girl identifies with the father and rejects the female role; or the girl identifies with neither and does not acquire any stable sexual identity) is clearly not valid today, as the change in gender-role definitions shows. Closer differentiation of the course of female development would have interesting implications for psychoanalytic theory, as well as for the treatment of disturbed cases.


## NOTES

1) Our interest is not in the linguistic parameters of the interview, but in the information exchanged. For this reason, German responses have been translated with a view to keeping content intact but providing a sense of the verbal qualities of the original. Since we are not interested in the language behavior of the mothers, the criticism often leveled by sociolinguistics against the interview as an instrument for obtaining natural linguistic data does not apply (Berens 1975; Schank 1979; Dittmann 1979; Steger 1971).

2) Psychologists and sociologists have long opposed the qualitative analysis of interviews (Jahoda, Deutsch and Cook 1974). If done at all, a qualitative analysis can only supplement a quantitative, statistical investigation. On the other hand, ethnomethodologists and symbolic interactionists — if they accept the interview at all — argue only for qualitative analyses (Cicourel 1971; Berger 1974; Filstead 1971).

3) A description of the sample is included in Table 5. The code numbers are used throughout the qualitative and quantitative study of the mother-daughter pairs, thus allowing the reader to go back and connect all necessary information with each example given. In addition, the most important descriptive data on the mothers and daughters (sociological parameters and answers to important questions) are included.

4) See the English version of the Giessen Test in Appendix III.

5) Protocols, in which an assessment of the nonverbal characteristics of the situation were recorded, were made immediately following each interview (with both mothers and daughters).

6) We should stress that we are not interested in discourse-analysis here, but only in the markers which are indicators of the impact of Motherese and of sex-specific socialization.

7) It is worth stressing that recent research in network theory indicates that *everyone* in the child's network is potentially influential upon the child's emotional well-being.

8) Adjectives were counted in the Austrian sample. We do not include an analysis of their use here, because no comparable phenomenon occurred in the U.S. data. Neither adjectives nor adverbs occurred in sufficient quantity to merit inclusion in the study.

# APPENDIX I

## CASE STUDIES

It was, naturally, difficult to choose which cases to discuss in depth. We decided to select one mother-daughter pair from each type of cluster. For these, we give the most important personality-variables from the Giessen Test taken by the mothers, and we interpret the central issues evident in the essay, especially those concerning the mother-daughter relationship and the educational style of the home. Then we present self-assessment information from the interviews with mothers and daughters. The sociological parameters for the case studies can be found in Table 13, and the Austrian essays are printed in full in Appendix IV (because of privacy requirements, essays cannot be photographically reproduced).

*CASE STUDY 1*: Masochistic Mothers
(Cluster 8)

[CNR 98]

(Austrian)

(Working Class, B-stream of public school; mother married, housewife; three older brothers; no caretaker in the afternoon; no wish for child, profession, or marriage; feels discriminated against as a girl)

The essay, written in a very untidy hand, is a long, reflective text, containing expressions of affection (the essay ends with a drawing of a big red heart with an arrow through it, with the inscription "My Mother and I") intermingled with feelings of loneliness and neglect. The argumentation shows frequent ruptures, and the writer uses many mitigating particles:

> In the summer I drive with my mother to the Old Danube. My mother suns herself there. Otherwise, I almost never see her. Her mood is changeable. Mostly, she is in a good mood, but if she says no, it's "No." I like her very much. Mostly, I am jealous that she is just [a typical rupture] . . . . But sometimes I don't like her and think that she is unfair. . . . She has to cook

for six people. . . . She has an uncle at the Old Danube [a boy friend?] . .
. . I don't look much like her, I don't have all her good habits.

The depiction of the mother in her role as mother is central to the essay, which goes on to discuss the mother's cooking, gardening, and housework. The girl closes her essay with a regressive "oral orgy" about what her mother can cook. Her self-image is as a girl whose feelings about the mother are ambivalent ("I think that my mother is very nice to me. I help her, too. Mostly I have to put things away"). She complains of the restrictive educational style of the home (her mother sometimes slaps her and refuses to let the girl do things her sister is allowed to do), and the daughter complains that her mother is unfair ("I would love to have a dog, but she won't let me. I am not even allowed to have a goldfish").

In the interview, the girl speaks openly about her feelings of loneliness and neglect. Even on weekends she does not see her mother but, rather, goes to visit a friend. She does not tell her mother everything; she says she discusses problems with her father, who is less strict than her mother. Asked whether she would like to be a boy, she replies, "Well, then I could do more, because they never take me with them."

The mother has quite a different picture of her relationship with her daughter ("Well, this is difficult, but I mean, we relate quite well"). She tells the interviewer that she is usually at home, that there are no complications in their relationship, and that her daughter talks openly about everything with her. It is the relationship between daughter and father that she characterizes as bad.

The contrast between her report and her daughter's illustrates well the differences that may exist between self- and other-assessment. Clearly, something is very wrong in this family, but neither daughter nor mother expresses it openly. Nothing turns up in the interview about the "uncle" and the "Old Danube," and the mother seems to have no sense of the loneliness of the child.

Her relationship with her own mother is good, but she does not believe herself to be much like her mother. She wishes her daughter to find happiness, but she has no picture of a future husband in mind. At first, she does not understand the question about whether or not she has told her daughter about the "facts of life"; then she replies "Yes, always, if she came with questions, of course; I waited and she came anyway with her questions."

The home is small and crowded (six people live in two and a half rooms), and during the interview the mother remains shy and uncomfortable, unable to sit still. She is not content with her life as a woman; she would like to have studied, gone on in school — but with so many children . . . (she laughs insecurely very often).

[CNR 1114]
(American)

Chicana, Working-class; two older sisters; mother married; mother works parttime, is caretaker after school; daughter wants to be a dentist, but does not expect to combine career with motherhood)

Ambivalence is signaled by the negative coordinator in the very first sentence of this girl's essay:

> Me and my mother get along well, but sometimes we do not. We sometimes get in an argument about how come she does not let me go to my friends house. I tell her I am twelve years old, but she will not listen to me. When me and my mother go somewhere, like the Del Amo Mall, she usually buys some clothes or takes me out to eat. . . . I like to do things with my mother because I can learn a lot from her. Like I could sew and cook dinner for my family, that only when I have to. I like my [mother] because I am taller than her. She is only five foot two, and I am five foot three. Well, I love my mom so much because she taught me everything I know.

This essay begins with a straightforward evaluation of the mother/daughter relationship, but then it loses focus as the girl seeks to elaborate on the initial generalization (that she and her mother get along well). There is an immediate contradiction, followed by an illustration; then there is an extended digression in which she discusses the size and scope of the shopping center they visit. Finally, she provides three positive statements about the mother ("I like to do things with [her]," "I like [her]," and "I love [her]"), each followed by a justification based not upon the mother's traits but upon the advantages felt by the girl ("because I can learn a lot from her," "because I am taller than her," and "because she taught me everything I know").

In the interview, the girl was friendly but reticent, giving short and often contradictory answers. A large, plump girl, mature for her age, she would choose to be a puppy "because they are cute." There is an apathy evident in many of the details she gives about her daily life: she watches reruns of cartoons after school (most children her age have moved beyond this); she listens to whatever music her sisters put on, expressing no favorites herself; asked what kind of books she likes to read, she replies "Ones that have chapters" and then asks, uncertainly, "Fiction?" Her answer may have represented an attempt to say what was expected of her; earlier in the interview she identified reading as a subject that gave her difficulty.

The mother is a second-generation American woman of Mexican descent. This was one of the mothers who preferred to talk about children other than the daughter participating in the case study. The two older daughters have given her a great deal of grief; this one is good-natured and popular. No problems.

She is unable to understand much that her daughters do or hope to do. One of them has attempted suicide, but the mother cannot understand why she would want to hurt herself ("She has a problem; she's nervous"). She hopes her daughters will go to college, but she has only a vague notion of what they will learn ("I think academic something"). When one daughter wanted to fight back against a bully, the mother wouldn't let her, fearing that it would go on the daughter's record (although she is not clear who keeps these records or who might eventually look at them). The daughter was furious. "And now she thinks I'm against her. She wanted me to be on her side." Although she tries to understand the problems of the current generation, she expresses little sympathy for them. They begin dating too young, they use unacceptable language ("Little kids: everybody says those bad words"), and they lack manners ("I try to tell them that they should respect people, but they don't . . . they don't want to listen . . . they don't know what respect is, really").

This mother has a great many fears for her daughters. There is too much "corruption or something"; she has heard that even very young children are being given LSD or PCP on stickers; and in explaining menstruation to her daughters, she has stressed the dangers of becoming pregnant. She faces such fears alone. Her mother does not live nearby, and when the interviewer inquires who she asks for help and advice when she has a problem, she replies, "I don't ask anybody. My husband, I guess" (this was her only reference to him in the interview). Nevertheless, she insists "It's good to be a woman. I'm really satisfied to be a woman."

## COMPARISON - AUSTRIA AND THE U.S.

The Giessen test showed the Austrian mother to have negative social resonance, to be submissive, passive, self-critical, only slightly open, and sociable — an extremely contradictory picture of a woman with masochistic tendencies. The American mother's profile was very much the same, except that she scores even lower on sociability.

Although their life styles are similar (both are working class and live with large families in crowded conditions), there are only a few similarities between the mothers and daughters in this case study. Neither mother is happy or confident in her life as a woman. Both are characterized as strict by their daughters, and both hit or slap when angry. Neither has a clear idea of what she hopes the future will bring for her daughter, but rather has only vague hopes that she will find happiness. Both have good relationships with their own mothers but consider themselves to be quite different from them.

Both daughters portray their mothers in the role of housekeeper/cook/ mother. Remarkable is the similar way that both express their ambivalent feelings about their mothers. The Austrian girl writes, "I like her very much. . . . But sometimes I don't like her and think that she is unfair." The American girl writes, "Me and my mother get along well, but sometimes we do not." And both write essays containing digressions which avoid the topic: the Austrian girl, about her mother's cooking; the American girl, about the shopping center to which they go.

## CASE STUDY 2: Active Mothers
## (Cluster 2)

### [CNR 7]
### (Austrian)

(Lower Middle Class, 16th district (School B); parents married; mother employed parttime; has one younger brother; mother is caretaker; daughter wishes to combine profession, marriage, and motherhood; does not feel discriminated against)

This girl wrote a long essay of an expository texttype. The argumentation is full of contradictions and contains stereotypes, adjectives, and particles.

> I have a very good relationship with my mother. She is a little strict. . . .
> She is very particular about what I do in school. She wants a lot from me.
> . . . She does not preach morals, but she does not have too much to fear
> from me. . . . I often go out at eight in the evening with friends and return
> at 9:00. [The mother seems very liberal here.] Of course, there are crises
> sometimes in the family; then we fight for a time. Afterwards we sit down
> and talk. . . . I have a good relationship with my mother, and I hope that
> I will get along with her in the future, too.

This relationship is clearly quite different from that in Case Number 1. Given the brevity of her essay and of her answers in the interview, it is striking how much energy the child invests in making every quality of the mother into a good one, justifying and explaining everything in a positive way, revealing no underlying negative feelings. It is almost too good to be true. In fact, the relationship is ambivalent; the daughter seems jealous. She tells her mother "almost everything," but she confides more in her best friend. She has quite a good relationship with the father. The educational style of the home is liberal: although her parents are strict, they do not punish her and they allow her quite a bit of freedom. Despite the freedom, she would like to be a bird. Why? "Because I would like to be free, to feel free." If she could transform her parents into animals, she would change her mother into a cat and her father into a horse.

The mother, too, is very brief and unrevealing in her interview. She has a good relationship with her husband; the apartment is pleasant and comfortable; the relationship with her daughter is "good, perhaps friendly"; and there are no complications. At least the daughter does not seem to have any problems. The relationship between father and daughter is good, but the child keeps to herself. Asked whether or not she has enough time for her daughter, she replies, "Well, actually, not now. I have been working for a year." In response to the question of whether or not she is content as a woman, she answers, "Well, yes, but I have too much to do now. It is difficult for a woman to find a parttime job."

She has quite definite ideas about her daughter's future career plans and about the kind of man she should marry (it should be someone who can take over responsibility for the house the parents have built). Her relationship with her own mother is ambivalent, but she finds that she is quite a bit like her. On the other hand, she behaves differently toward her own daughter, or would like to.

[CNR 1107]
(American)

(Anglo, Middle Class; two older sisters; parents married; mother is fulltime caretaker, works at home for her husband's business; daughter is vague on marriage and career plans)

The daughter's essay shows the degree to which the mother is involved with her children. Although no affection is expressed in this essay (no protestations of loving or liking the mother), her mother's positive influence is clear.

> My mother and me always do stuff together. Like we talk about school and about my problems. My mother teaches me how to cook and shows me how to put in the other stuff in the cake, how to barbeque a steak, and all kinds of other foods. My mother takes me places that I like to go like to the grocery store and the beauty shop to see all her friends. She helps us with our candy sales. She helps us with our problems like if I get in trouble at school.

The daughter's interview continues the theme of closeness with the mother: in speaking of the children she wants to have, she says she wants to have a girl first "because my mom says that is what she wanted it to be." The mother refers to her as "the baby" rather than by name in the interview, and Leslie says she would like to be a rabbit "because they're cute."

A striking stylistic feature of the interview with the daughter is her use of reported dialogue throughout. In the anecdote about her birth, she quotes her mother's supposed decision ("Okay, her name's gonna be Lester"). Asked whether she has ever known anyone else with her name, she quotes what she said when she first heard of a boy also named "Leslie" (not her real name). In answering why she does not get an allowance, how she is punished, and why she wants a girl baby first, she quotes her mother. In telling about waking up during a frightening movie and in discussing what she does when her mother lets her have candy, she quotes herself.

In a similar way, the mother's speech is full of "So she said," and "Then I said." An important difference between the daughter's interview and the mother's, however, typifies the tendency of mothers to report the relationships between their children as being better than they are. The mother says Leslie and one of her sisters are "bosom buddies"; Leslie acknowledges that her sister is nice to her sometimes, but she lumps both older sisters together as bullies on whom she threatens to tattle to her mother.

Comparing their conversation also gives us a clue to how mothers and daughters view their behavior differently. The daughter says that, although she doesn't get an allowance, her mother sometimes offers to buy her whatever she wants. She says she always chooses very little. Her mother sees things quite differently. She says that the daughter always insists upon *quid pro quo*, citing an instance of taking her out to lunch to make up for having done something for the older sisters a short time earlier.

The mother expresses quite a few ambivalent feelings. She is one of the mothers who preferred to talk about a child other than the one participating in the study. She and her oldest daughter have been locked into combat for years. That is the relationship she would prefer to talk about. Her first comment about the daughter in our study is a negative evaluation ("She's the baby. And she's the whiner"). She says the relationship with her husband is good, but she says tentatively "Sometimes . . . sometimes . . . I tell him" — leaving unsaid the equivocation implied. When discussing having given up her work to have a family, she laughs ruefully ("About that, I don't know"). She has deliberately carved out a life different from her mother's, believing that she does the opposite of what her mother did. Their family is very close: they work together (all of them painting the ceramics the father sells); they play together (ice skating, camping); all participate in church work.

She wants her daughters to prosper and neither to become, nor to marry what she calls "doughnut pushers," warning them that "doughnut pushers" will not "buy them the clothes nor do the things they want."

## COMPARISON - AUSTRIA AND THE U.S.

The Giessen test of the Austrian mother indicates a woman with negative social resonance, who is impatient, boisterous, happy, open and sociable. The American mother's profile suggests that she is more patient and has more social resonance. Otherwise the two are very much alike.

The Austrian and American mothers in Case Study 2 both have ambivalent feelings about their own mothers (the American mother is still in conflict with hers), and both strive to behave differently toward their own daughters. Both have good relationships with their husbands and characterize the father-daughter relationship as being good. And both want their daughters to marry men who will be able to take care of them.

The daughters, although they describe the positive qualities of their mothers at great length, speak more frankly than their mothers about family problems. The Austrian girl writes of "crises" that occur in the family, and the American girl, asked about punishment in the home, answers:

> She puts me on restriction for like a month or something. A long time. . . .
> And sometimes she smacks me, too. And so my dad does too. And my
> mom says, "I don't want you to be like your big sister," cause my sister is
> real // bad mouths my mom and everything.

Both daughters describe the mother in their essays rather than discussing their feelings for her. And although they say they talk freely with their mothers, both acknowledge that they have best friends they are more frank with. The negative side of their relationships slips out in the interviews with both girls.

## CASE STUDY 3: Passive Mothers
### (Cluster 1)

### [CNR 4]
### (Austrian)

(Middle Class, 16th District (School B); mother married, employed fulltime; other caretakers; no other children; child has no professional, child, or marriage wish; feels discriminated against as a girl)

The text, a medium length expository essay containing contradictions, stereotypes, and particles, uses an unusual number of adjectives (both positive and negative). The mother is pictured as a housewife and the girl as a daughter in opposition.

> My mother is a very nice woman. She understands many problems . . . . I have a lot of confidence in her. . . . My parents explain everything that I do not understand to me. . . . What I don't like is that she makes me do a lot of work that isn't necessary. . . . She has a really unrealistic way of cleaning things up. She has a lot of patience, but if she sees my "mess" (that's what she calls my way of keeping things), then she insists on cleaning it up. I like her in spite of this.

The educational style of the home is restrictive, and the girl feels ambivalent about her relationship with her mother, expressing feelings of both hate and guilt. Both parents are teachers. Her father is often away from home, and she does not answer the question about what animals she would transform her parents into. Asked what she tells her mother, she answers "Whatever is her business."

Her answers are very short, and it is clear that she is a lonely child. Although she views her mother's passivity negatively, the daughter, too, comes across as passive. She often does nothing but hang around, and she feels restricted as a girl ("Boys have different opportunities; I think that isn't fair"). She was very closed in the interview, but she would like to be a bird, to fly free in the air.

Her mother was very friendly, but also closed, quiet, and controlled. She considers her relationship with her daughter to be quite good (although she did not tell her the facts of life), and she characterizes the relationship between the father and daughter as the same. Of her relationship with her husband, she says, "Good. There is nothing to say." She has an ambivalent relationship with her own mother, but she finds that she behaves in similar ways. In response to the question about whether or not she is content with her life as a woman, she answers uncertainly: "I mean, . . . I mean with the general life of a woman, I'm actually not content. . . . " But she prefers to talk about school — the subjects and grades of her daughter.

## [CNR 1109]
## (American)

(Chicana, lower middle class; oldest (has a younger brother); parents married; mother works fulltime; relatives serve as caretakers; ambivalent about marriage; wants to be a nurse)

The American girl's essay is full of clichés, but a negative undercurrent is quite apparent. Although she wishes to see her relationship with her mother as one of equality ("[We] are like a team," "We always stick together"), the daughter's essay betrays her excessive concern for maintaining harmony with her mother. To achieve this she takes on the mother-role, doing things that she hopes will please the mother and make her happy.

> Me and my mother are like a team. Whenever she comes home from work I always ask her how was your day and she would ask me the same thing, too. Sometimes I clean the house for her to make her happy. I like to see her come home happy. I really like to see my mom happy because then I get happy, but when she is depressed, I am depressed. Me and my mom go a lot of places. We always stick together. We go shopping, go to a restaurant. If she needs me to go to the store, I go, and when my mom tells me something, I do not argue. I just do it. She is the best mom I ever had, and she is also kind to others.

The American girl is ambivalent about whether it is a good thing to be a girl. She pauses before acknowledging that she is happy to be a girl. She sees the difference between her and her brother as revolving around how much trouble he gets into; compared with him she is obedient and well-behaved ("I do not argue," she writes). He receives physical punishment, but she apparently does not. If she does something wrong, she is sent to her room.

The Mother sees herself as strict, saying "I have to know where they're at all the time. I just want to hold her back as much as I can." She objects to the lyrics of rock music, complaining of "the stuff they're trying to pass off as being okay," and she fears that one of her daughter's older friends will lead the girl into trouble. She is attempting to emphasize Christian values as a means of counteracting cultural pressures upon her daughter, and she is trying to interest her daughter in Christian "soft rock" music. They have also bought a home computer, hoping that it will wean their children away from television and make them content to play at home.

Her relationship to her own mother was disturbed when she married quite young (she was pregnant at the time), but it has improved. Although her relationship with her husband was troubled in the early years — he was not yet ready to settle down when they married — it has improved, and she characterizes the family relationships as good in all respects. She is not particularly content with her life at the moment. Although she returned to work eagerly when her children entered school, she finds her job repetitive and boring.

There are many similarities between this mother and daughter. The mother, who is overweight, is concerned about her daughter's weight. She mentions the girl's loneliness, characterizing her as moody, sensitive, and easily upset (the daughter sees her mother in a similar light). The mother is conscious of the mothering qualities in her daughter's behavior toward her; she says, "I think Maria has a lot of mother in her, because she sometimes thinks she's mother instead of me." She appears not to sense that this reversal of roles is likely to engender resentment and anger in her daughter.

## COMPARISON - AUSTRIA AND THE U.S.

According to the Giessen test, the Austrian mother has negative social resonance, is submissive, controlled, gloomy, frank, but rarely sociable. The American mother is very similar, but has somewhat more positive social resonance.

It is difficult to compare the two cases because all four participants were closed in the interview. There is a remarkable similarity in concern with tidiness in both of these cases. Both mothers are disturbed by disorder in the household. The Austrian girl complains about her mother's impatience with her messiness and insistence that things be kept in order. In much the same way, the American mother becomes grumpy when things are in a mess. Her daughter pacifies her by cleaning the house.

*CASE STUDY 4*: Hysterical Mothers
(Cluster 5)

[CNR 22]
(Austrian)

(Lower Middle Class, 16th district (School B); mother married, house-wife, fulltime caretaker; oldest child; wishes for marriage and children; feels no discrimination as a girl)

The girl's essay is of medium length, a narrative containing contradic-tions and stereotypes, but without negative particles. The text is unusually interesting. It consists of two events revealing the behavior of her mother in two different situations given as examples of their relationship. Although other essays containing narratives appear in the sample, none is as clever and skillfully written as this one:

> I just got my English test back, mark "5" [the lowest grade]. This time I needed more time than usual to think of what to say. What will my mother say? I had told her that it would probably be a "3." . . . My mother looks at me and says, "Well, great, now you will have to learn more for the next test." I thought I was dreaming because she did not scold me. . . . But my mother can also be different. I was listening quietly to music in the room that I share with my brother. Suddenly she came into the room and turned off the radio. I complained. . . . Then I said, "Just because you weren't allowed to listen, I'm not allowed to. What an education! Good night!" This was too much for my mother and — wham — I had her hand on my face. . . . Five minutes later, I stood at her bed, my face red, my eyes swollen, and I apologized. . . . My mother hates lies. If I lie, she punishes me and does not let me invite friends over or to go to parties. She takes these restric-tions very seriously and does not forgive me so quickly . . . . I love my mother and hope that she stays as she is.

This essay really describes the character of the mother very clearly: she is inconsistent and unpredictable. She can be very sweet, but she is also very severe. The educational style, therefore, is strict and the relationship, ambi-valent, with the feeling of guilt dominant. (The guilt mechanism is nicely exposed here.)

The girl has a little brother with whom she fights sometimes. She has many interests; she likes sports and is learning to play the guitar. She says she can tell her mother everything, but not her father ("I have less contact with him"). Asked if she is punished often, she replies, "Not really, even if

I do something bad. My mother gets angry, but five minutes later she apologizes and everything is forgotten — unless I lie!" The father is more severe and more traditional in attitudes toward makeup and friends. She answers quite openly and is not at all shy. If she has children, she would like to continue to work (unlike her mother). She would like to transform her whole family into dogs because it is her favorite animal. The impression of a clever and creative child is underscored by the self-confidence displayed in the interview.

The mother, very shy at first, is quite pretty. She laughs a lot and speaks with animated gestures. Of her daughter she says, "She is a child without problems, a *really* unproblematic child." Punishment is rare, and the daughter talks freely with her mother about everything. She confirms the daughter's view that they are like friends, but she contradicts the daughter's characterization of the relationship to the father: she insists that it is very good.

Although her childhood was stormy, her relationship to her own mother is good now ("but I see her very seldom"). She tries to be different from her mother. She hopes her daughter will be as happy as she is, and she has quite definite ideas about the sort of husband the daughter should marry (among other things, he should be smarter than her daughter).

Her relationship with her husband is very good, and she is content with her life as a woman: "Only at the beginning, it was difficult to stay home from the office. . . . I'm really happy and don't want to go to work any more." Then she describes everyday life in detail and how much she is needed; she is proud about being essential to the family and does not want to think about the future when the children will be grown up. Her answers generally are exaggerated ("fantastic," "wonderful"). She describes herself in such positive terms that one wonders what she is covering up.

[CNR 6120]
(American)

(Anglo, Middle Class; mother married, works fulltime; youngest; hopes to combine marriage, motherhood, and career)

This girl opens and closes her essay with very positive remarks about the relationship with her mother, but the main body contradicts her generalizations, illustrating the difficulties they have and blaming those difficulties on the mother. It illustrates well the "shadow text" finding its way to the page despite the writer's attempt to suppress it (and, judging by the coda, her belief that she has succeeded in suppressing it):

> My mother and I have a really good relationship. We talk about problems and go places together. Sometimes we get into little arguments. For instance, when she asks me to do something and I don't do it. Also when she's in a grumpy mood because of work, she'll tend to get upset at me for no reasons, but she makes up right away and I know she doesn't mean it. We have never gotten into a huge argument and don't think we ever will. So all in all my mother and I have a great relationship.

The daughter confides more in her mother than her father, and she feels closer to the mother. If her parents are displeased with her, they respond quite differently: her mother "yells at me just a little and then she'll make up with me, but my dad would ground me and stuff." She prefers the mother's way, although she believes that her father's method of punishment is probably more effective.

Like many younger children, she resents the fact that her older sisters can do things she cannot do ("They can go out at night and stuff"). She considers the educational style of her home to be strict, at least so far as she is concerned.

The mother, a teacher who returned to work when this daughter started to school, worries that her daughter is trying to keep up with the older sisters. She is also concerned that her daughter has few interests other than going to the beach, jogging, and playing volleyball. She wishes the girl had a greater interest in intellectual or artistic pursuits, since these would "fill that void when she complains of nothing to do." The girl has some musical talent, but she lacks the discipline to practice regularly, according to her mother. Although the father and daughter "just cannot get along," she sees her own relationship to the daughter as a good one, believing that they are on friendly, easy terms, although "we have little in common. She's nothing like me."

Her relationship to her own mother is "all right, but not spectacular," and she believes it is helped by the fact that her mother lives several thousand miles away. "We see each other every three or four years, and that is really enough right now." She thinks she is nothing like her mother and insists, in fact, to the contrary, "My husband is more like her than I am." She is quick to add that she gets along very well with him despite the similarity. "I am lucky to be so happy," she says.

## COMPARISON - AUSTRIA AND THE U.S.

The Austrian mother's Giessen test reveals the mother to be attractive, extremely patient, controlled, open, slightly sociable, and hypomaniacal (easily upset and excited). There is an absolute rupture between the patience and hypomaniacy. One wonders whether, in fact, she is hiding from herself more impatience than she can acknowledge. The American mother's profile differs chiefly in the degree of patience reported: her report on this item places her more toward dominance than toward patience. An interesting contrast between the two mothers is the Austrian girl's report that it is *she* who apologizes after the mother has lost her temper. According to the American girl, the *mother* comes around and apologizes later.

Both mothers counteract for their daughters the severity of the father by expressing affection and emotional support openly. Both daughters, despite the undercurrent of anger expressed in each essay, appear on the surface to feel good about themselves and about their family relationships.

*CASE STUDY 5*: Modern Mothers
(Cluster 7)

[CNR 48]
(Austrian)

(Middle Class, 19th district (School C); parents married; mother employed fulltime; youngest child; other caretaker in the afternoon; wishes for career, marriage, and children; is satisfied to be a girl)

The daughter's essay is reflective, contains some contradictions and particles, and is moderately long. The mother's work seems to be central for the daughter (the mother is a successful doctor). The daughter perceives herself as a woman and is in opposition to her mother:

> I am similar to my mother in some respects. I do not only mean in looks, the same brown eyes, the same nose, but also in things which we like. My mother invests a lot of money in clothes, which I would do too if my pocket money would allow it. She is a doctor and works a lot, sometimes too much. Then she has to lie down and nobody may disturb her. . . . She always comes home late. . . . But I have to be punctual. She is very intelligent, but very impatient. When she used to study with my brother, she would begin after

a while to scream at him because he did not understand everything (but now he has outside help and it doesn't happen anymore). In the evenings she often goes out with my father, but sometimes we have a "family evening"; this is where we are all at home, and she cooks. That she often is away does not mean that we do not have a family life. She is also willing to go somewhere with my father if I have a party in the evening. She has a lot of sympathy for me, and we understand each other very well.

This essay is full of contradictions, reproaches, and justifications. Although she understands (on a cognitive level) that her mother could not bear to stay at home (the girl wants the same life for herself), she must rationalize her feelings of neglect, arguing that she does have a family life and that her mother does understand her. The "very well" at the end may be a cliché, or it may be designed to convince the researcher that despite her equivocations the relationship is good. On the one hand, she is hiding her hurt. On the other, she seems very grownup and independent. The educational style of the home is liberal, permitting her to act independently. Despite the good relationship with her mother, the daughter expresses rivalry and jealousy. They get along well, but she says, "I don't know. It depends on her mood. Then I can, sometimes she does not have time, I mean ..." She finds it impossible to express the nuances of her mother's moods.

The mother is small, thin, friendly, and very interested in our study. She laughs often and easily, is secure, resolute, but not overly controlled. Her answers are long, and clever, and the argumentation is logical. Although she does not think that her children have a very good relationship, she attributes this to the age of both. About her own relationship with her daughter she says: "I think, I hope it is good, that she is as good as she should be. . . . I don't control her. . . . There are no problems, whatsoever."

She has separated from her daughter, but it may have been too soon. The daughter demonstrates in her essay that she has not yet arrived at this stage of separation. The mother perceives her daughter as being very independent — perhaps too independent. She does not guess at what profession will be appropriate for the daughter, but she emphasizes that women must have jobs: "It is my real and honest opinion that a mother who is at home and just takes care of the children and cleans their shoes — that this is not fruitful — not even for the children."

What about a husband for the daughter? She does think about it, but she does not want to meddle in the children's lives. She knows that the man her daughter marries will have a difficult life because the daughter is clever and good-looking.

This woman sees herself as being completely different from her own traditional, long-suffering mother. Since she could never talk about problems with her mother, she wants to be more of a friend to her daughter. But she also wants to have her own life. Is she content with her life as a woman?

> Very, very. Yes, absolutely. I know one should never say these things so loud, but I say this to school friends who also married at the same time as I (or earlier) and asked me why I studied and said that I should stay home with my children, and one now, she sits alone and actually a lot of friends envy me because of my job, which really fulfills me and because our family functions in spite of it.

Asked whether she has enough time for her daughter, she replies: "Well, I must say yes, yes, yes. . . . It is not the *quantity* of the togetherness, but the quality . . . !" She enjoys their family dinners and cooks superb meals, but she doesn't do it every day.

This mother lives quite a liberated life. Clearly such a mother (liberal and unpossessive) may be difficult for a daughter to compete with. But the family members seem to have found a comfortable compromise. Her relationship to her husband is very good. She talks a lot about it, and she is quite aware that men have difficulties living with successful women. But they have found a workable compromise and are very open with each other. The father and daughter have a very good relationship, as well. He is very proud of her. There are no contradictions in her narrative, the picture is of a very self-confident woman who lives her own life in addition to fulfilling her roles as wife and mother.

## [CNR 1110]
### (American)

(Anglo, Middle Class; parents married; mother works fulltime; a twin, also has a younger sister; wants to be a teacher, marry, and have children; is satisfied with being a girl)

The American girl's essay is a competently written, reflective essay. It handles in an organized fashion three separate themes: 1) things the girl does with her mother; 2) nurturance provided by the girl when the mother is angry; and 3) nurturance provided by the girl when the mother is sick. The abstract sets forth the first theme ("My mother and me do a lot of things together") and the coda echoes it ("we do things that I would like to do with the kids when I grow up").

> My mother and me do a lot of things together, like we go places together, and we clean our house together . . . . When we shop together my mother gets a lot of things for me. So I do a lot of things for her to thank her for what she does for me. When my mom gets mad at my little sister, I help her to be calm, and I ask her to be nice. But when she gets mad, she is usually angry at someone (her sisters, her mother, or her boss). But she gets over it because I help her to try not to be mean to them. So I ask her to say sorry to whoever she is mad at. When my mom is sick I feel sad for her. She gets sick a lot, too. . . . When she is sick, I help out around the house and do my chores so when she gets better she will have a clean house to look at. So now you have heard things that me and my mom do. I hope that I can be just like my mom because we do things that I would like to do with my kids when I grow up. . . .

The opening and closing illustrate the kinds of clichés that occur throughout the U.S. essays. Since the substance of the essay concerns things the daughter does for the mother, the coda (in which she expresses the wish to be just like her mother when she grows up) seems somewhat ironic, especially following the discussion of how she must nurture an irritable, hypochondriacal mother. This girl already sees herself as performing the maternal role far better than her mother. The daughter is the nurturant one: she helps calm and sooth, she advises, and she cleans for her mother — all of these services are explicitly described and are attributed to the gratitude for the unstated things that mother does for her. (The only one of these the girl chooses to name typifies the American essays: "When we shop together, she gets me lots of things").

The affectivity of the essay is complex. The girl expresses solidarity, but she is in competition with her mother. There is no overt expression of ambivalence, but it is implicit in the strange disjunction between the girl's professed admiration and the pitiable portrait she draws.

The mother who appeared for the interview bore little resemblance to the mother depicted in this essay, nor did her self-assessment agree with the daughter's view of her. She is self-confident and outgoing, sure of her skills as a mother, except for her relationship with the youngest (seven-year-old) daughter. She acknowledges that there is an unresolved conflict with the youngest, but she attributes the difficulty to her daughter's personality ("I would rather have another set of twins, if they had the personalities and temperament of those two, than to have another single child like my youngest. Yes. Definitely.") She admits, however, that the difficult daughter is the one most like her. She realizes that she is excitable and has a tendency to "go flying [off the handle]," but she goes on to say proudly: "But when it's something that is very big and very important, or something that would devastate another mother into tears, I can easily handle it. . . . I'm the type of person who is great in an emergency." [Her daughter is as proud of her ability to handle the little, everyday problems as the mother is of her ability to handle the big ones.]

This mother is proud that her daughters are learning to be independent. She is eager to help them become more self-sufficient and to separate from her, and she believes that working has facilitated their growth: "I started working parttime, and they started doing extra little chores around the house and helping me there, and that's how one of my daughters got busy in the kitchen, cause she helped me get dinner . . . It's a lot easier . . . when you *need* for them to take the responsibility. Definitely. Oh yes."

She is quite different from her own mother, with whom she was in sufficient conflict that she left home at sixteen. When she was growing up, she and her sister had full care of the younger ones while her mother (who was a single parent) was at work. "My mother was so busy surviving that there was not a lot of affection . . . my children, we enjoy each other's company. I never enjoyed my mother's company." As a result of her early practice, she feels absolute self-confidence in her abilities as a mother. She laughs and says, "I've already been through the rebellion things with my sister, you know." (But she acknowledges that she hopes her own daughters do not rebel.)

She hopes that they will go to college because they are intelligent and because she believes they will have to work throughout their adult lives. However, she feels that it will be good for them to do so. Her own days as a housewife quickly became oppressive to her, and she found it difficult to fill her time. She is happier with her life now. Asked what was the worst thing about living in Los Angeles, she replied: "The fear! I think the fear. Especially with daughters. Uh, I dunno if it's — because it's just ingrained in us, you know, that boys can take care of themselves, but you know girls must be watched over. And they can't take care of themselves . . . it's a constant fear."

## COMPARISON - AUSTRIA AND THE U.S.

The Giessen profile for the Austrian mother included the traits "very attractive, dominant, boisterous, aggressive, frank, and sociable". The American mother had the Giessen cluster closest to that identified as [7], one which occurred only once in the Viennese sample. The U.S. mother differs in Giessen profile only in the lesser degree to which she thinks of herself as socially accommodating.

Despite the cultural and family differences between the two cases, there are striking similarities between the mothers and daughters in Case Study 5. Both mothers gave lively, definite answers. Both mothers see themselves as different from their own mothers. They value their lives as working women, and yet are proud that their own mothering skills are superior to those of their mothers. Their answers to the question about telling the daughters the facts of life were strikingly similar. The Austrian mother replied, "Well, actually I waited, and that is, she came with all the questions she had." The American mother said, "Whenever . . . they've worked up enough courage to ask me that question, I'll give them an honest answer." (These oblique strategies are in keeping with the response of liberal mothers, generally.) Both express some disdain for housework and find pleasure in having been able to create lives for themselves separate from those of their children. Both are eager to foster self-sufficiency in their daughters. And both have worked out partnerships with their husbands. (This, apparently, is almost essential to a happily functioning home where the mother works.)

Their daughters, too, share many similarities. Both model after their mothers (the Austrian daughter in looks, clothes, and profession; the American daughter in nurturance). Both feel some rivalry with the mother and want to compete with her (the Austrian daughter expresses it in terms of her mother's appearance and rationalizes her own failure to measure up; the American daughter implies it in her successful "mothering" of her mother). Both daughters are content to be female and are confident that they will be able to manage career, marriage, and children simultaneously, just as their mothers have done.

*CASE STUDY 6*: Positive Mothers
(Cluster 4)


[CNR 42]
(Austrian)

(Upper Class, 19th district (School C); oldest daughter; parents married; mother, housewife and caretaker; wishes for profession, marriage, and children; feels no discrimination against her as a girl)

This represents the largest cluster of mothers in the Austrian sample, and it includes mothers from all social classes. The essay is chiefly a description of the mother using positive adjectives, avoiding stereotypes,and without particles or counterstatements that might reveal contradictory feelings.

> My mother is as tall as I am, blond and 35 years old. She is always smartly dressed, not very spectacular, but also not traditional. My mother must be very courageous sometimes, because my father often makes cool remarks which would make another woman cry. But she says nothing, stays quiet. But I don't want you to misunderstand my father. He is always funny and joking around [a contradiction and rationalization about the father]. . . . My mother is, as already mentioned, very quiet and patient. She is strict, if she has to be strict, because she cannot let us do everything we want. Otherwise, she gives my sister and me a lot of freedom. When my parents were first married, they had little money. My father was a salesman in a computer firm. But now they have gone a long way and my father has worked his way up to the director of the firm. . . . My mother is a good housewife, who likes to rest sometimes, as well. My parents enjoy sports. . . . My mother and I like going into town together or other places. . . My mother likes animals very much . . . She loves her husband and the family [this was added later] holds together in all situations.

Clearly, the atmosphere at home is not the best. The daughter sides with her mother and is understanding and sensible, perhaps too sensible for her age. Although it remains hidden, she must feel great aggression against her father, and she must also think that her mother should be less patient and fight more for her rights. Any feelings of jealousy, opposition, or aggression are hidden both in the essay and interview. She says that she sometimes fights with her sister, that her mother scolds, but does not punish, and that she would like to transform her father into a dog or lion (something fierce), her mother into a cat or bird. She confides more in her mother than in her best friend, telling the mother "everything about school and friends and special events," but she tells her father only about school. Yet, later in the interview, she insists that she confides in both parents equally (a contradiction). Since she is one of the very few girls to write so much about her father, she may be competing with her mother, feeling rivalry for the affection of the father. She would like to be a bird (the bird wish is common among children who feel closed in).

If she has children, she would stop working (like her mother). Asked why she would study for a profession in this case, she answers: "One can start again, when the children are grown up and independent." Asked if she thinks that the life of her mother is dull, she replies that her mother goes to art lessons, goes to town, visits friends, and has a busy social life.

The mother is young, with long hair, very pretty and distinguished-looking. She is thoughtful and seems calm, with controlled gestures. After the interview, she talks about the courses she is taking and the problematic situation of women in some families. She defines the relationship between the sisters as very good. Of her own relationship to her daughter she says: "I have, I think, a very good relationship and a very friendly relationship. . . . I am pleased that she has come to the stage where she really comes to me: where I can help her and she can help me." She says that she has no difficulties with the daughter; she has plenty of time for her and they talk freely about everything. In addition, she characterizes the relationship between the daughter and husband as very good (a contradiction). She calls the relationship between her husband and herself "a warm partnership," adding "I think we have a good marriage" [the mitigation of "I think" is evident].

Her relationship with her own mother is not good; she was educated in a restrictive way and always went to her father with her problems. Although she tries very hard to be different from her mother, seeing herself as more tolerant, she discovers similarities sometimes. She has not thought about her daughter's future yet, but of course she wants her daughter to be happy. (Such an attitude indicates that she is not possessive, dominating, or ambitious for her daughter.)

Asked whether she is content with her life as a woman, she replies:

> Yes, I am actually very content right now. I have found a way which makes me happy. . . . While the children were small, I had a parttime job for two years. I was able to do that because I worked only two hours a day. . . . And I found out that I — maybe — could do more than housework. But I also found out that I felt closed in, and I actually couldn't do justice to my interests. And so . . . I chose: "You are a housewife and mother and stay with the children." I do it so that in the mornings — the time when my children are taken care of — I have for myself.

Surprisingly, it was the father who told the daughter the facts of life, and she is concerned that the daughter does not talk about these things with her (a contradiction of her earlier claim). She favors open discussions about everything with the children, believing that is why the daughter is so sensible. Having been poor (she is now Upper Class), the mother has some status problems which she discusses quite openly. She does not want her children to be as spoiled as the others in the same school.

After a long discussion about the school, she mentions another problem (which illustrates how happy some women are to be able to talk with a stranger, a therapist perhaps): she has broken a friendship of long-standing because the woman attacked her husband. The mother has found it difficult to explain this to the children, who liked the woman very much.

This case illustrates great differences between self- and other-assessment. The mother seems happy and active, but the daughter perceives her as suffering and finds the father very dominant. This may be a result of the oedipal phase, or it may be a manifestation of the interview-bias.

### [CNR 3105]
### (American)

(Upper Middle Class, Jewish; parents married; mother fulltime caretaker, an active volunteer, especially at school; oldest daughter; wants to be a doctor, continue her profession after marriage and children)

Both the mother and the daughter characterize their relationship as ideal. The daughter's short essay is free of particles which might indicate contradictory feelings (although it ends in a stereotypical expression of love), and her discussion of home and family simply recounts rituals of her daily life.

> My mom and I do a lot of things together. My mom takes my sister and me to gymnastics, dancing, and also sometimes on Saturdays I go with her to the store and help her shop. In the summer we go swimming every morning .... In the afternoons we go to the Science and Industry Museum, Natural History [Museum], or LaBrea Tar Pits. We also go clothes shopping .... My mom also cares for me when I am sick, like she makes my meals and talks to me when I am lonely. My mother and I love each other very much, we will never stop loving each other for as long as we live.

She is a high achiever, the sort of child adults and teachers like very well (of this her mother remarks "first born stuff, you know"). She has above average intelligence; she has broad interests; she has parents who see to it that she frequents the city's museums; and she appears to go willingly with them.

Her father is unusual. Before becoming parents, he and his wife traded off: she worked while he went to school and then he worked while she went to school. He assisted at the birth of both daughters, and he remains a partial caretaker. He is home when she comes in from school and, in fact, he sometimes prepares dinner.

There is an interesting generational shift in attitudes toward the combining of motherhood and a profession in this family. The grandmother was bitter at being unable to pursue a career seriously while being a mother, and that bitterness led to resentment of her children. This mother quit work when her children were born and expresses no wish to return (although she occasionally does some volunteer work and part time teaching). The daughter wants it all: she hopes to continue with her career after marriage and motherhood. When the interviewer mentioned that her mother had not attempted both at the same time, the daughter insisted that the mother planned to go to work: "She's going to work. She's getting ready for 1984, the Olympics. She's going to — she's kind of like, uh, getting people to buy houses or they're going to set up apartments for people who are coming to see the Olympics or participating." Like her mother, she praises the openness within the family. She talks, she says, as freely to her parents as to her own friends.

The mother, in this interview, was much more frank than the daughter, but she spoke less about her present life as a mother than of her childhood. Before her children were born, the mother had studied for her doctorate in psychology. She was attracted to the field "because I wanted to help other people; I wanted to help myself." She believes it helped her come to terms with her feelings about her own mother (although in the interview she remains obsessed with them):

> I had a terrible relationship with my mother, and I was unaware of a lot of why it was terrible until I was older and in therapy and in school. . . . My mother died last June — before she died, within the six months before her death, we had worked out our things. And — oh! it was lovely — and I was left with a very good feeling. No guilt. None of the bad feelings I could have been left with.

She says that she has set out to create for her own children a very different life from that which she experienced in growing up, but she recognizes that she replicates much that her mother did.

> There have been times . . . when I have become acutely aware of things coming out of my mouth or even entering my mind that were so my mother, and I think "My God, where did that come from?" Of course, I knew where it came from. It came from her. I was just astounded, because a lot of the things that were coming out had basic truth and wisdom. Of course, besides, some of them had anger and hostility, too. When I react to my children, I know, I can feel a lot of my mother in me.

In fact, she differs less in her mothering than she acknowledges. She praises her parents for the freedom allowed to her and her brother, and she wishes to provide the same for her own children. She insists that hers "was a warm and loving home, but [contradiction] we had very few restrictions."

Asked how her own childhood differed from that of her daughters, she speaks in terms of time and personal attention. The crucial complaint about her own childhood seems to have involved distance from her mother. She was her father's daughter, they shared a close relationship, one she believed paralleled by her brother's relationship with her mother. About this she expresses a rivalry which is replicated by her younger daughter, whose behavior reveals a similar jealousy of the older sister. Although she characterizes the sisters' relationship as "a very reasonable sibling rivalry," insisting that the daughters "like each other very much," she notes that the younger one has always tried to fill the shoes of the older, a difficult task, since the older "is a gifted child."

> They are really very loving, but the older one would like very much, in terms of a career, to be a pediatrician. She loves children. She would like to make them more healthy. The younger, now. We went past Cedars [a very large hospital in Los Angeles] one day and she looked at those towers and she said, "What is that place?" And I said it was a place for doctors, and she said, "Oh! You mean if Barbara [not her real name] gets to be a doctor she can have an office in a place like that?" And I said, "Right." And she said, "I want to *own* that building!"

This mother has greater ambitions for her daughters than does the mother in CNR 42. Although she begins in a similar fashion, hoping merely for happiness for her daughters, it becomes clear that she has rather specific goals for them. Asked what kind of husband she wished for her daughters, she answered: "I think, and I certainly would like to see, people who would change and help them to grow and experience joy in living. You know, God, it's great! This is it! Let's make the most of what we've got. We've tried quite hard to give our kids that feeling. . . . Not just a career but whatever. I'd just like to see a, you know, a male counterpart."

## COMPARISON - AUSTRIA AND THE U.S.

The Austrian mother's Giessen profile shows her to be impatient, controlled, cheerful, frank, only slightly socially accommodating. The picture is a bit contradictory, in fact, the low self-confidence coupled with the high satisfaction. The American mother differs only in that she has much greater self-confidence and sociability.

There are strong similarities between the two mothers in Case Study 6. Both had difficult relationships with their own mothers, finding greater happiness in their fathers than their mothers. Both find that they resemble their mothers, despite their wish to reject the model. Both have husbands who are on frank and friendly terms with the daughter (each father, indeed, participated in the discussion of the facts of life with the daughter: the Austrian father entirely alone, the American father in conjunction with the mother). Both women express great contentment with their lives and wish the same for their daughters.

Although both daughters wrote positive essays discussing virtues of the mother, both were somewhat closed in the interview. The Austrian girl was slightly less frank than her mother. The American girl was quite reticent; she spoke little about her family, replying to most questions with one or two word answers.

### CASE STUDY 7: Negative Mothers
### (Cluster 6)

### [CNR 75]
### (Austrian)

(Lower Middle Class, A-stream of public school; mother married, housewife; only child; mother caretaker; wishes for profession and children but not marriage; feels no discrimination as a girl)

The text is reflective, of medium length, containing ruptures and stereotypes, but no particles. The daughter perceives her mother as a housewife and herself as a woman full of insight.

> My mother does not work. She used to work, but when I started school, she stopped. If we are alone, she is almost like a friend. She often puts in a good word with my father if I want something. . . . As we also have a small place in the country, she helps there when she can. . . . To be a mother is no pleasure. As I have no sisters or brothers, it is okay. There are no secrets between us. I think we have a very good mother-daughter relationship.

The stereotypes and jargon seem to hide a lot. Striking is the sentence, "To be a mother is no pleasure." Asked why she wrote the sentence, she replied, "Well, it's certainly not easy. . . . There are children who are a problem. Maybe they get sick. And there are children who . . . how shall I put it? It's just not easy to be a mother."

She seems to pity her mother. Although she rationalizes about her situation, she feels ambivalent, guilty, and jealous. In the interview the source of her guilt comes out even more clearly. When she was in an all-day school, her mother was able to work, but now that she is going to a different school, the mother has to stay at home.

Her mother does not punish her and is much less severe and restrictive than her father. He forbids her to watch TV and does not give her any pocket money. She does not understand why he punishes her, nor does she try to explain. Asked if she tells her father as much as her mother, she answers, "No. Not out of fear, but I don't have any real contact . . . . I like to be with my mother much more than with my father."

She would like to be a teacher and have a child of her own — without marriage. She knows that it must be difficult to raise a child by herself, but she argues "It would be dull to be with one man all my life." Asked if she thinks it is dull for her mother, she answers, "Well, not actually dull, but I notice that my father, he does not want my mother to go away very often if he has to be alone, . . . he is mostly at home, and my mother just has to go away sometimes and so . . . and he does not." Asked if her parents fight often, she replies, "No, actually not. My mother is too forgiving." Clearly the father is a tyrant, and the daughter will require time and help to be able to find normal relationships with men. It is not being a mother that is difficult, but rather being the wife of such a man.

The mother is very friendly, but she keeps a distance between herself and the interviewer. She is very controlled, but after the interview she feels more at ease. Then she says that she and her daughter are completely different. She perceives herself as closed, whereas her daughter is extroverted. The daughter tells her everything, she says. Although she understands that there are difficulties at this age, she insists "I think that our relationship is good" (her answers were all rather short). She quite rightly perceives that the relationship between her husband and daughter is not good. Of her own relationship to him she says, "Well, normal." Pressed on the question of whether she finds him (as the daughter does) insensitive, she answers, "Well, actually not, but, as I mentioned, it is difficult." She tries to explain and rationalize this by telling about her husband's youth (difficulties with his sisters and aunts).

She characterizes her own relationship to her mother as follows: "Well, this is difficult, I mean, as a child one feels misunderstood, but I must say, the older I got, the better the relationship got." But she has never talked frankly with her mother ("I am not a talkative person"). She does discover similarities between herself and her mother, but she does not like them.

She hopes that her daughter will have an active, sensible future and will make something out of her life (perhaps making up for what the mother has missed). But she has not (unsurprisingly) thought about a future husband for her daughter at all.

## [CNR4103]
### (American)

(Black, Lower Middle Class; mother divorced, remarried; mother employed; has infant half-sister; mother and step-father caretakers after school; wants career; ambivalent about marriage and children)

The essay is of medium length, full of stereotypes and contradictions. Unusual is the daughter's elaborate plan for taking care of her mother when she grows up:

> My mother and I are very close. . . . My mother can be very grumpy like me, or she can be very cheerful and fun like me. . . . She knows what I like and how I feel about clothes. My mother and I get along like sisters. We fight over things and rarely agree about anything. My mother and I talk a lot about growing up. When I grow up I am going to be a wealthy doctor. I am going to buy my mother a big house next door to me. She is going to have an elevator in her house. (I insist.) I will have a big brick house. I will also have a motorcycle, a Porsche, and a Mercedes. My mother and I often talk about the facts of life. She could be a doctor because she knows so much. My mother and I make a great team. I am glad she is my mother.

In her interview, the girl was more straightforward about her relationship with her mother. Asked if they get along pretty well, she replied, "Ummmm. Sometimes. Well, I guess so." Asked who she talked to about her problems, she answered, "My cats." (If she could transform herself into an animal, it would be a cat because she likes them best.)

On the question of satisfaction in being a girl she is ambivalent. She used to think it was better to be a boy, since they can do things girls can't do. Tied to this is resentment against her father (her step-father?):

> Because when I was small I wanted a skate board and my mother, my mother kept on — no it was my father, my father kept on saying it was too dangerous, and stuff like that, and like when I want to do certain things like when I used to want to play baseball or all kinds of stuff like that they used to say

like you know "It's too rough for you if you're a girl." And I could have gotten a skate board this Christmas if it wasn't for my dad. It made me so mad.

The mother considers her daughter to be rebellious, stubborn, and hostile. She feels that she has never been as close to this daughter as she is with the younger one. When the daughter was a baby, her marriage was breaking up, and she was too involved in her own problems to take pleasure in motherhood. Now there is a distance between them that she can't bridge. Both she and the step-father are very close to the younger sister (his natural child). In fact, he has always been so undemonstrative to her and to her daughter that she was astonished to find that he was able to express love to their baby. She tries to console her daughter for the indifference of the step-father, but she can only do this by pointing out that he is not warm and loving to her, either. In fact, she says of living with such a husband, "I think it's Hell. It really is. It's terrible." This may account for the daughter's wish for a child (she can see that they give pleasure) coupled with her reluctance to marry (men do not give pleasure to their wives).

The mother has a bad relationship with her own mother, difficulties resulting from her divorce and her failure to go to church. She complains that her mother was strict with her but spoils her grandchildren. Despite her resentment (and, perhaps, jealousy), this mother, in fact, resembles her own. She is strict and controlling (monitoring phone calls, choosing her daughter's friends), and she has quite definite ideas about her daughter's future. It is mandatory that the daughter go to college. When the daughter voiced a desire to get a clerical job like her mother's, she insisted, "You don't want to do that. It's a living. I don't want you to make just a living." The daughter, clearly, must make up for the mother's lost opportunities: "I spent so much time and probably still am spending time trying to find some direction, I would like for her to have very definite goals so she won't be wandering around aimlessly, going from one thing to the other, trying to figure out what she wants."

## COMPARISON - AUSTRIA AND THE U.S.

The Austrian mother's Giessen profile suggests that she is unattractive, impatient, relaxed, dissatisfied, closed, and unsociable — clearly the profile of a depressed person. The American mother is astonishingly similar, both in profile and in her present situation.

Neither mother in this case study is in sufficient control of her own life to be helpful to her daughter. The Austrian mother is closed in upon her own problems (although she does not say so openly). The American mother says quite frankly that she does not provide a model for her daughter: "I'm not really sure I've given her much of a pattern because I've been wandering around aimlessly trying to find some direction myself." Neither woman has found a satisfying marriage, and their daughters are internalizing strange notions of the role husbands play. The Austrian girl sees the husband as a tyrant; the American girl sees a tyrant who is undemonstrative and aloof, but who hands down rules governing her life; and neither expresses a wish to marry (although both would like to have children).

### CASE STUDY 8: Introverted Mothers
### (Cluster 3)

#### [CNR 21]
#### (Austrian)

(Lower Middle Class, 16th District (School B); mother married, works full time; only child; other caretakers; wishes for career, child, and marriage; feels no discrimination against her as a girl)

The text, written in an untidy way, is reflective, containing ruptures and particles, but no stereotypes. The central role of the mother is as mother, and the writer perceives herself as a naughty daughter.

> My mother is 27 years older than me. She does not always dress after the newest style but is always pretty. I get along well with her, although she often scolds me about bad marks. If I talk, she says I scream. I play a lot of sports and play five instruments . . . . It is possible to talk about anything with her. . . . She thinks one must always study hard and be good at school. . . . Before going to work, she went to a higher school, made the Matura in evening courses, where she got to know my father. Now she has a leading position. For twelve years I have endured my mother and this is the way it will stay.

She found it hard to write the essay, she says. In it her feelings are suppressed but not hidden very well; every short sentence tells a whole story. The relationship is ambivalent and although the essay as a whole is very unemotional, cool, and serious, it is touching in that it reveals a great deal of hatred of the mother.

The answers in the interview were also short. She would like to transform her parents into horses because she enjoys riding [them?], and she would like to be a horse, herself. Asked what she tells her mother, she responds "Everything, I don't know" and laughs insecurely. She tells her father less, and she talks to a friend about "things that don't interest my mother." Although both are equally strict, she is not punished, and she is allowed to do everything ("everything" means, in this instance, athletics).

We have already mentioned this case. This was the only mother who came to visit the researcher at the university, wanting to see her daughter's essay because she feared what the daughter may have said. Naturally, she was not shown the essay, but she was permitted to talk informally.

It turns out that she is an extremely dominating, self-confident, hard-working and ambitious mother, who has worked her way up (typical of the Lower Middle Class), and she wants her daughter to learn to play several musical instruments, to skate professionally, and so forth. She is disappointed that her daughter did not make the best marks possible in school, but an explanation that children at this age need some time for themselves seems to calm her.

The mother is tall, wears a traditional suit, and appears somewhat old-fashioned. She is very kind and seems secure and self-confident; however she remains distant. She talks a lot about her job and thinks that her daughter is very proud of her. During the conversation, she keeps knocking on the table very energetically.

Asked about her relationship with her daughter, she replies, "Very good. We fight quite often, but in spite of that, it is very good I think, and I think she accepts me completely." The daughter tells her everything, so she was very hurt when the daughter did not tell her about her first menstruation until three days after its onset (after she had purchased everything she needed by herself). Although this reveals how little the girl confides in her mother, especially on a matter which usually ties mother and daughter together, she rationalizes this as showing how independent the daughter is.

She says of the relationship between her husband and the daughter, "My husband, he is not — he loves her very much; he does everything for her," and then goes on to talk about his difficult childhood, justifying his rigidity and traditional views. She gets along with him very well.

Although her relationship to her own mother was good, she tries to be very different as a mother — more modern and open. But she is quite controlling and has specific ideas about the future she would like her daughter to have (she hopes it will be better than her own). She complains again about the daughter's grades (actually they are above average, but the mother is not satisfied).

Is she content with her life as a woman?

> Yes, I am actually content. I mean, I have a child, where . . . I find . . . except some small things but I mean, with whom I am content, only the marks could be better. . . . I am content with my husband. I have a job rare for women. I fought my way up in a man's world, if you want to see it that way, and have a good income. Thus, I could not wish for more.

She doesn't have as much time for her daughter as she would like, "but what can I do?" she asks.

## [CNR 3101]
## (American)

(Middle Class, Black; mother divorced and remarried; infant half-brother; mother works full time but at home; hopes to combine career with marriage and children)

The essay is very short and full of particles. The self-image is of a naughty child, and the mother hardly appears at all:

> My mother is a real nice person. It is just when I am bad like when I am bad at school or something like that. She will get mad and I probably get a whipping or get on punishment for a weekend. I never get on punishment any longer than that. But now I understand why she does that. It is because I have a bad attitude and a smart mouth. I know that it is that I just when people tell me that when I already know it she does that a lot. I know I do things to make her mad, and I just have to take the punishment.

The girl expresses ambivalence about all the members of her household. Her step-brother, whom she frequently has to care for, is good at "messing up the house." She calls the step-father (whom the mother identifies as her husband) "my mother's boyfriend." She continues to do this even after her step-father has made a point of urging her to call him "Daddy" and has assured her that he thinks of her as his daughter. And, as her essay makes clear, she has a great many problems with her mother. If she could be an animal she would be a bird "because they can go anywhere they want to."

She has several responsibilities in the home — caring for her brother, cleaning, cooking for him when her mother goes to get her hair done, washing dishes. She does not simply say that these are her chores; these are things she *has* to do: "Well, before my mom comes home, the dishes have to be washed, and I have to keep my room clean all the time." She hopes for a glamorous career (stewardess) and wants to marry and have children (twin girls). Asked why she prefers girls, she answers, "Because I like to comb their hair. I don't like combing boys' hair [her brother's?]."

In the interview she says her punishment is having her activities restricted, although the essay mentioned whippings. (The mother confirms the physical punishment; at one point she says that she told her daughter that if she were to run away, "I would just have to come after you, and then I would beat you up!")

The mother has a great many unresolved problems. One is the girl's relationship to her step-father. When he reprimanded her one day she answered, "You're not my daddy." The mother told her, "As long as he's here, he's my husband, so you've gotta respect him. You don't have to like anybody. But you will respect him until you get to be eighteen or are out on your own. But if you can't respect him, you stay out of this house."

She has a continuing conflict with her own mother. In fact, one day she told her mother about all the things she didn't like; she thinks it released some of her anger and made her feel better afterwards. But she had to get several thousand miles away before she could get up nerve to tell her mother (on the telephone). She complains that as a child she had to make her bed before going to school and wash the dishes and she couldn't come home from school late (ironically, complaints very much like her daughter's). She believes that she does not push her own daughter so hard: "So I try to make her pick up after herself, but not to the point where, you know, not the way my mother did." However, later in the interview she acknowledges that one of their arguments revolves around just this question:

> I say she can't go any of those places, 'cause she didn't clean her room. She didn't keep — you know — her part of the house. . . . And she will be angry. And I told her, "I don't care. I know at this point that you probably don't like me very much, but I don't like you either when I have to ask you every day to clean your room, clean your room, and you don't do it. . . ." When I was her age, I was so much older in mind than she is, and so much more responsible, you know, as far as // uh // doin' whatever chores my mother asked me to do. . . .

She resents the fact that her mother is less strict with the daughter than she was with her when she was a girl, and she insists that she is less strict than her mother. It is clear from the interviews, however, that her daughter views her much as she views her mother (the arguments in which her daughter complains that her friends call her "mean" are discussed in detail in Chapter 7 above). She says that she does not make her daughter baby-sit for her: "If I go out, I ask her if she wants to babysit, and if she says 'No,' then I get somebody else. . . . Cause my mother treated me like that, I mean [laughs] 'You've gotta take your sister!'" This woman makes few decisions in her life without reference to her earlier problems, and although she believes she is doing everything differently, it is clear that she is repeating the patterns of her own mother's behavior.

She resents the fact that other mothers do not have the same rules that she does, and she is determined to control the daughter's friendships and to postpone her friendships with boys ("If I pick up the phone [while she is talking to someone] and find that some little girl has called so that some little boy can talk to her, then that little girl can't talk to her any more on the phone!"). She opposes makeup and tells the girl, "I told her, I don't care if you're in college! [Laughs]. I will come up to the school, and I will embarrass you in front of all your friends, so your best thing is to get all your business straight before it comes to me. . . You have to be on your best behavior." And like I told her, "I'm coming up to the school today. I might pop in your classroom and I might not."

She complains that her daughter has a "bad mouth" (the daughter acknowledges this in her essay):

> One day she said, "You make me sick!" And so I said, "I don't care. You make me sick, too." And her eyes grew big, and so I said, "You think I like you all the time?" And she couldn't believe it. She said, "You mean you don't like me?" And I said, "No. You have ugly ways. You talk ugly. You act ugly. And you think I should like you just because I'm your mother?" I said, "You don't like me when I do something you don't want." So I said, it's okay, but she knows that underneath, you know, that I love her.

Although she insists that she will support her daughter in whatever she wants to do with her life, she is certain that her daughter will come to grief unless she follows the mother's advice. She especially fears that the daughter may lose her opportunities through early pregnancy ("I have told her, 'You will not have a boy come and you will not talk on the phone to a boy!'"), and she acknowledges that she would probably urge an abortion upon her daughter if that were the case. She speaks of a friend who made that difficult choice for her own daughter.

## COMPARISON - AUSTRIA AND THE U.S.

The Giessen test indicates that the Austrian mother is unattractive, impatient, compulsive, self-critical, closed, and unsociable. The profile of the American mother is quite similar, although she scores more highly on attractiveness.

There are many differences in these two cases, perhaps attributable to the extreme authoritarianism and the continuing enmeshment of the American mother in her relationship with her own mother (the Austrian mother, on the contrary, had a good relationship with her mother). However, both mothers are extremely controlling (the Austrian mother wanting even to know what her daughter had written in the essay), and both daughters feel sufficient guilt to depict themselves as naughty.

# APPENDIX II

## TABLE 1

Stages of the Fieldwork (in Austria and the U.S.)

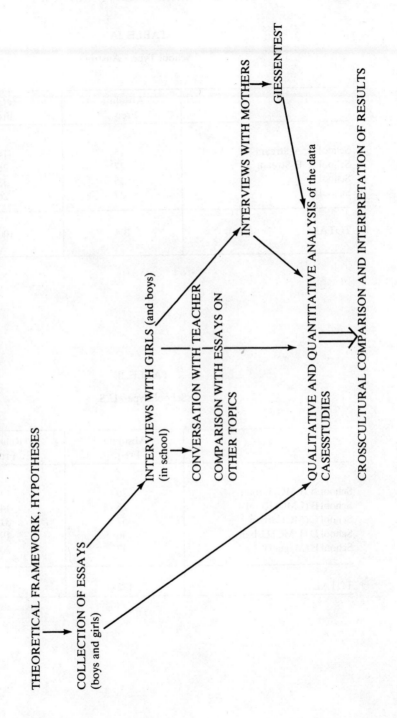

## TABLE 2A

### School Type - Austria

|  | Absolute Freq. | Relative Freq. |
|---|---|---|
| School A, A-Stream | 15 | 14.4 |
| School A, B-Stream | 27 | 26.0 |
| School B | 35 | 33.7 |
| School C | 27 | 26.0 |
| TOTAL | 104 | 100.0 |

## TABLE 2B

### School Type - U.S.

|  | Absolute Freq. | Relative Freq. |
|---|---|---|
| School A (LMC) Urban | 26 | 14.3 |
| School B (LMC) Rural | 26 | 14.3 |
| School C (MC) Urban | 57 | 31.3 |
| School D (UMC) Urban | 36 | 19.8 |
| School E (Magnet) | 37 | 20.3 |
| TOTAL | 182 | 100.0 |

## TABLE 2C

### School Type/Sex - Austria

|                      | Girls | | Boys | |
| --- | --- | --- | --- | --- |
|                      | Absolute Freq. | Relative Freq. | Absolute Freq. | Relative Freq. |
| School A, A-Stream   | 10 | 66.7 | 5  | 33.3 |
| School A, B-Stream   | 7  | 25.9 | 20 | 74.1 |
| School B             | 28 | 80.0 | 7  | 20.0 |
| School C             | 17 | 63.0 | 10 | 37.0 |
| TOTAL                | 62 | 59.6 | 42 | 40.4 |

## TABLE 2D

### School Type/Sex - U.S.

|            | Girls | | Boys | |
| --- | --- | --- | --- | --- |
|            | Absolute Freq. | Relative Freq. | Absolute Freq. | Relative Freq. |
| School A   | 15 | 57.7 | 11 | 42.3 |
| School B   | 14 | 53.8 | 12 | 46.2 |
| School C   | 30 | 52.6 | 27 | 47.4 |
| School D   | 20 | 55.6 | 16 | 44.7 |
| School E   | 20 | 54.1 | 17 | 45.9 |
| TOTAL      | 99 | 54.4 | 83 | 45.6 |

## TABLE 3A

### Social Class - Austria

|  | Absolute Freq. | Relative Freq. |
|---|---|---|
| Working Class (WC) | 31 | 29.8 |
| Lower Middle Class (LMC) | 35 | 33.7 |
| Middle Class (MC) | 25 | 24.0 |
| Upper Class (UC) | 13 | 12.5 |
| TOTAL | 104 | 100.0 |

## TABLE 3B

### Ethnicity - U.S.

|  | Absolute Freq. | Relative Freq. |
|---|---|---|
| Anglo | 66 | 36.3 |
| Chicano | 25 | 13.7 |
| Black | 43 | 23.6 |
| Jewish | 12 | 6.6 |
| Other | 36 | 19.8 |
| TOTAL | 182 | 100.0 |

## TABLE 4A

### Mother/Class - Austria

|  | Absolute Freq. | Relative Freq. |
|---|---|---|
| Working Class (WC) | 4 | 13.3 |
| Lower Middle Class (LMC) | 12 | 40.0 |
| Middle Class (MC) | 10 | 33.3 |
| Upper Class (UC) | 4 | 13.3 |
| TOTAL | 30 | 100.0 |

## TABLE 4B

### Mother/Ethnicity U.S.

|  | Absolute Freq. | Relative Freq. |
|---|---|---|
| Anglo | 5 | 33.3 |
| Chicano | 4 | 26.7 |
| Black | 3 | 20.0 |
| Jewish | 3 | 20.0 |
| Other | 0 | 0.0 |
| TOTAL | 15 | 100.0 |

TABLE 5

| CNR | Class | Mar | Prof | CL | MOTHERS RD | RM | RH | Est | Cluster | School |
|---|---|---|---|---|---|---|---|---|---|---|
| 4 | MC | m | f | n | Am | Am | Am | V | 1(1) | B,C |
| 5 | MC | m | Hw | n | Af | C | N | V | 1(1) | |
| 7 | LMC | m | p | n | S | Am | P | V | 2(2) | |
| 8 | LMC | m | Hw | n | Af | C | P | V | 3(3) | |
| 14 | LMC | m | p | y | Am | Am | A | V | 4(2) | |
| 15 | LMC | m | Hw | n | Am | Am | A | V | 1(1) | |
| 18 | LMC | m | p | y | Af | S | P | V | 4(1) | |
| 21 | LMC | m | f | y | Af | Am | P | V | 3(3) | |
| 22 | LMC | m | Hw | y | S | Am | P | V | 5(4) | |
| 26 | MC | m | Hw | n | Af | Am | A | V | 6(1) | |
| 36 | UC | m | p | y | Am | C | P | V | 4(2) | |
| 37 | MC | m | p | n | Am | Af | A | V | / | |
| 38 | MC | m | f | y | Af | Am | P | V | 5(4) | |
| 39 | MC | m | p | y | Am | C | N | V | 3(3) | |
| 41 | MC | m | Hw | n | Af | Am | A | V | 2(2) | |
| 42 | UC | m | Hw | y | Am | C | P | V | 4(2) | |
| 47 | MC | m | Hw | n | S | Af | P | V | 1(1) | |
| 48 | MC | m | f | y | Am | Am | P | V | 7(4) | |
| 49 | MC | m | Hw | y | S | C | P | V | 4(2) | |
| 51 | UC | m | p | n | S | Am | A | V | 6(1) | |
| 52 | UC | m | Hw | y | Am | Am | P | V | / | |
| 71 | WC | m | p | y | Am | Af | A | V | 4(2) | A |
| 72 | LMC | m | p | y | Af | Am | A | V | 5(4) | |
| 74 | LMC | d | f | n | S | Am | N | V | 6(1) | |
| 75 | LMC | m | Hw | n | Am | Am | A | V | 6(1) | |
| 77 | LMC | m | p | n | Af | Am | P | V | 4(2) | |
| 98 | WC | m | Hw | n | Am | Af | A | V | 8(1) | |
| 101 | WC | d+m | f | n | Af | C | A | V | 8(1) | |
| 103 | WC | m | Hw | n | Am | C | A | V | 4(2) | |
| 104 | LMC | d | f | n | S | C | N | V | 3(3) | |

## TABLE 5

### DAUGHTERS

| Sibl | Car | PW | C | M | Dis | RME | RMI | A | Est1 | Est2 |
|------|-----|-----|---|---|-----|-----|-----|---|------|------|
| n | O | n | n | n | y | Am | L | H | S | S |
| y | M | y | n | n | n | R | E | L | L | L |
| y | M | y | y | y | n | Am | E | J | L | S |
| y | M | y | y | y | y | Am | E | H | S | S |
| y | O | n | y | y | n | Am | E | G | S | L |
| y | M | y | y | n | n | R | E | J | S | L |
| y | M | y | y | y | y | Am | L | J | L | L |
| n | O | y | y | y | n | Am | E | H | S | S |
| y | M | y | y | y | n | Am | E | G | S | L |
| n | M | y | y | y | n | Am | L | H | S | S |
| n | M | n | y | y | n | Am | E | J | L | L |
| y | M | n | y | y | n | Am | E | H | S | S |
| y | M | y | y | y | n | R | E | J | S | L |
| y | M | y | y | y | y | Af | L | G | L | S |
| y | M | y | y | y | y | Am | E | G | L | L |
| y | M | y | y | y | n | R | L | J | L | L |
| y | M | y | y | y | n | Am | L | J | L | L |
| y | O | y | y | y | n | R | L | J | L | L |
| y | M | y | y | y | n | Af | E | G | L | L |
| y | M | y | y | y | n | Am | E | G | S | L |
| y | M | n | y | y | n | R | L | L | L | L |
| y | M | y | y | y | y | R | E | J | L | L |
| n | O | y | y | y | y | Am | E | J | S | L |
| n | O | y | n | n | n | Af | E | L | L | L |
| n | M | y | n | y | n | Am | E | J | L | L |
| y | M | y | n | n | y | Am | E | G | L | L |
| y | O | n | n | n | y | Am | L | J | S | L |
| y | O | y | n | n | y | Am | N | H | S | S |
| y | O | y | y | y | n | Am | E | H | S | L |
| y | O | y | n | y | n | Af | E | L | L | L |

LEGEND:

Class: Working Class, Lower Middle Class, Middle Class, Upper Class (WC, LMC, MC, UC).

Mar(ital Status): married, divorced, widowed, separated (m, d).

Prof(ession): Housewife, Part Time, Full Time, (Hw, p. f).

Contentment with Life (CL): yes, no (y, n).

R(elationship)-D(aughter): Affection, Solidarity, Ambivalence Conflict (Af, S, Am, C).

R(elationship)-M(other): Affection, Solidarity, Ambivalence, Conflict (Af, S, Am, C).

R(elationship)-H(usband): Positive, Ambivalent, Negative (P, A, N).

E(ducational) St(yle): V(erbal), N(onverbal).

Cluster: 1, 2, 3, 4, 5, 6, 7, 8: (passive, active, introverted, positive, hysterical, negative, modern, masochistic) the second number corresponds to the contracted 4 clusters.

School: A (A-stream, B-stream), B, C.

Siblings: yes, no (y,n).

(Afternoon) Car(etaker): M(other), O(ther).

P(rofessional) W(ish): yes, no (y, n).

(Wish for) C(hildren): yes, no (y, n).

(Wish for) M(arriage): yes, no (y, n).

Dis(crimination as Girl): yes, no (y, n).

R(elationship)-M(other)-E(ssay): Affection, Ambivalence, Rivalry (Af, Am, R)

R(elationship)-M(other)-I(nterview): (What do you tell her?): Everything, Little, Nothing (E, L, N).

A(ffectivity-Essay): Love, Guilt, Hate, Jealousy (L, G, H, J).

E(ducational) St(yle) 1 (Essay): Strict, Liberal (S, L).

E(ducational) St(yle) 2 (Interview): Strict, Liberal (S, L).

## TABLE 6

### Sociological Parameters (Essay Analysis)

| | | |
|---|---|---|
| **SEX:** | Female | 1 |
| | Male | 2 |
| **CLASS:** | WC | 1 |
| | LMC | 2 |
| | MC | 3 |
| | UC | 4 |
| **SCHOOL TYPE** | A, A-Stream | 1 |
| | A, B-Stream | 2 |
| | B | 3 |
| | C | 4 |
| **MARITAL STATUS** | Married | 1 |
| **OF MOTHER** | Separated | 2 |
| | Divorced | 3 |
| | Widowed | 4 |
| | Second Marriage | 5 |
| **PROFESSION OF MOTHER** | Full Time | 1 |
| | Part Time | 2 |
| | Housewife | 3 |
| **SIBLING POSITION** | None | 1 |
| | Youngest | 2 |
| | Middle | 3 |
| | Oldest | 4 |
| **AFTERNOON CARE** | Mother | 1 |
| | Father | 2 |
| | Day Care | 3 |
| | Other | 4 |
| | None | 5 |
| **PROFESSIONAL WISH** | Yes | 1 |
| | No | 2 |
| **WISH FOR MARRIAGE** | Yes | 1 |
| | No | 2 |
| **WISH FOR CHILDREN** | Yes | 1 |
| | No | 2 |
| **GLAD TO BE FEMALE?*** | Yes | 1 |
| | Ambivalent | 2 |
| | No | 3 |

* In Austria, this was coded as "Discrimination as woman", following the question "Do you feel discriminated against". "Yes" in the Austrian sample thus means "No" in the American Sample.

TABLE 7

Categories for the Analysis of Essays


TEXT TYPE      1Reflective  2Unreflective  (3Poem)
COHERENCE      1Consistency  2Illogicalities  3Contradictions
CLICHÉS      1Yes  2None
LENGTH      1Short(up to 90 words/24 clauses)   2Average(165/40)
               3Long (more than 165/40)
SEMIOTIC      1Picture  2Other  3None
PARTICLES      1Yes  2None
SELF-IMAGE      1Daughter/Son  2Girl/Boy  3Adult
MOTHER ROLE      1Mother 2Housewife 3Wife 4Daughter 5Lover
               6Working Woman
SELF-ASSESSMENT      1Obedient  2Naughty  3Defiant  (None)
EDUCATIONAL STYLE      1Strict  2Liberal  3Neglect  (None)
QUALITY OF SANCTIONS      1Verbally Explained   2Verbally
               Unexplained  3Inconsistent
RELATIONSHIP TO MOTHER      1Affection 2Solidarity 3Admiration
               4Rivalry  5Conflict, Ambivalence  6Confidence
               7Distance
AFFECTIVITY      1Hate  2Love  3Guilt  4Jealousy  5Fear
RELATIONSHIP TO THE RESEARCHER      1Positive (open)  2Ra-
               tionalization  3Regression  4Projection  5Denial
               6Negative

TABLE 8A

## RELATIONSHIP TO MOTHER/SEX (Austrian Sample)

| | | Male | Female | Row Total |
|---|---|---|---|---|
| | Affection | 21 | 5 | 26 |
| | | 80.8 | 19.2 | 25.0 |
| | | 50.0 | 8.1 | |
| | | 20.2 | 4.8 | |
| Solidary | Solidarity | 6 | 4 | 10 |
| | | 60.0 | 40.0 | 9.6 |
| | | 14.3 | 6.5 | |
| | | 5.8 | 3.8 | |
| | Admiration | 9 | 10 | 19 |
| | | 47.4 | 52.6 | 18.3 |
| | | 21.4 | 16.1 | |
| | | 8.7 | 9.6 | |
| Enmeshed - | Rivalry: | 1 | 14 | 15 |
| | | 6.7 | 93.3 | 14.4 |
| | | 2.4 | 22.6 | |
| | | 1.0 | 13.5 | |
| | Ambivalence, | 5 | 29 | 34 |
| Separate - | Conflict | 14.7 | 85.3 | 32.7 |
| | Distance | 11.9 | 46.8 | |
| | | 4.8 | 27.9 | |
| | Column | 42 | 62 | 104 |
| | Total | 40.4 | 59.6 | 100.0 |

$x^2 = 35.99152$     df = 4     $\alpha = 0.00001$

TABLE 8B

RELATIONSHIP TO MOTHER/SEX (American Sample)

|          | Solidary | Enmeshed | Separate | Row Total |
|----------|----------|----------|----------|-----------|
| Female   | 40       | 10       | 45       | 95        |
|          | 23.26    | 5.81     | 26.16    | 55.23     |
|          | 42.11    | 10.53    | 47.37    |           |
|          | 45.98    | 90.91    | 60.81    |           |
| Male     | 47       | 1        | 29       | 77        |
|          | 27.33    | 0.58     | 16.86    | 44.77     |
|          | 61.04    | 1.30     | 37.66    |           |
|          | 54.02    | 9.09     | 39.19    |           |
| Column   | 87       | 11       | 74       | 172       |
| Total    | 50.58    | 6.40     | 43.02    | 100.00    |

$$X^2 = 9.608 \qquad df = 2 \qquad \alpha = 0.0082$$

TABLE 9A

TEXT TYPE/SEX (Austrian Sample)

| Text type: | | Male | Female | Row Total |
|---|---|---|---|---|
| Un-Reflective | Description of everyday life: | 21<br>100.0<br>50.0<br>20.2 | 0<br>0<br>0<br>0 | 21<br>20.2 |
| | Description of person: | 13<br>65.0<br>31.0<br>12.5 | 7<br>35.0<br>11.3<br>6.7 | 20<br>19.2 |
| Reflective | Narrative: | 4<br>44.4<br>9.5<br>3.8 | 5<br>55.6<br>8.1<br>4.8 | 9<br>8.7 |
| | Reflexion: | 4<br>7.4<br>9.5<br>3.8 | 50<br>92.6<br>80.6<br>48.1 | 54<br>51.9 |
| | Column Total | 42<br>40.4 | 62<br>59.6 | 104<br>100.0 |

$x^2 = 60.48709$ \qquad df = 3 \qquad $\alpha = 0.00001$

## TABLE 9B: TEXT TYPE/SEX (American Sample)

Reflective    Un-Reflective

| Text type | | | Row Total |
|-----------|------|------|-----------|
| Female | 77 | 18 | 95 |
| | 44.77 | 10.47 | 55.23 |
| | 81.05 | 18.95 | |
| | 64.71 | 33.96 | |
| Male | 42 | 35 | 77 |
| | 24.42 | 20.35 | 44.77 |
| | 54.55 | 45.45 | |
| | 35.29 | 66.04 | |
| Column Total | 119 | 53 | 172 |
| | 69.19 | 30.81 | 100.0 |

$x^2 = 14.027$      df = 1      $\alpha = 0.0002$

## TABLE 10
### Daughter interview

1. SEX       1Female   2Male
2. CLASS      1WC   2LMC   3MC   4UMC
3. ETHNICITY      1Anglo   2Black   3Chicano   4Jewish   5Other
4. MARITAL STATUS      1Married   2Separated   3Divorced
                       4Widowed   5Second Marriage
5. MOTHER WORKS      1Full Time   2Part Time   3Housewife
6. SIBLING POSITION      1None   2Youngest   3Middle   4Oldest
7. AFTERNOON CARE      1Mother   2Father   3Day Care   4Relative
                       5None
8. PROFESSIONAL WISH      1Yes   2No
9. MARRY?      1Yes   2No
10. CHILDREN?      1Yes   2No
11. GLAD TO BE FEMALE?*      1Yes   2Ambivalent   3No
12. CONTACT CAPABILITY      1Yes   2No
13. FREE TIME      1Read   2TV   3Play
14. TELL MOTHER      1Everything   2Little   3Nothing
15. TELL FATHER      1Everything   2Little   3Nothing
16. PUNISHMENT      1Verbal   2Restrictions   3Physical   4None
17. EDUCATIONAL STYLE      1Strict   2Liberal
18. SIBLING FEELING      1Rivalry   2Friends   3None
19. LING. FORM OF ANSWER      1Generalization   2Story
                             3Description   4Short   5Yes-No

* In Austria, this was asked as "Do you feel discriminated against" ("Fühlst Du Dich als Mädchen benachteiligt") - the translation into 11 (Glad to be female?) seemed better and more understandable.

## TABLE 11

### Mother Interview

1. MOTHER-DAUGHTER    1Affection  2Friends  3Ambivalence  4Conflict
2. TEXT TYPE    1Expository  2Story  3Description  4Short
3. HUSBAND RELATIONSHIP    1Positive  2Ambivalent  3Negative
4. FATHER-DAUGHTER    1Positive  2Negative
5. OWN MOTHER    1Affection  2Friends  3Ambivalence  4Conflict
6. SIMILAR TO MOTHER?    1Yes  2No
7. SEX INSTRUCTION    1Mother  2Others
8. SANCTIONS    1Verbal  2Nonverbal
9. PUNISHMENT    1Verbal  2Restrictions
10. COMPLICATIONS WITH DAUGHTERS?    1Yes  2No
11. CONFIDENCE OF DAUGHTER?    1Yes  2No
12. WISH FOR DAUGHTER    1Luck  2Carrier
13. PROF. WISH FOR DAUGHTER    1Yes  2No
14. SON-IN-LAW    1Status  2Nice  3No idea yet
15. CONTENTMENT AS WOMAN    1Yes  2No
16. CONTACT CAPABILITY OF DAUGHTER    1Yes  2No
17. PARTICLES    1Yes  2No
18. ADJECTIVES    1Yes  2No
19. ARGUMENTATION    1Logical  2Ruptures  3Contradictions
20. SCHOOL    1Good  2Bad

## TABLE 12

The GIESSENCATEGORIES

| | |
|---|---|
| Social Resonance: | very unattractive   unattractive   negative   popular   very popular |
| Dominance: | very dominant   dominant   impatient   submissive   very submissive   overly patient |
| Control: | very vivacious   vivacious   relaxed   controlled   too controlled   compulsive |
| Basic Mood: | hypomaniacal   cheerful   satisfied   dissatisfied   self doubts   depressed |
| Permeability: (Self-disclosure) | very open   frank   trusting   reticent   closed   fearful |
| Social Potential: | very sociable   sociable   little sociable   rarely sociable   unsociable   isolated |

CLUSTERS (Case-Studies): A Typology of Mothers

Cluster 1: Passive Mothers
Cluster 2: Active Mothers (lacking self-confidence)
Cluster 3: Introverted Mothers
Cluster 4: Positive Mothers
Cluster 5: Hysterical Mothers
Cluster 6: Negative Mothers
Cluster 7: Modern Mothers
Cluster 8: Masochistic Mothers

CLUSTERS (Quantitative Analysis):

Cluster A: (1+6+8) = Negative Mothers
Cluster B: (4+2)   = Positive Mothers
Cluster C: (3)     = Introverted Mothers
Cluster D: (5+7)   = Hypomaniacal Mothers

TABLE 13: CASE STUDIES - AUSTRIA AND U.S. COMPARED

| | ≅1 (CLUSTER 8) | | ≅2 (CLUSTER 2) | | ≅3 (CLUSTER 1) | | ≅4 (CLUSTER 5) | | ≅5 (CLUSTER 7) | | ≅6 (CLUSTER 4) | | ≅7 (CLUSTER 6) | | ≅8 (CLUSTER 3) | |
|---|---|---|---|---|---|---|---|---|---|---|---|---|---|---|---|---|
| | 98 | 1114 | 7 | 1107 | 4 | 1109 | 22 | 6120 | 48 | 1110 | 42 | 3105 | 75 | 4103 | 21 | 3101 |
| Class/Ethnicity | WC | CH | LMC | AN | MC | CH | LMC | MC | MC | AN | UC | J | LMC | BL | LMC | BL |
| Marital Status | M | M | M | M₂ | M | M | M | M | M | M | M | M | M | M₂ | M | M₂ |
| Mother Employed? | No | No | No | No | Yes | Yes | No | Yes | Yes | No | No | No | No | Yes | Yes | Yes |
| Siblings? | Yes | Yes | Yes | Yes | No | Yes | Yes | Yes | Yes | Yes | Yes | Yes | Yes | Yes | Yes | Yes |
| Wish for Profession? | No | No | No | Amb. | No | Amb. | Yes | Yes | Yes | Yes | Yes | Yes | No | No | Yes | Yes |
| Wish to Marry? | No | No | Yes | Amb. | No | Amb. | Yes | Yes | Yes | Yes | Yes | Yes | No | No | Yes | Yes |
| Wish for children? | No | No | No | Amb. | No | Amb. | Yes | Yes | Yes | Yes | Yes | Yes | No | No | Yes | Yes |
| Glad to be female? | No | – | No | Amb. | No | Amb. | Yes | Yes | Yes | Yes | Yes | Yes | No | No | No | No |
| Text Type | R | R | R | R | R | R | NR | R | R | R | NR | NR | R | R | R | R |
| Clichés used? | No | Yes | Yes | Yes | Yes | No | Yes | Yes | Yes | Yes | No | No | No | No | Yes | Yes |
| Negative Particles? | Yes | Yes | Yes | Yes | Yes | No | Yes | Yes | Yes | Yes | No | No | Yes | Yes | Yes | Yes |
| Mother-Relationship | Amb. | Amb. | Amb. | Aff. | Amb. | Aff. | Amb. | Amb. | Riv. | Riv. | Riv. | Aff. | Aff. | Riv. | Amb. | Amb. |
| Educational Style | Str. | Str. | Lib. | Lib. | Str. | Lib. | Str. | Str. | Lib. | Lib. | Lib. | Lib. | Lib. | Lib. | Str. | Str. |
| Affectivity--Girl | Jeal. | Jeal. | Jeal. | Love | Hate | Love | Guilt | Love | Jeal. | Jeal. | Jeal. | Love | Jeal. | Jeal. | Hate | Hate |
| Self-Image | Girl | Girl | ---- | Dau. | Dau. | Dau. | --- | --- | Ad. | Ad. | Dau. | Dau. | Ad. | Girl | Dau. | Girl |

Ethnicity: CH=Chicano; AN=Anglo; BL=Black; J=Jewish

Marital Status: M₂=Second Marriage

Text Type: R=Reflection; NR=Non-Reflective

Mother-Relationship: Amb.=Ambivalent; Aff.=Affection; Riv.:Rivalry

Educational Style: Str.=Strict; Lib=Liberal

Affectivity: Jeal.=Jealousy

Self-Image: Dau.=Daughter; Ad.=Adult

# APPENDIX III

## GIESSEN TEST - ENGLISH VERSION

These questions concern how you see yourself in relationship to others. Please give your impression of yourself on the scale marking "0" if you think you are just like others. When you think you differ from others, mark "1," "2" or "3," depending upon how strong you feel the difference to be.

| | | |
|---|---|---|
| 1) I think I am less patient | 3 2 1 0 1 2 3 | or more patient than other people |
| 2) I believe I seek, or | 3 2 1 0 1 2 3 | avoid companionship. |
| 3) I think I prefer to lead others, or | 3 2 1 0 1 2 3 | to be lead by others. |
| 4) I think that if my life style changed, my disposition would change a lot | 3 2 1 0 1 2 3 | or would change only a little |
| 5) I feel that I hardly ever worry about my inner problems | 3 2 1 0 1 2 3 | or that I often worry about my inner problems. |
| 6) It seems that I tend to hold in my anger | 3 2 1 0 1 2 3 | or that I let my anger out. |
| 7) I think I have a strong interest in doing better than others | 3 2 1 0 1 2 3 | or hardly any interest in doing better than others. |
| 8) I believe I have only a little anxiety | 3 2 1 0 1 2 3 | or too much anxiety. |
| 9) It seems to me that others are quite satisfied with the job I do | 3 2 1 0 1 2 3 | or dissatisfied with the job I do (as homemaker or professional). |
| 10) I suppose I tend to trust others too much | 3 2 1 0 1 2 3 | or too little. |
| 11) I think I show my need for love openly | 3 2 1 0 1 2 3 | or that I do not show it very much. |

12) It seems to me that I        3 2 1 0 1 2 3        or that I seek close
    avoid close attach-                                attachments to
    ments                                             people.

13) I belive, compared           3 2 1 0 1 2 3        or bad at handling
    with others, I am good                            money.
    at handling money

14) I think I seldom feel         3 2 1 0 1 2 3        or I often feel
    depressed                                          depressed.

15) I believe I reveal too        3 2 1 0 1 2 3        or too little about
    much                                               myself.

16) It seems to me I find it      3 2 1 0 1 2 3        or easy to make others
    hard to make others                                like me.
    like me

17) I feel it is easy for me      3 2 1 0 1 2 3        or hard for me to main-
    to maintain close rela-                            tain close relationships
    tionships                                          for a long time.

18) I believe that I tell too     3 2 1 0 1 2 3        or too little of the
    much of                                            truth.

19) I think it is easy for me     3 2 1 0 1 2 3        or hard for me to come
    to come out of my shell                            out of my shell.

20) I believe I act younger       3 2 1 0 1 2 3        or older than others
                                                       my age.

21) I believe that I am too       3 2 1 0 1 2 3        or too sloppy.
    neat

22) I think I often get into      3 2 1 0 1 2 3        seldom get into argu-
    arguments or                                       ments with other
                                                       people.

23) I believe I am more           3 2 1 0 1 2 3        or overrate me.
    comfortable when
    people underrate me

24) I think that I take           3 2 1 0 1 2 3        or less trouble in life
    more trouble                                       than I should

25) I seem to feel detached       3 2 1 0 1 2 3        or close to other
    from other people                                  people.

26) I believe that in com-    3 2 1 0 1 2 3    or not very much
    parison with others I                       imagination.
    have a lot of imagina-
    tion

27) I believe I care more     3 2 1 0 1 2 3    or less than they about
    than others about                           looking good.
    looking good

28) I feel that it is hard for 3 2 1 0 1 2 3    or easy for me to work
    me to work closely                          closely with other
    with other people                           people.

29) I think I seldom blame    3 2 1 0 1 2 3    or frequently blame
    myself                                      myself.

30) I believe I can show a    3 2 1 0 1 2 3    or very little love to a
    lot of love                                 partner.

31) Compared with others,     3 2 1 0 1 2 3    usually try to get my
    I think I give in to                        own way.
    people or

32) I feel that I tend         3 2 1 0 1 2 3    or often to think
    seldom to think about                       about other people's
    other people's prob-                        problems.
    lems

33) I believe that it is hard  3 2 1 0 1 2 3    or easy for me to get
    for me to get what I                        what I want.
    want

34) I think in comparison     3 2 1 0 1 2 3    or less capable of deep
    with others I am more                       love.
    capable of deep love

35) I think I am a very        3 2 1 0 1 2 3    or not a very good
    good actress                                actress.

36) I believe that people     3 2 1 0 1 2 3    or as weak.
    tend to see me as
    strong

37) I find that it is hard for 3 2 1 0 1 2 3    or easy to be attractive
    me to be attractive to                      to others.
    others

38) I believe it is easier for         3 2 1 0 1 2 3          or harder than for
    me to stick to one thing                                  others to stick to one
                                                              thing.

39) I think it is hard for             3 2 1 0 1 2 3          or easy for me to be
    me to be relaxed with                                     relaxed with people.
    people

40) I feel at ease when I              3 2 1 0 1 2 3          or that I am self-
    am with men                                               conscious when I am
                                                              with men.

# APPENDIX IV
## Austrian Essays*
CNR 4

## Meine Mutter und ich

Meine Mutter ist eine sehr nette Frau. Sie versteht sehr viele Probleme. Ich vertraue ihr fast alles an, da sie dies bei sich behält. Ich habe viel Vertrauen zu meinen Eltern, da sie mit mir über jedes Problem reden und nicht so tun, als wären alle Probleme, die ich ihnen vorlege nur meine Probleme.

Meine Eltern erklären mir alles, was ich nicht verstehe. Wenn mein Vater dabei die Geduld verliert, erklärt es mir meine Mutter. Sie hat sehr viel Ausdauer und Geschicklichkeit.

Leider macht sie viele Arbeiten, die gar nicht notwendig sind, doch mein Vater und ich haben ihr einen Großteil schon abgewöhnt z.B. früher hat sie das Doppelbett jeden Tag zu einer Bank gemacht, heute macht sie das nur mehr, wenn Besuch kommt. Manche Sachen die sie macht, stören mich: z.B.: sie saugt täglich den Boden und hat eine sehr, sehr unpraktische Ordnung.

Sie hat zwar viel Geduld, aber wenn sie meine "Unordnung" (so nennt sie meine Ordnung) sieht, dann muß sie immer ihre Pfoten dranhaben. Ich habe sie trotzdem sehr gern.

---

* The essays are arranged chronologically. They are presented with all the original errors and with original margins, as far as possible.

CNR 7

Meine Mutter und ich

Ich habe ein (ziemlich sehr) gutes Verhältnis zu meiner Mutter. Sie ist aber ziemlich streng, aber nicht nachtragend. In Sachen Schule ist sie sehr genau. Sie verlangt ziemlich viel von mir, weil sie genau weiß, daß ich sehr gut sein kann in der Schule und deshalb nehme ich es ihr nicht übel. Meine Mutter arbeitet vormittags, aber nur bis 1 Uhr, deswegen stört es mich auch nicht, weil sie immer schon Zuhause ist, wenn ich heimkomme. Sie ist keine Moral-predigerin und hat auch nie panische Angst um uns. (z.B. "Ja, jetzt kannst du aber nicht mehr weggehen, es ist ja schon dunkel. Da kann dich ja wer mit-nehmen ......") So ist sie auf keinen Fall. Ich gehe öfters erst um 8 Uhr abends mit meiner Freundin spazieren und komme um 9 Uhr zurück. Das macht ihr nichts aus. Die einzige Bedingung ist, daß ich nicht unbedingt im Wienerwald spazieren gehe. Wir haben ausgemacht daß ich mir einmal in der Woche etwas im Abendprogramm (20.15 h.) ansehen darf (Fernsehen). Sie mag das nicht, wenn mein Bruder und ich ewig vor der Kiste sitzen. Wenn Ferien sind oder Samstag ist, dann darf ich mir schon ansehen was ich will, aber, unter der Schulzeit mag sie das nicht, weil wir dann am nächsten Morgen nicht ausgeschlafen sind.

Meine Mutter ist sehr tierlieb. Zur Zeit haben wir den 4 Monate alten Spaniel meiner Tante bei uns. Den liebt sie aus ganzen Herzen. Wenn ich mit Rini (der Spaniel) spazierengehen will dan kann ich sogar das Lernen aufschieben.

Meine Mutter behandelt mich eigentlich nicht wie ein Kind. Ich habe meine Rechte, darf meistens machen was ich will und kann über meine Freizeit frei verfügen. Wenn ich einmal etwas unternehmen will, brauche ich es ihr nur mitzuteilen. Wenn sie etwas dagegen hat, dann sagt sie es mir und dann tue ich eben etwas anderes und bin ihr böse, weil sie mir doch meistens alles erlaubt.

CNR 21

Meine Mutter und ich

Meine Mutter ist 27 Jahre älter als ich.
Sie zieht sich nicht immer nach der neuesten Mode an, aber immer hübsch.
Ich verstehe mich gut mit ihr, obwohl sie öfter keppelt, z.B. über schlechte Noten.
Wenn ich rede, behauptet sie, ich schreie sie an.
Ich betreibe sehr viel Sport und spiele fünf Instrumente (Geige, Klavier, C- und F- Flöte, Trompete).
Meine Mutter spielt Klavier.
Sie holt mich meistens von den Stunden mit dem Auto ab, des öfteren muß ich aber mit der U-Bahn fahren.
Wir streiten nur selten, dann ist eine von uns angefressen, was sich aber bald gibt.
Man kann mit meiner Mutter über alles reden.
Sie glaubt man muß immer strebern um in der Schule gut zu sein.
Sie will, daß ich lauter gute Noten habe, so wie sie früher.
Befor sie arbeiten ging, hat sie die HAG (Handelsakademie) besucht. Später hat sie die Matura in Abendkursen nachgemacht, wo sie auch meinen Vater kennenlernte. Jetzt hat sie eine Leitende Stellung.
Ich bin Schülerin in einer AHS und möchte auf die HAG gehen und nach der Matura in das Büro meines Vaters.
12 Jahre habe ich meine Mutter ausgehalten, und so wird es auch weiter bleiben.

CNR 22


Meine Mutter und ich


Ich habe gerade die Englischschularbeit zurück bekommen, Ergebnis "5". Diesmal brauche ich viel länger nach Hause als sonst. Was wird wohl meine Mutter dazu sagen? Ich hatte zu ihr gesagt, daß es wahrscheinlich eine "3" werden würde. Ich drücke ganz kurz die Klingel, meine Mutter macht auf und fragt. "Was hast du auf die Englisch Schularbeit?" — "Verhaut." Meine Mutter starrt mich an und sagt: "Na, toll, du mußt aber für die nächste Schularbeit mehr lernen!" Ich glaubte zu träumen, denn sie schimpfte gar nicht. Nicht einmal das Wort "Trottel" hörte ich. Aus lauter Freude fiel ich ihr um den Hals und weinte. Sie tröstete mich, das beruhigte mich sehr.
Aber meine Mutter kann auch anders sein:
Ich hörte leise in meinem Zimmer, das ich mit meinem Bruder teile, Musik. Es war ca. halb zehn. Plötzlich kam meine Mutter ins Zimmer und stellte das Radio ab. Ich wehrte mich und sagte, daß ich hören wolle, doch es half nichts. Da sagte ich frech: "Weil du als Kind nicht hören durftest, darf ich wohl auch nicht, tolle Erziehung. Gute Nacht!" Das war meiner Mutter zuviel, patsch, und ich hatte die Hand mitten im Gesicht. Sie verließ das Zimmer und schloß die Tür. Ich war mir im klaren, daß ich etwas Gemeines gesagt hatte. Fünf Minuten später stand ich schon am Bett meiner Mutter, das Gesicht rot und die Augen verheult und entschuldigte mich. Meine Mutter sah, daß es mir sehr am Herzen liegt, daß ihre Tochter sich entschuldigen will, und sie verzieh mir. Sie gab mir einen Kuß und ich versprach ihr nie wieder so etwas Gemeines zu sagen, denn ich wußte, daß sie ihr bestes gab um uns richtig zu erziehen.
Lügen haßt meine Mutter sehr. Wenn ich lüge, straft mich meine Mutter indem sie mir verbietet, Freundinnen einzuladen oder auf die nächsten Parties zu gehen. Diese Strafe nimmt sie sehr ernst und sie verzeiht nicht so schnell. Ihr Versprechen, daß sie mich straft, hält sie. Da gibt es kein bitten und betteln. Sie möchte mit den Strafen erreichen, daß ich nie wieder lüge. Meistens gelingt ihr das.
Ich liebe meine Mutter und möchte, daß sie so bleibt wie sie ist. Sie hat viel Verständnis und ich kann ihr alle Problemchen anvertrauen.

CNR 42

## Meine Mutter und ich

Meine Mutter ist so groß wie ich, blond und 35 Jahre alt. Sie ist immer schick gekleidet, nicht so auffällig, aber auch nicht altmodisch. Meine Mutter muß manchmal sehr tapfer sein, da mein Vater öfter kühle Bemerkungen macht, bei denen eine andere Fraue sofort losheulen würde. Sie aber sagt nichts, bleibt ruhig. Ich möchte aber nicht, daß Sie meinen Vater falsch verstehen. Er ist immer lustig und zu Späßen aufgelegt.

Meine Mutter und ich stehen in einem sehr guten Verhältnis. Mit allen meinen Problemen kann ich zu ihr gehen, ich habe vor ihr nichts zu verbergen. Besonders jetzt, wo die Pubertät beginnt, habe ich öfters Schwierigkeiten. Meine Mutter ist, wie schon erwähnt, sehr ruhig und geduldig. Sie ist streng, wenn sie streng sein muß, denn alles kann sie uns nicht durchgehen lassen. Sonst aber läßt sie mir und meiner 9-jährigen Schwester Verena viel Freiheit.

Meine Mutter ist nicht eine Frau, die bei allen möglichen Organisationen dabeisein muß, sie ist aber interessiert an der Malerei und an der französischen Sprache.

Bei der Heirat meiner Eltern hatten sie wenig Geld, mein Vater war Verkäufer in einer Computer-Firma, inzwischen haben sie einen langen Weg zurückgelegt, und mein Vater hat sich bis zum Direktor dieser Firma hinaufgearbeitet. Meine Mutter hat viel Erfahrung gesammelt und sparen gelernt.

Meine Mutter ist eine tüchtige, gute Hausfrau, die sie aber auch gerne einmal ausruht.

Meine Eltern sind sehr sportlich. Beide spielen gut Tennis, fahren hervorragend Schi, schwimmen und segeln gern.

Meine Mutter und ich gehen gerne zusammen in die Stadt oder sonst irgendwohin. Meine Mutter ist auch sehr anpassungsfähig, kann sich also auch in andere Personen hineindenken und Personen nach ihrer Art behandeln.

Meine Mutter ist sehr tierliebend (wir haben schon 3 Meerschweinchen gehabt) und zärtlich. Sie liebt ihren Mann und unsere Familie hält in allen Situationen fest zusammen.

CNR 48


Meine Mutter und ich

Meiner Mutter bin ich in mancher Hinsicht ähnlich. Ich meine nicht nur das
Aussehen, die braunen Augen, die Nase, sondern auch zum Beispiel in den
Dingen, die uns gefallen. Meine Mutter investiert ziemlich viel Geld in
Kleidern, was ich auch tun würde, wenn mein Taschengeld reichte. Aber sie
kauft nicht nur sich, sondern auch mir schöne teure Kleider. Sie hört meistens
nur klassische Musik, aber wenn ich die Beatles spiele, hat sie nicht dagegen.
Sie fordert mich sogar manchmal dazu auf.
Sie ist Ärztin und arbeitet sehr viel, manchmal zu viel. Dann muß sie sich
hinlegen, und niemand darf sie stören. Doch das passiert eher selten. Sie ver-
spätet sich prinzipiell, doch ich sollte immer pünktlich sein. Aber wenn ich
mich verspäte, sagt sie, daß es diesmal nichts macht. Sie ist sehr intelligent,
aber sehr ungeduldig. Wenn sie früher mit meinem Bruder gelernt hat,
begann sie nach einiger Zeit, ihn anzuschreien, weil er manches nicht
kapierte. (Doch jetzt hat er Nachhilfe; da ergibt sich die Sache.). Zu Mittag
ist sie nie zu Hause, mein Vater auch nicht, sondern meine Omi oder die
Bedienerin. Am Abend geht sie oft mit meinem Vater aus, aber manchmal
haben wir auch einen "Familienabend", das ist, wenn wir alle zu Hause sind,
und sie gekocht hat. Daß sie so oft weg ist, heißt aber nicht, daß wir kein
Familienleben haben. Wir gehen oft zusammen in die Stadt, und wir verstehen uns sehr gut. Sie erlaubt mir sehr viel, zum Beispiel bei einer Freundin zu
übernachten, oder auf Feste zu gehen. Ich selbst darf auch jedes Jahr ein-
zwei Feste machen. Sie ist auch bereit, mit meinem Vater wegzugehen, wenn
ich eine Party am Abend mache. Sie zeigt sehr viel Verständnis für mich, und
wir verstehen uns blendend. Manchmal haber wir auchKrisen in der Familie,
dann streiten wir uns eine Weile, aber nachher setzen wir uns alle zusammen,
diskutieren das Problem, jeder sagt was er davon hält und wir einigen uns
wieder, weil man sich doch nicht ewig und 3 Tage streiten kann. Im Urlaub
kann meine Mutter fast nichts aus der Ruhe bringen. Sie genießt ihren
Urlaub und läßt sich von uns nicht stören. Wir haben immer ein eigenes Zimmer und dürfen meistens die Umgebung selbst erkunden. Was aber auf
keinen Fall heißt, daß unsere Mutter uns vernachlässigt, ich glaube eher, daß
sie will, daß wir selbständig denken und leben lernen.
Wenn meine Mutter guter Laune ist, und sie sieht, daß ich in letzter Zeit viel

gearbeitet habe (für die Schule), dann sagt sie einfach: "Jetzt gehst du zur Tante Anneliese hinauf, sie hat dich auf einen Irish Coffee eingeladen." oder sie geht mit mir in der Stadt bummeln. Ich habe ein sehr gutes Verhältnis zu meiner Mutter, und ich hoffe, daß ich mich weiterhin mit ihr so gut verstehe.

CNR 75

## Meine Mutter und ich

Meine Mutter ist nicht berufstätig, früher hatte sie gearbeitet, doch seit ich in die Hauptschule kam, hörte sie auf. Ich kann meine Mutter gut leiden. Wenn wir alleine sind, ist sie fast wie eine Freundin. Oft legt sie ein gutes Wort bei meinen Vater ein, wenn ich etwas will. Meistens erreicht sie auch das was sie will. Wenn ich mich bei einer Hausaufgabe nicht auskenne, erklärt sie mir alles. Oft besser und leichter zu verstehen als in die Schule. Meine Mutter will natürlich nicht immer nur zu Hause sitzen und den Haushalt versorgen, sie will auch hinaus, wo sie uns ein paar Stunden vergessen kann. Sie geht turnen und lernt Bauernmahlen. Da wir auch einen Bauernhof haben hilft sie auch dort wo sie kann. Da er noch nicht fertig ist, gibt es immer was zum reinigen. Auch in unserer Wohnung gibt es viel zu putzen, da wir einen Hund haben, wir haben überall Hundehaare. Auf jeden Kleidungsstück! Früher, wie ich noch kleiner war, gingen meine Eltern reiten. Das ist jetzt auch vorbei. Mutter sein ist kein VERGNÜGEN. Da ich aber keine Geschwister habe, geht es ja noch. Zwischen uns gibt es keine Geheimnisse, ich finde, es herrscht ein gutes "Mutter-Kind Verhältniss".

CNR 98

## Meine Mutter und ich

Im Sommer fahr ich mit meiner Mutter an die Alte Donau. Dort baden wir. Meine Mutter sonnt sich dort. Ansonsten komme ich fast nie mit meiner Mutter zusammen. Früher haben wir Berge bestiegen und Seen besucht. Meiner Mutter ihr Gemüt ist ziemlich wechselseitig. Meistens ist sie guter Laune. Jedoch auch wenn sie guter Laune ist, wenn sie "Nein" sagt, dann ist es "Nein". Ich habe meine Mutter sehr gern.
Am meisten beneide ich sie darum daß sie gerecht ist. Wenn meine drei Brüder und ich einen Streit haben dann schlichtet sie ihn meist gerecht. Allerdings habe ich manchmal meine Mutter nicht sehr gern und finde sie ungerecht. Denn ich würde so gerne einen Hund haben aber sie erlaubt es nicht. Nicht einmal einen Goldfisch darf ich haben, obwohl der überhaupt keinen Schmutz macht. Meine Mutter hat es sehr schwer denn sie muß für sechs Personen kochen: für sich, für meinen Vater, für meine drei Brüder und für mich. Sie muß auch waschen und aufräumen und kann nur jede zweite Woche die Waschmaschine einmal benützen. Meine Mutter ist meist an der Alten Donau. Manchmal übernächtigt sie dort. Aber nur im Sommer. Sie hilft dort in einem Betrieb meinem Onkel und meiner Tante beim Dienst. Sie geht sehr selten Baden. Ich sehe meiner Mutter nur zur Hälfte ähnlich. Ich habe auch noch nicht all die guten Eigenschaften meiner Mutter. Besonders die Geduld und Ausdauer habe ich noch nicht. Auch kann meine Mutter sehr hübsch zeichnen und malen. Am liebsten zeichnet sie mit Bleistift und Tusche. Meine Mutter ist auch sonst sehr geschickt in Handwerkssachen. Sie kann zum Beispiel einem Kamin (im Freien zum Grillen und rösten) selber mit meinem Onkel basteln. Darüber hinaus kann meine Mutter auch sehr gut kochen und backen. Zu Weihnachten bäckt sie uns immer einen guten Gugelhupf und viel Bäckerei.
Meine Mutter macht auch selber Windbäckerei und macht allen Christbaumschmuck selbst. Manchmal macht sie auch noch selber Topfengolatschen, gebackene Mäuse and Striezel.

# REFERENCES

Abramovitch, Rona, Carl Carter and Debra J. Pepler. (1980). Observations of mixed-sex sibling dyads. *Child Development*. 51, 1268-71.

Adorno, Theodor W., Max Horkheimer, and Jürgen Habermas. (1969). *Der Positivismusstreit in der deutschen Soziologie*. Berlin: Luchterhand.

Ammon, Ulrich. (1973). *Dialekt, soziale Ungleichheit und Schule*. Weinheim: Beltz.

Andersen, Elaine. (1977). Young children's knowledge of role-related speech differences: A mommy is not a daddy is not a baby. *Papers and Reports on Child Language Development*. 13 (August), 83-90.

Anisfeld, Moshe, N. Bogo, and W. E. Lambert. (1962). Evaluational reactions to accented English speech. *Journal of Abnormal and Social Psychology*. 65,223-31.

Anthony, James E. and Therese Benedek (eds.). (1970). *Parenthood*. Boston: Little, Brown.

Argyle, Michael. (1969). *Social Interaction*. N.Y.: Atherton.

Augst, Gerhard (ed.). (1978). *Spracherwerb von 6-16. Linguistische, psychologische, soziologische Grundlagen*. Düsseldorf: Schwann.

Ausubel, David Paul. (1954). *Theory and Problems of Adolescent Development*. N.Y.: Grune & Stratton.

Autorinnengruppe Uni Wien. (1981). *Das ewige Klischee*. Vienna: Böhlau.

Bardwick, Judith M. (ed.). (1972). *Readings on the Psychology of Women*. N.Y.: Harper & Row.

Barnes, J. A. (1971). Some ethical problems in modern fieldwork. In W. J. Filstead (ed.). 235-51.

Bartlett, F. C. (1932). *Remembering: A Study in Experimental and Social Psychology*. Cambridge: Cambridge Univ. Press.

Bates, Elizabeth. (1971). The development of conversational skill in 2, 3, and 4 year olds. Unpublished master's thesis, Univ. of Chicago.

Baumrind, Diana. (1971). Current patterns of parental authority. *Developmental Psychology Monograph*. 4(1). Part 2, 1-103.

Baumrind, Diana. (1980). New directions in socialization research. *American Psychologist*, 35, 639-52.

Beaugrande, Robert de and Wolfgang U. Dressler. (1980). *Introduction to Textlinguistics*. London: Longman. Published in German (1981): *Einführung in die Textlinguistik*. Tübingen: Niemeyer.

Becker, Howard S. and Blanche Geer. (1975). Participant observation and interviewing. *Human Organization.* 16(3), 28-32.

Beckmann, Dieter and Horst-Eberhard Richter. (1975). *Giessen-Test (GT). Ein Test für Individual- und Gruppendiagnostik.* Stuttgart: Hans Huber.

Beckwith, Leila. (1971). Relationships between attributes of mothers and their infants' IQ scores. *Child Development.* 42, 1083-97.

Bell, R. Q., G. M. Weller, and M. F. Waldrop. (1971). Newborn and preschooler: Organization of behavior and relations between periods. *Monographs of the Society for Research in Child Development.* Vol. 36.

Bellinger, David. (1979). Changes in the explicitness of mothers' directives as children age. *Journal of Child Language.* 6, 443-58.

Belotti, Elena Gianini. (1973). *Dalla parte delle bambine.* Milan: Giangiacomo Feltrinelli. Translated into English (1975) by L. Appignanesi, A. Fletcher, T. Shimura, S. Williams, and J. Wordsworth, as *Little Girls.* London: Writers and Readers.

Belsky, Jay. (1981). Early human experience: A family perspective. *Developmental Psychology.* 17, 3-23.

Berens, Franz-Josef. (1975). Analyse des Sprachverhaltens im Redekonstellationstyp "Interview." *Heutiges Deutsch.* I/6. München: Hueber.

Berger, Hartwig. (1974). *Untersuchungsmethode und soziale Wirklichkeit.* Frankfurt/M.: Suhrkamp.

Bergmann, Anni. (1980). *Die Entwicklung des kleinen Mädchens während der Loslösungs-Individuations-Periode.* Ms.

Bernard, Jesse. (1974). *The Future of Motherhood.* N.Y.: Dial.

Bernard, Jesse. (1981). *The Female World.* N.Y.: Free Press.

Bernstein, Basil. (1970). Familiales Rollensystem, Kommunikation und Sozialisation. In B. Bernstein (ed.). 117-33.

Bernstein, Basil. (ed.). (1970). *Soziale Struktur, Sozialisation und Sprachverhalten.* Amsterdam: De Munter.

Bernstein, Basil *et al.* (1970). *Lernen und soziale Struktur.* Amsterdam: De Munter.

Bernstein, Basil. (1971). *Class, Codes, and Control.* Vol. 1. London: Routledge & Kegan Paul.

Bierschenk, Inger. (1977). Computer-based content analysis: Coding manual. *Pedagogic Dokumentation.* (In Swedish).

Bierschenk, Bernhard. (1974). A computer-based content analysis of interview data: Some problems in the construction and application of coding rules. ERIC 110045.

Bierschenk, Bernhard. (1977). A computer-based content analysis of interview texts: Numeric description and multivariate analysis. *Didakometry*. 53. ERIC 152223.

Bingham, N. E. (1971). Maternal speech to pre-linguistic infants: Differences related to maternal judgments of infant language competence. Unpublished paper. Cornell Univ. Mimeo.

Block, Jeanne H. (1976). Another look at sex differentiation in the socialization behavior of mothers and fathers. In F. Denmark and J. Sherman (eds.) *Psychology of Women: Future Directions of Research*. N.Y.: Psychological Dimensions. 57-83.

Blom, G. E., R. R. Waite, and S. G. Zimet. (1970). A motivational content analysis of children's primers. In Harry Levin and J. F. Williams (eds.) *Basic Studies on Reading*. N.Y.: Basic Books.

Blom, Jan-Peter and John J. Gumperz. (1972). Social meaning in linguistic structure: Code-switching in Norway. In J. Gumperz and D. Hymes (eds.). 407-33.

Blos, Peter. (1962). *On Adolescence: A Psychoanalytic Interpretation*. N.Y.: Free Press. Translated into German (1978) as *Adoleszenz. Eine psychoanalytische Interpretation*. Stuttgart: Klett.

Blount, Ben G. (1973). Parental speech and language acquisition: Some Luo and Samoan Examples. *Southwestern Journal of Anthropology*. 27, 41-50.

Blount, Ben G. and Elise J. Padgug. (1976). Mother and father speech: Distribution of parental speech features in English and Spanish. *Papers and Reports on Child Language Development*. 12 (December), 47-59.

Blumer, Herbert. (1962). Society as symbolic interactionism. In A. M. Rose (ed.). 187-201.

Bock, J. Kathryn and Mary E. Hornsby. (1981). The development of directives: How children ask and tell. *Journal of Child Language*. 8, 151-63.

Bodkin, Anne. (1975). Observed sex differences in the written expressions of boys and girls in the writing processes of students. Paper presented at the Annual Conference on Language Arts. Buffalo. 71-76.

Bolognese-Leuchtenmüller, Birgit. (1981). Zwischen Anforderung, Anpassung und Alternativen. Uberlegungen zur gegenwärtigen Rollenverteilung in der Familie. In Autorinnengruppe Uni Wien. 108-32.

Bönner, Karl H. (ed.). (1973). *Die Geschlechterrolle*. München: Hueber.

Borker, Ruth. (1980). Anthropology: Social and cultural perspectives. In S. McConnell-Ginet, R. Borker, and N. Furman (eds.). 26-44.

Brim, O. (1959). The parent-child relation as a social system: (1) Parent-child roles. *Child Development*. 28, 343-64.

Brody, Sylvia and Sidney Axelrad. (1978). *Mothers, Fathers and Children. Explorations in the Formation of Character in the First Seven Years.* N.Y.: International Universities Press, Inc.

Broen, Patricia. (1972). The verbal environment of the language-learning child. *Monograph of ASHA*. No. 17. December. Washington, D.C.: American Speech and Hearing Association.

Bronstein-Burrows, Phyllis. (1981). Patterns of parent behavior: A cross-cultural study. *Merrill-Palmer Quarterly*. 27(2),137-43.

Brooks-Gunn, Jeanne and Wendy Schempp Matthews. (1979). *He & She: How Children Develop their Sex-role Identity.* Englewood Cliffs, N.J.: Prentice-Hall, Inc.

Brown, Penelope. (1980). How and why are women more polite: Some evidence from a Mayan community. In S. McConnell-Ginet, R. Borker, and N. Furman (eds.). 111-36.

Brown, Roger. (1977). Introduction to C. Snow and C. Ferguson (eds.). 1-27.

Brown, Roger and C. Hanlon. (1970). Deprivational complexity and order of acquisition in children's speech. In J. Hayes (ed.). 11-53.

Bruner, Jerome S. (1978). From communication to language: A psychological perspective. In I. Markova (ed.). *The Social Context.* Chichester, N.Y.: John Wiley & Sons. 17-48. Also translated by Karin Martens (1979) as *Von der Kommunikation zur Sprache — Überlegungen aus psychologischer Sicht.* In K. Martens (ed.). 9-60.

Caesar, Beatrice. (1974). *Autorität in der Familie.* Hamburg: Rowohlt.

Carroll, John B. and Roy Freedle (eds.). (1972). *Language Comprehension and the Acquisition of Knowledge.* Washington, D.C.: Winston; Wiley Distrib.

Cater, Libby and Anne Scott (eds.). (1977). *Women and Men: Changing Roles, Relationships and Perceptions.* N.Y.: Praeger.

Cherry, Louise. (1974). *Sex Differences in Preschool Teacher-child Verbal Interaction.* Unpublished dissertation. Harvard Univ.

Cherry, Louise. (1975). Sex differences in child speech: McCarthy revisited. ETS RB-75-3. Educational Testing Service, Princeton, N.J.

Cherry, Louise and Michael Lewis. (1976). Mothers and two-year-olds: A study of sex-differentiated aspects of verbal interaction. *Developmental Psychology*. 12, 278-82.

Cherry, Louise and Michael Lewis. (1978). Differential socialization of girls and boys: Implications for sex differences in language development. In N. Waterson and C. Snow (eds.). 189-97.

Cheshire, Jane. (1974). Present tense verbs in reading. In P. Trudgill (ed.). 52-68.

Chodorow, Nancy. (1974). Family structure and female personality. In M. Rosaldo and L. Lamphere (eds.). *Woman, Culture, and Society*. Palo Alto, Ca.: Stanford Univ. Press. 43-66.

Chodorow, Nancy. (1978). *The Reproduction of Mothering: Psychoanalysis and the Sociology of Gender*. Berkeley, Ca.: Univ. of California Press.

Cicirelli, Victor G. (1978). Effect of sibling presence on mother-child interaction. *Developmental Psychology*. 14, 315-16.

Cicourel, Aaron. (1970). *Methode und Messung in der Soziologie*. Frankfurt/M.: Suhrkamp.

Cicourel, Aaron. (1975). Discourse and text: Cognitive and linguistic process in studies of social structure. *Versus*. 12,33-84.

Cicourel, Aaron. (1978). Interpretation and summarization issues in the child's acquisition of social structure. In J. Glick and C. Clark-Stewart (eds.). *The Development of Social Understanding*. N.Y.: Gardner Press. 251-81.

Clarke-Stewart, Alison. (1973). Interactions between mothers and their young children: Characteristics and consequences. *Monographs of the Society for Research in Child Development*. Vol. 38, No. 6-7, Serial No. 153. Chicago: Univ. of Chicago Press.

Clarke-Stewart, Alison. (1978). And daddy makes three: The father's impact on mother and young. *Child Development*. 49, 466-78.

Cochran, Moncrieff M. and Jane Anthony Brassard. (1979). Child development and personal social networks. *Child Development*. 50,601-16.

Cohler, Bertram J. and Henry U. Grunebaum. (1981). *Mothers, Grandmothers, and Daughters: Personality and Childcare in Three-generation Families*. N.Y.: John Wiley & Sons.

Coleman, James. (1961). *The Adolescent Society*. N.Y.: Free Press.

Collis, G. M. and H. R. Schaffer. (1975). Synchronization of visual attention in mother-infant pairs. *Journal of Child Psychology and Psychiatry*. 16, 315-20.

Condry, John and Sandra Condry. (1976). Sex differences: A study of the eye of the beholder. *Child Development*. 47, 812-19.

Conrad, Cynthia G. (1979). On the relation between sex differences in children's writing and neurolinguistic sex differences: Problems and possibilities. *OBST*. 13, 61-78.

Cook-Gumperz, Jenny. (1973). *Social Control and Socialization: A Study of Class Differences in the Language of Maternal Control*. London: Routledge & Kegan Paul.

Cook-Gumperz, Jenny. (1977). Situated instructions: Language socialization of school age children. In S. Ervin-Tripp and C. Mitchell-Kernan (eds.). 103-21.

Cook-Gumperz, Jenny and John Gumperz. (1978). Context in children's speech. In N. Waterson and C. Snow (eds.). 3-23.

Corsaro, William. (1977). The clarification request as a feature of adult interactive styles with young children. *Language in Society*. 6,183-207.

Corsaro, William. (1979). Sociolinguistic patterns in adult-child interaction. In E. Ochs and B. Schieffelin (eds.). 373-89.

Cross, Toni G. (1979). Mothers' speech adjustments and child language learning. *Language Sciences*. 1(1), 3-25.

Cross, Toni G., Jenny E. Johnson-Morris and Terry G. Nienhuys. (1980). Linguistic feedback and maternal speech: Comparisons of mothers addressing hearing and hearing-impaired children. *First Language*. 1, 163-89.

Crothers, Edward J. (1972). Memory structure and the recall of discourse. In J. Carroll and R. Freedle (eds.). 247-83.

Crumrine, Lynne S. (1968). An ethnography of Mayo speaking. *Anthropological Linguistics*. 10(2),19-31.

Dally, Ann. (1976). *Mothers: Their Power and Influence*. London: Wiedenfeld and Nicolson. Translated into German as *Die Macht unserer Mütter*. (1977) Stuttgart: Klett.

Dascal, M. and A. Margalit. (1974). A new "revolution" in linguistics: "Text grammars" vs. "sentence grammars." *Theoretical Linguistics*. 1(1/2),195-213.

Delamont, Sara. (1976). *Interaction in the Classroom*. London: Methuen.

Derwing, Bruce L. (1977). Is the child really a "little linguist"? In J. Macnamara (ed.). 79-84.

Deutsch, Helene. (1944 and 1945). *The Psychology of Women*. Vols. I and II. N.Y.: Grune & Stratton.

Deutscher, Irwin. (1971). Words and deeds: Social science and social policy. In W. J. Filstead (ed.). 27-51.

Dewey, John. (1933). *How We Think*. Boston, N.Y.: D. C. Heath.

van Dijk, Teun A. (1972). *Some Aspects of Text Grammars. A Study in Theoretical Linguistics and Poetics*. The Hague: Mouton.

van Dijk, Teun A. (1976). Philosophy of action and theory of narrative. *Poe-

*tics*. 6,287-338.

van Dijk, Teun A. (1977). *Text and Context. Explorations in the Semantics and Pragmatics of Discourse*. London: Longmans.

van Dijk, Teun A., and Walter Kintsch. (1977). Cognitive psychology and discourse: Recalling and summarizing stories. In W. U. Dressler (ed.). 61-80.

Dinnerstein, Dorothy. (1977). *The Mermaid and the Minotaur*. N.Y.: Harper & Row.

Dittmann, Jürgen. (1979a). Einleitung - Was ist, zu welchen Zwecken and wie treiben wir Konversationsanalyse? In J. Dittmann (ed.). 1-12.

Dittman, Jürgen (ed.). (1979b). *Arbeiten zur Konversationsanalyse*. Tübingen: Niemeyer.

Dittmar, Norbert. (1973). *Soziolinguistik. Eine Einführung und kommentierte Bibliographie*. Frankfurt/M: Fischer-Athenäum.

Dixon, W. J. and M. B. Brown. (1977). *BMDP-77. Biomedical Computer Program*. Berkeley, Ca: Univ. of California Press. P-Series.

Dooling, J. L. and R. Lachman. (1971). Effects of comprehension on retention of prose. *Journal of Experimental Psychology*. 88, 216-22.

Douvan, E. and J. Adelson. (1966). *The Adolescent Experience*. N.Y.: John Wiley & Sons.

Drachman, Gaberell. (1973). Baby talk in Greek. *Working Papers in Linguistics*. No. 15. Ohio State Univ..

Dressler, Wolfgang (ed.). (1977). *Current Trends in Textlinguistics*. Berlin: de Gruyter.

Dressler, Wolfgang and Ruth Wodak. (1982). Sociophonological methods in the study of sociolinguistic variation in Viennese German. *Language in Society*. 11, 339-70.

Dubois, Betty L. and Isabel Crouch (eds.). (1976). *The Sociology of the Languages of American Women*. San Antonio, Texas: Trinity Univ. Press.

Dunedin Collective for Women. (1973). *First Sex, Second Sex: Images of Male and Female in Infant Readers*. Dunedin, New Zealand.

Eder, Alois. (1976). Texttheoretisches zum Aufsatzunterricht. *WLG* 12, 25-56.

Edwards, John R. (1979). Social class differences and the identification of sex in children's speech. *Journal of Child Language*. 6, 121-28.

Elardo, Richard, Robert Bradley, and Bettye M. Caldwell. (1977). A longitudinal study of the relation of infants' home environment to language development at age three. *Child Development*. 48, 595-603.

Ellis, Allan and Audie F. Favat. (1966). From computer to criticism. An application of automatic content analysis to the study of literature. In P. Stone, D. Dunphy, M. Smith, and D. Ogilvie (eds.). 628-38.

Endsley, Richard C., M. Ann Hutcherson, Anita P. Garner, and Michael J. Martin. (1979). Interrelationships among selected maternal behaviors, authoritarianism, and preschool children's verbal and nonverbal curiosity. *Child Development*. 50, 331-39.

Engle, Marianne. (1980). Family influences on the language development of young children. In C. Kramarae (ed.). 259-66.

Erickson, Bonnie, Bruce C. Johnson, E. Allan Lind, and William O'Barr. (1978). Speech style and impression formation in a court setting: The effects of "powerful" and "powerless" speech. *Journal of Experimental and Social Psychology*. 14, 266-79.

Ervin-Tripp, Susan. (1976). "Is Sybil there?" The structure of some American English directives. *Language in Society*. 5, 25-66.

Ervin-Tripp, Susan. (1978). Some features of early child-adult dialogues. *Language in Society*. 7, 357-73.

Ervin-Tripp, Susan. (1980). Speech acts, social meaning and social learning. In H. Giles, W. P. Robinson, and P. M. Smith (eds.). 389-96.

Ervin-Tripp, Susan and Claudia Mitchell-Kernan (eds.). (1977). *Child Discourse*. N.Y.: Academic Press.

Ervin-Tripp, Susan, Catherine O'Connor and Jarrett Rosenberg. (1984). Language and power in the family. In C. Kramarae *et al*. 116-35.

Etaugh, C. (1974). Effects of maternal employment on children: A review of recent research. *Merrill-Palmer Quarterly*. 20,71-98.

Ferguson, Charles A. (1964). Baby talk in six languages. *American Anthropologist*. 66, 103-14.

Ferguson, Charles A. (1975). Toward a characterization of English foreigner talk. *Anthropological Linguistics*. 17, 1-14.

Ferguson, Charles A. (1977). Baby talk as a simplified register. In C. Snow and C. Ferguson (eds.). 209-35.

Ferguson, Charles A. and Dan I. Slobin (eds.). (1973). *Studies of Child Language Development*. N.Y.:Holt, Rinehart & Winston.

Fillmore, Charles, David Kempler, and W. S.-Y. Wang (eds.). (1979). *Individual Differences in Language Ability and Language Behavior*. N.Y.: Academic Press.

Filstead, William J. (ed.). (1971). *Qualitative Methodology. Firsthand Involvement with the Social World.* Chicago: Markham.

Fischer, John L. (1970). Linguistic socialization: Japan and the United States. In R. Hill and R. Koenig (eds.). *Families in East and West*. The Hague: Mouton. 107-19.

Flower, Linda. (1979). Writer-based prose: A cognitive basis for problems in writing. *College English*. 41,19-37.

Fowler, William. (1981). A strategy for stimulating infant learning. In R. L. Schiefelbusch and D. B. Bricker (eds.). 517-57.

Franck, Barbara. (1979). *Ich schau in den Spiegel und sehe meine Mutter*. Hamburg: Hoffmann u. Campe.

Fraser, Colin and Naomi Roberts. (1975). Mother's speech to children of four different ages. *Journal of Psycholinguistic Research*. 4, 9-16.

Freedle, Roy. (1972). Language users as fallible information processors: Implications for measuring and modeling comprehension. In J. Carroll and R. Freedle (eds.). 196-209.

Freedle, Roy (ed.). (1977). *Discourse Production and Comprehension*. Norwood, N.J.: Ablex.

Freedle, Roy (ed.). (1979). *New Directions in Discourse Processing*. Norwood, N.J.: Ablex.

Freedle, Roy and Richard P. Duran. (1979). Sociological approaches to dialogue with suggested applications to cognitive science. In R. Freedle (ed.), 197-206.

Freud, Sigmund. (1931). Über die weibliche Sexualität. *Ges. Werke (1976)*. Bd. 14. Frankfurt/M: S. Fischer. 517-37. Translated into English by James Strachey as "Female sexuality." In *The Standard Edition of the Complete Psychological Works of Sigmund Freud*. Vol. XXI, 225-43.

Friday, Nancy. (1977). *My Mother/My Self*. N.Y.: Dell. German translation, *Wie meine Mutter*. (1979). Frankfurt/M: S. Fischer.

Friedrichs, Jürgen. (1973). *Methoden empirischer Sozialforschung*. Hamburg: Fischer.

Friedlander, Bernard Z., Antoinette C. Jacobs, Barbara B. Davis, and Harriet S. Wetstone. (1972). Time sampling analysis of infant's natural language environments in the home. *Child Development*. 43, 730-40.

Frisch, Hannah L. (1977). Sex stereotypes in adult-infant play. *Child Development*. 48, 1671-75.

Garnica, Olga K. (1977). Some prosodic and paralinguistic features of speech to young children. In C. Snow and C. Ferguson (eds.). 63-88.

Garnica, Olga K. (1979). The boys have the muscles and the girls have the sexy legs: Adult-child speech and the use of generic labels. In O. Garnica and M. King (eds.). 135-48.

Garnica, Olga K. and Martha L. King (eds.). (1979). *Language, Children and Society*. N.Y.: Pergamon Press.

Garvey, Catherine. (1975). Requests and responses in children's speech. *Journal of Child Language*. 2, 41-63. Also translated by Peter Huth (1979) as Aufforderungen und ihre Beantwortung im kindlichen Sprachgebrauch. In K. Martens (ed.). 133-67.

Gerbner, George, *et al.* (eds.). (1969). *The Analysis of Communication Content*. N.Y.: John Wiley & Sons.

Gethmann, Christian. (1979). *Protologik. Untersuchungen zur formalen Pragmatik von Begründungsdiskursen*. Frankfurt/M: Suhrkamp.

Gethmann, Christian. (ed.). (1980). *Theorie des wissenschaftlichen Argumentierens*. Frankfurt/M.: Suhrkamp.

Giles, Howard, W. P. Robinson, and P. M. Smith (eds.). (1980). *Language: Social Psychological Perspectives*. Oxford: Pergamon Press.

Givon, Talmy (ed.). (1979). *Discourse and Syntax*. Volume 12 of *Syntax and Semantics*. N.Y.: Academic Press.

Gleason, Jean Berko. (1973). Code-switching in children's language. In T. E. Moore (ed.). *Cognitive Development and the Acquisition of Language*. N.Y.: Academic Press. 159-68.

Gleason, Jean Berko. (1975). Fathers and other strangers; Men's speech to young children. In Daniel Dato (ed.). *Developmental Psycholinguistics: Theory and Application*. Washington, D.C. 289-97.

Gleason, Jean Berko. (1977). Talking to children: Some notes on feedback. In C. Snow and C. Ferguson (eds.). 199-205.

Gleason, Jean Berko. (1980). The acquisition of social speech: Routines and politeness formulas. In H. Giles, W. P. Robinson, and P. M. Smith (eds.). 21-27.

Goeppert, Herma (ed.). (1979). *Sprachverhalten im Unterricht*. München: UTB Fink.

Goffman, Erving. (1961). *Asylums: Essays on the Social Situation of Mental Patients and Other Inmates*. N.Y.: Garden City.

Goffman, Erving. (1979). Footing. *Semiotica*. 25,1-29. Reprinted in *Forms of Talk*. Philadelphia: Univ. of Pennsylvania Press. (1981).

Goffman, Erving. (1976). *Gender Advertisements*. N.Y.: Harper & Row.

Goldberg, Susan and Michael Lewis. (1972). Play behavior in the year-old infant: Early sex differences. In J. Bardwick (ed.). 30-34.

Gooch, G. P. (1965). *Maria Theresa and Other Studies*. N.Y.: Archon Books.

Goodwin, Marjorie Harness. (1980). Directive-response speech sequences in girls' and boys' task activities. In S. McConnell-Ginet, R. Borker, and N. Furman (eds.). 157-73.

Gordon, Susan. (1969). The relationship between the English language abilities and home language experiences in first-grade children from three ethnic groups, of varying socioeconomic status and varying degrees of bilingualism. Unpublished dissertation. The Univ. of New Mexico.

Graber, Gustav H. (1973). *Tiefenpsychologie der Frau*. München: Piper.

Grasso, Laura. (1979). *Madri e figlie*. Speccio contro specchio. L'identificazione 'obligata' fra madri e figlie impedisce la vera singola identità. Florence: Nuova Guaraldi.

Graves, Donald. (1975). An examination of the writing processes of seven-year-old children. *Research in the Teaching of English*. 9, 227-41.

Gray, Bennison. (1977). *The Grammatical Foundations of Rhetoric: Discourse Analysis*. The Hague: Mouton.

Green, J. and C. Wallat. (1981). Mapping instructional conversations: A sociolinguistic ethnography. In. J. Green and C. Wallat (eds.). *Ethnography and Language in Educational Settings*. Norwood, N.J.: Ablex.

Greif, Esther B. (1980). Sex differences in parent-child conversations. In C. Kramarae (ed.). 253-58.

Greif, Esther B. and Jean B. Gleason. (1980). Hi, thanks, and goodbye: More routine information. *Language in Society*. 9, 159-66.

Grewendorf, Günther (ed.). (1979). *Sprachakttheorie und Semantik*. Frankfurt/M: Suhrkamp.

Gülich, Elisabeth and Wolfgang Raible. (1977). *Linguistische Textmodelle*. Stuttgart: UTB.

Gumperz, John. (1964). Linguistic and social interaction in two communities. Supplement to *American Anthropologist*. 9(2).

Gumperz, John. (1972). Sociolinguistics and communication in small groups. In J. B. Pride and J. Holmes (eds.). *Sociolinguistics*. 203-24.

Gumperz, John. (1976). The sociolinguistic significance of conversational code-switching. Language Behavior, Research Laboratory, Berkeley, Working Paper 46.

Gumperz, John. (1977). Sociocultural knowledge in conversational inference. In M. Saville-Troike (ed.). *Linguistics and Anthropology*. Washington, D.C.: Georgetown Univ. Press. 191-211.

Gumperz, John. (1982). *Discourse Strategies*. Cambridge: Cambridge Univ. Press.

Gumperz, John and Dell Hymes (eds.). (1972). *Directions in Sociolinguistics.* N.Y.:Holt, Rinehart & Winston.

Gumperz, John and Deborah Tannen. (1979). Individual and social differ-Gumperz, John and Deborah Tannen. (1979). Individual and social difference in language use. In C. J. Fillmore, D. Kempler, and W. S.-Y. Wang (eds.). 305-25.

Gunnar, Megan R. and Margaret Donahue. (1980). Sex differences in social responsiveness between six months and twelve months. *Child Development.* 51, 262-65.

Guntrip, Harry. (1961). *Personality Structure and Human Interaction: The Developing Synthesis of Psycho-dynamic Theory.* N.Y.: International Universities Press.

Guttentag, Marcia and Helen Bray. (1977). Teachers as mediators of sex-role standards. In A. Sargent (ed.). *Beyond Sex Roles.* St. Paul, Minn.: West. 395-411.

Habermas, Jürgen. (1970). *Zur Logik der Sozialwissenschaften.* Frankfurt/ M.: Suhrkamp.

Habermas, Jürgen. (1973). Wahrheitstheorie. In H. Fahrenback (ed.). *Wirklichkeit und Reflexion.* Pfulbingen: Naske. 50-84.

Habermas, Jürgen. (1977). *Erkenntnis und Interesse.* Frankfurt/M.: Suhrkamp.

Halliday, Michael A. K. (1976). Early language learning: A sociolinguistic approach. In W. C. McCormack and S. A. Wurm (eds.). 97-124.

Halpern, Howard. (1976). *Cutting Loose. An Adult Guide to Coming to Terms with Your Parents.* N.Y.: Simon and Schuster. Translated into German (1978) as *Abschied von den Eltern.* Hamburg: ISKO Press.

Halverson, Charles F. and Mary F. Waldrop. (1970). Maternal behavior toward own and other preschool children: The problem of "ownness." *Child Development.* 41, 839-45.

Hammer, Signe. (1975). *Daughters and Mothers. Mothers and Daughters.* N.Y.: Quadrangle/The New York Times.

Harkness, Sara. (1976). Mother's language. *Neurolinguistics.* 5, 110-11.

Harkness, Sara. (1977). Aspects of social environment and first language acquisition in rural Africa. In C. Snow and C. Ferguson (eds.). 309-16.

Harper, Edward B. (1969). Fear and the status of women. *Southwestern Journal of Anthropology.* 25, 81-95.

Hartnett, D. (1974). The relation of cognitive style and hemispheric preference to deductive and inductive second-language learning. Paper presented at the Neurosciences meeting. Brain Research Institute. UCLA. September 27, 1974.

Hatano, Giyoo, Kazuo Miyake, and Nobumoto Tajima. (1980). Mother behavior in an unstructured situation and child's acquisition of number conservation. *Child Development*. 51, 379-85.

Hayes, John R. (ed.). (1970). *Cognition and the Development of Language*. N.Y.: John Wiley & Sons.

Hellinger, Marlis. (1979). For men must work, and women must weep: Sexism in English language textbooks used in German schools. *Women's Studies International Quarterly*. 3, 267-75.

Hess, Robert D. and Virginia Shipman. (1965). Early experience and the socialization of cognitive modes in children. *Child Development*. 36, 869-86.

Hess, Robert D. and Virginia Shipman. (1968). Maternal influences upon early learning. In R. D. Hess and R. M. Bear (eds.). *Early Education*. Chicago: Aldine. 91-103.

Hirsch, Marianne. (1981). Review essay: Mothers and daughters. *Signs*. 7(1), 200-21.

Hoffman, Lois. (1974a). The effects of maternal employment on the child. A review of the research. *Developmental Psychology*. 10,204-28.

Hoffman, Lois. (1974b). Effects on Child. In L. W. Hoffman and F. I. Nye (eds.). *Working Mothers*. San Francisco: Jossey-Bass.

Holenstein, Elmar. (1975). *Roman Jakobsons phänomenologischer Strukturalismus*. Frankfurt/M.: Suhrkamp.

Holenstein, Elmar. (1976). *Linguistik, Semiotik, Hermeneutik*. Plädoyer für eine strukturale Phänomenologie. (Roman Jakobson zum 80. Geburtstag). Frankfurt/M.: Suhrkamp.

Hollos, Marida and William Beeman. (1978). The development of directives among Norwegian and Hungarian children: An example of communicative style in culture. *Language in Society*. 7, 345-55.

Holsti, Ole R. (1969). *Content Analysis for the Social Sciences and Humanities*. Reading, Mass.: Addison-Wesley.

Holzman, Mathilda, E. Masur, L. Ferrier, J. Goldner, K. O'Leary, and J. Morse. (1983). How the human infant becomes a language user. Unpublished manuscript.

Horney, Karin. (1928). Zur Genese des weiblichen Kastrationskomplexes. *Internationale Zeitschrift für Psychologie*.

Hymes, Dell. (1974). *Foundations in Sociolinguistics*. Philadelphia: Univ. of

Pennsylvania Press.

Iben, G. (1979). "Abweichende" und "defizitäre" Sozialisation. In G. Neidhardt (ed.). 114-61.

Jacobs, Blanche S. and Howard A. Moss. (1976). Birth order and sex of sibling as determinants of mother-infant interaction. *Child Development.* 45, 315-22.

Jaeger, Karl H. (1976). Zur Argumentation in Texten gesprochener Sprache. *Deutschunterricht.* 28,33-50.

Jahoda, Marie, Merton Deutsch, and Stuart Cook. (1974). Die Technik der Auswertung: Analyse und Interpretation. In R. König (ed.). *Das Interview.* Köln: Kiepenheuer & Witsch. 271-89.

Jocić, M. (1978). Adaptation in adult speech during communication with children. In N. Waterson and C. Snow (eds.). 159-71.

Jochens, Birgit. (1979). "Fragen" im Mutter-Kind-Dialog: Zur Strategie der Gesprächsorganisation von Müttern. In K. Martens (ed.). 110-33.

Jung, Carl G. and Carl Kerenyi. (1969). The psychological aspects of the Kore. *Essays on a Science of Mythology: The Myths of the Divine Child and the Mysteries of Eleusis.* Princeton, N.J.: Princeton Univ. Press.

Kagan, Jerome and H. A. Moss. (1962). *From Birth to Maturity: A Study in Psychological Development.* N.Y.: John Wiley & Sons.

Kagan, Jerome and Marion Freeman. (1963). Relations of childhood intelligence, maternal behavior, and social class to behavior during adolescence. *Child Development.* 34, 899-911.

Kallmeyer, Werner, *et. al.* (1974). *Lektürekolleg zur Textlinguistik. Bd. I, Einführung.* Frankfurt/M.: Fischer Athenäum.

Keller, Helmut (ed.). (1979). *Geschlechtsunterschiede.* Weinheim: Beltz.

Keseling, Gisbert. (1978). "Gut" und "schlecht": Affektive und emotionale Bestandteile in der Sprache des Schulkindes. Versuch einer ontogenetischen Rekonstruktion. In G. Augst (ed.). 192-208.

Kintsch, Walter. (1974). *The Representation of Meaning in Memory.* N.Y.: John Wiley & Sons.

Kintsch, Walter. (1977). *Memory, Language, and Thinking.* N.Y.: John Wiley & Sons.

Kintsch, Walter and Teun van Dijk. (1978). Toward a model of text comprehension and production. Ms.

Klann-Delius, Gisela. (1979). Welchen Einfluss hat die Geschlechtszugehörigkeit auf den Spracherwerb des Kindes? Habilitationsvortrag,

Free Univ. of Berlin. English translation (1981), as Sex and language acquisition--Is there any influence? *Journal of Pragmatics*. 5, 1-25.

Klein, Norma. (1975). *Girls Can Be Anything*. N.Y.: Dutton.

Kohlberg, Laurence. (1966). A cognitive developmental analysis of children's sex-role concepts and attitudes. In E. Maccoby (ed.). *The Development of Sex Differences*. Palo Alto, Ca.: Stanford Univ. Press. 82-173.

Kopperschmidt, Jürgen. (1980). *Argumentation, Sprache und Vernunft*. II. Teil. Stuttgart: Kohlhammer.

Kracauer, Siegfried. (1959). The challenge of qualitative content analysis. *Public Opinion Quarterly*. 16(4),631-41.

Kramarae, Cheris (ed.). (1980). *The Voices and Words of Women and Men*. Oxford: Pergamon Press.

Kramarae, Cheris. (1981). *Women and Men Speaking*. Rowley, Mass.: Newbury House.

Kramarae, Cheris, Muriel Schulz, and William M. O'Barr (eds.). (1984). *Language and Power*. Beverly Hills: Sage.

Krappmann, Lothar. (1972). *Dimensionen von Identität*. Stuttgart: Klett.

Krashen, S., H. Seliger, and D. Hartnett. (n.d.). Two studies in adult second-language learning. Manuscript.

Krippendorff, Klaus. (1980). *Content Analysis. An Introduction to Its Methodology*. Beverly Hills: Sage.

Kuhn, Elisabeth. (1980). *Geschlechtsspezifische Unterschiede in der Sprachverwendung*. Frankfurt/M. M.A. Thesis.

Kummer, Ingrid. (1978). The formation of role concepts in texts: The concept "mother" in German schoolbooks. *Journal of Pragmatics*. 2,207-23.

Kunkel, Peter and Sara Sue Kennard. (1971). *Spout Spring: A Black Community*. N.Y.:Holt, Rinehart & Winston.

Kürthy, Thomas. (1978). *Geschlechtsspezifische Sozialisation 1,2*. Paderborn: UTB.

Labov, William. (1966). *The Social Stratification of English in New York City*. Washington D.C.: Center for Applied Linguistics.

Labov, William. (1970). The study of language in its social context. *Studium Generale*. 23/1, 30-88.

Labov, William. (1972). The transformation of experience in narrative syntax. In *Language in the Inner City*. Philadelphia: Univ. of Pennsylvania Press. 354-96.

Labov, William and Daniel Fanshel. (1977). *Therapeutic Discourse: Psychotherapy as Conversation*. N.Y.: Academic Press.

Labov, William and J. Waletzky. (1967). Narrative analysis: Oral versions of personal experience. In J. Helm (ed.). *Essays on the Verbal and Visual Arts*. Seattle, Washington: Univ. of Washington Press. 12-44.

Lachman, R. and D. J. Dooling. (1965). Connected discourse and random strings: Effects of numbers of inputs on recognition and recall. *Journal of Experimental Psychology*. 77, 507-22.

Lakoff, Robin. (1975). *Language and Woman's Place*. N.Y.: Harper & Row.

Lamb, Michael E. (1976). The role of the father: An overview. In M. Lamb (ed.). 1-63.

Lamb, Michael E. (ed.). (1976). *The Role of the Father in Child Development*. N.Y.: John Wiley & Sons.

Lamb, Michael E. (1977). Father-infant and mother-infant interaction in the first year of life. *Child Development*. 48, 167-81.

Langlois, Judith H. and A. Chris Downs. (1980). Mothers, fathers, and peers as socialization agents of sex-typed play behaviors in young children. *Child Development*. 51, 1237-47.

Larson, Karen. (1978). Role-playing and the real thing: Socialization and standard speech in Norway. Paper presented at the Ninth World Congress of Sociologists, Uppsala, Sweden.

Lasswell, Harold D. *et al.* (1965). *Language of Politics: Studies in Quantitative Semantics*. Cambridge, Mass.: MIT Press.

Lazarsfeld, Paul F. (1944). The controversy over detailed interviews. An offer for negotiation. *Public Opinion Quarterly*. 8,38-60.

Lee, Paul and Robert Stewart (eds.). (1976). *Sex Differences: Cultural and Developmental Dimensions*. New York.

Lehr, Ursula. (1979). Die mütterliche Berufstätigkeit und mögliche Auswirkungen auf das Kind. In F. Neidhardt (ed.). 230-69.

Leodolter, Ruth (=WODAK). (1975a). *Das Sprachverhalten von Angeklagten bei Gericht*. Kronberg/Ts.: Scriptor.

Leodolter, Ruth. (1975b). Gestörte Sprache oder Privatsprache: Kommunikation bei Schizophrenen. *WLG (Wiener Linguistische Gazette)*. 10/11, 75-95.

Levy, David M. (1979). Communicative goals and strategies: Between discourse and syntax. In T. Givón (ed.). 183-210.

Lewis, Diane. (1975). The black family: Socialization and sex roles. *Phylon*. 36(3) Fall, 221-37.

Lewis, Michael and Louise Cherry. (1977). Social behavior and language acquisition. In M. Lewis and L. Rosenblum (eds.). 227-45.

Lewis, Michael and S. Goldberg. (1969). Perceptual-cognitive development in infancy: A generalized expectancy model as a function of the mother-infant interaction. *Merrill-Palmer Quarterly.* 15(1),81-100.

Lewis, Michael and Roy Freedle. (1973). Mother-infant dyad: The cradle of meaning. In P. Pliner, L. Krames, and T. Alloway (eds.). *Communication and Affect, Language and Thought.* N.Y.: Academic Press.

Lewis, Michael and Leonard A. Rosenblum (eds.). (1977). *Interaction, Conversation, and the Development of Language.* N.Y.: John Wiley & Sons.

Lewis, Michael and Leonard A. Rosenblum (eds.). (1980). *The Development of Affect.* N.Y.: Plenum Press.

Lewis, Michael and Leonard A. Rosenblum. (1980). Introduction. Lewis and Rosenblum (eds.). 1-10.

Lewis, Michael, Marsha Weinraub, and P. Ban. (1972). Mothers and fathers, girls and boys: Attachment behavior in the first two years of life. Research Bulletin RB - 72 - 60. Princeton, N.J.: Educational Testing Service.

Lewis, Michael and Marsha Weinraub. (1976). The father's role in the child's social network. In M. Lamb (ed.). 157-84.

Lewis, Michael and C. D. Wilson. (1972). Infant development in lower-class American families. *Human Development.* 15, 112-17.

Lieven, E. V. M. (1978). Conversations between mothers and young children: Individual differences and their possible implication for the study of language learning. In N. Waterson and C. Snow (eds.). 173-87.

Linde, Charlotte and William Labov. (1975). Spatial networks as a site for the study of language and thought. *Language.* 5(4),924-39.

Loeb, Roger C., Leslie Horst and Patricia Horton. (1980). Family interaction patterns associated with self-esteem in preadolescent girls and boys. *Merrill-Palmer Quarterly.* 26,205-17.

Lorber, Judith, Rose Coser, Alice Rossi and Nancy Chodorow. (1981). *On The Reproduction of Mothering*: A Methodological Debate. *Signs.* 6,482-514.

Lorenzer, Alfred. (1972). *Sprachzerstörung und Rekonstruktion.* Frankfurt/Main: Suhrkamp.

Lott, Bernice. (1981). *Becoming a Woman: The Socialization of Gender.* Springfield, Ill.: Charles C. Thomas Publisher.

Lynn, David B. (1974). *The Father: His Role in Child Development.* Monterey, CA: Brooks/Cole.

Lynn, David B. (1979). *Daughters and Parents.* Monterey, CA: Brooks/Cole.

Macaulay, Ronald K. S. (1978). The myth of female superiority in language.

*Journal of Child Language.* 5, 353-63.

Maccoby, Eleanor E. (1980). *Social Development: Psychological Growth and the Parent-child Relationship.* N.Y.: Harcourt Brace Jovanovich.

Maccoby, Eleanor and Carol Jacklin. (1974). *The Psychology of Sex Differences.* Palo Alto, Cal.: Stanford Univ. Press.

Maccoby, Eleanor and Carol Jacklin. (1980). Sex differences in aggression: A rejoinder and reprise. *Child Development.* 51, 964-80.

McConnell-Ginet, Sally, Ruth Borker, and Nelly Furman (eds.). (1980). *Women and Language in Literature and Society.* N.Y.: Praeger.

McCormack, William C. and Stephen A. Wurm (eds.). (1976). *Language and Man: Anthropological Issues.* The Hague: Mouton.

Mack, John E. and Holly Hickler. (1982). *The Life and Suicide of an Adolescent Girl.* Boston, Mass.: Little Brown.

McLaughlin, Barry, Caleb Schutz, and David White. (1980). Parental speech to five-year old children in a game-playing situation. *Child Development.* 51, 580-82.

Mack-Brunswick, Ruth. (n.d.). Die prä-ödipale Phase in der Libidoentwicklung. (Unpublished Manuscript)

Macnamara, John. (1972). Cognitive basis of language learning in infants. *Psychological Review.* 79, 1-13.

Macnamara, John (ed.). (1977b). *Language, Learning and Thought.* N.Y.: Academic Press.

McNeill, David. (1966). Developmental psycholinguistics. In Frank Smith and George Miller (eds.). *The Genesis of Language.* Cambridge, Mass.: The M.I.T. Press, 15-84.

Magrab, Phyllis R. (1979). Mothers and daughters. In C. B. Kopp (ed.). *Becoming Female: Perspectives on Development.* N.Y.: Plenum Press. 113-29.

Maher, Brendan A., Kathryn O. McKean, and Berry McLaughlin. (1966). Studies in psychotic language. In P. Stone, D. Dunphy, M. Smith, and D. Ogilvie (eds.). 469-503.

Mahler, Margaret. (1972). *Symbiose und Individuation.* Stuttgart: Klett.

Mahler, Margaret, Fred Pine, and Anni Bergman. (1975). *The Psychological Birth of the Human Infant.* N.Y.: Basic Books; translated into German 1980: *Die psychische Geburt des Menschen,* Fischer, Frankfurt/M.

Marantz, Sonia A. and Annick F. Mansfield. (1977). Maternal employment and the development of sex-role stereotyping in five- to eleven-year-old girls. *Child Development.* 48, 668-73.

Martens, Karin (ed.). (1979). *Kindliche Kommunikation. Theoretische Perspektiven, empirische Analysen, methodologische Grundlagen.* Frankfurt/M.: Suhrkamp.

Martin, Carolyn Lynn and Charles F. Halverson. (1981). A schematic processing model of sex typing and stereotyping in children. *Child Development.* 52(4),1119-34.

Masur, Elise Frank and Jean Berko Gleason. (1980). Parent-child interaction and the acquisition of lexical information during play. *Developmental Psychology.* 16, 404-09.

Matarazzo, Joseph D. *et al.* (1970). Interviewee speech behavior under different content conditions. *Journal of Applied Psycholinguistics.* 1,15-26.

Mayer, Dorothy M. (1968). *The Tragic Queen: Marie Antoinette.* London: Weidenfeld and Nicolson.

Medinius, G. R. (1969). *Child and Adolescent Psychological Behavior and Development.* N.Y.: John Wiley & Sons.

Messer, David J. (1980). The episodic structure of maternal speech to young children. *Journal of Child Language.* 7, 29-40.

Milroy, Leslie. (1980). *Language and Social Networks.* London: Blackwells.

Milroy, Leslie and Susanne Margrain. (1980). Vernacular language loyalty and social network. *Language in Society.* 9,43-70.

Minton, C., J. Kagan, and J. A. Levine. (1971). Maternal control and obedience in the two year old. *Child Development.* 42, 1873-94.

Minturn, Leigh and John T. Hitchcock. (1963). The Rajputs of Khalapur, India. In B. Whiting (ed.). *Six Cultures: Studies in Child Rearing.* N.Y.: John Wiley & Sons.

Mischel, W. (1966). A social-learning view of sex differences in behavior. In E. E. Maccoby (ed.). *The Development of Sex Differences.* Stanford, CA: Stanford Univ. Press. 56-81.

Mitchell, Juliet. (1974). *Psychoanalysis and Feminism.* N.Y.: Pantheon Books; translated into German 1976: *Psychoanalyse und Feminismus.* Frankfurt/M.: Suhrkamp.

Mitchell-Kernan, Claudia and Keith Kernan. (1977). Pragmatics of directive choice among children. In S. Ervin-Tripp and C. Mitchell-Kernan (eds.). 189-208.

Moeller-Gambarov, Marina. (1977). Emanzipation macht Angst. *Kursbuch 47.* Berlin: Rotbuch Verlag. 1-26.

Moerk, Ernest L. (1972). Principles of interaction in language learning. *Merrill-Palmer Quarterly.* 18, 229-57.

Moerk, Ernest L. (1974). Changes in verbal child-mother interactions with increasing language skills of the child. *Journal of Psycholinguistic Research*. 3, 101-16.

Moerk, Ernest L. (1980). Relationship between parental input frequencies and children's language acquisition: A reanalysis of Brown's data. *Journal of Child Language*. 7, 105-18.

Moss, Howard A. (1972). Sex, age, and state as determinants of mother-infant interaction. In J. Bardwick (ed.). 22-29.

Mussen, Paul and Eldred Rutherford. (1963). Parent-child relations and the parental personality in relation to young children's sex-role preferences. *Child Development*. 34, 589-607.

Nebes, Robert D. (1975). Man's so-called "minor" hemisphere. *UCLA Educator*. 17(2),13-16.

Neidhardt, Fritz (ed.). (1979). *Frühkindliche Sozialisation*. Stuttgart: Enke.

Neisser, Edith. (1973). *Mothers and Daughters: A Lifelong Relationship*. Revised Edition. N.Y.: Harper & Row.

Nelson, Katherine. (1975). The nominal shift in semantic-syntactic development. *Cognitive Psychology*. 7, 461-79.

Nelson, Katherine. (1977). The conceptual basis for naming. In J. Macnamara (ed.). 117-36.

Nelson, Katherine. (1981). Individual differences in language development: Implications for development and language. *Developmental Psychology*. 17, 170-87.

Newport, Elissa L., Henry Gleitman and Lila R. Gleitman. (1977). Mother, I'd rather do it myself: Some effects and non-effects of maternal speech style. In C. Snow and C. Ferguson (eds.). 109-49.

Nichols, Patricia C. (1978). Black women in the rural South: Conservative and innovative. In B. L. Dubois and I. Crouch (eds.). 103-14.

Nichols, Patricia C. (1980). Women in their speech communities. In S. McConnell-Ginet, R. Borker, and N. Furman (eds.). 75-93.

Nichols, Patricia C. (1984). Networks and hierarchies: Language and social stratification. In C. Kramarae *et al.* (eds.). 23-42.

Ninio, Anat and Jerome Bruner. (1978). The achievement and antecedents of labelling. *Journal of Child Language*. 5(1),1-15.

N'Namdi, George R. (1978). *Analysis of Parent-child Interaction in the Two-child Black Family*. Unpublished Dissertation, Wayne State Univ., Detroit, Michigan.

Noller, Patricia. (1978). Sex differences in the socialization of affectionate expression. *Developmental Psychology*. 14, 317-19.

Noller, Patricia. (1980). Cross-gender effect in two-child families. *Develop-*

*mental Psychology*. 16, 159-60.

Norman, Daniel and Daniel Rumelhart (eds.). (1975). *Explorations in cognition*. San Francisco: Freeman.

O'Barr, William M. and Bowman K. Atkins. (1980). "Women's language" or "powerless language"? In S. McConnell-Ginet, R. Borker, and N. Furman (eds.). 93-110.

Ochs, Elinor. (1979). Planned and unplanned discourse. In Givon (ed.). 51-80.

Ochs, Elinor. (1980). Growing up in Samoa: A sociolinguist's perspective. Public lecture, Univ. of Southern California. May, 1980.

Ochs, Elinor and Bambi Schieffelin (eds.). (1979). *Developmental Pragmatics*. N.Y.: Academic Press.

Odell, Lee. (1980). Teaching writing by teaching the process of discovery: An interdisciplinary enterprise. In L. Gregg and E. Steinberg (eds.). *Cognitive Processes In Writing: An Interdisciplinary Approach*. Hillsdale, N.J.: Lawrence Erlbaum.

Oevermann, Ulrich. (1970). Einige Thesen über den Zusammenhang von Identifikationsprozessen und Sprachentwicklung. In B. Bernstein, U. Oevermann, R. Reichrein and H. Roth (eds.). 79-90.

Oevermann, Ulrich. (1972). *Sprache und soziale Herkunft*. Frankfurt/M.: Suhrkamp.

Oevermann, Ulrich, *et al.* (1979). *Die Methodologie einer objektiven Hermeneutik*. In Soeffner (ed.). 352-434.

Ogilvie, Daniel H., Philip J. Stone, and Edwin S. Shneidman. (1966). Some characteristics of genuine versus simulated suicide notes. In Stone *et. al.* (eds.). 527-35.

Oksaar, Els. (1977). *Spracherwerb im Vorschulalter: Einführung in die Pädolinguistik*. Stuttgart: Kohlhammer.

Olson, David R. (1977a). Oral and written language and the cognitive processes of children. *Journal of Communication* 27(3),10-26.

Olson, David R. (1977b). From utterance to text: The bias of language in speech and writing. *Harvard Educational Review*. 47,257-81.

Olson, David R. (1977c). The formalization of linguistic rules. In John Macnamara (ed.). *Language, Learning, and Thought*. N.Y.: Academic Press. 111-16.

Osofsky, Joy D. and Edward J. O'Connell. (1972). Parent-child interaction: Daughters' effects upon mothers' and fathers' behavior. *Developmental Psychology*. 7(2),157-68.

Ostermann, Fredrick. (1973). *Kreative Prozesse im "Aufsatzunterricht."* Paderborn: UTB.

Paige, Jeffrey M. (1966). Letters from Jenny: An approach to the clinical analysis of personality structure by computer. In Stone *et al.* (ed.). 431-51.

Parsons, Talcott. (1968). *The Social System.* N.Y.: Free Press.

Perelman, Charles and Anna Olbrechts-Tyteca. (1958). Traité de l'argumentation, la nouvelle rhétorique. Paris.

Peters, Ann M. (1977). Language learning strategies: Does the whole equal the sum of the parts? *Language.* 53, 560-73.

Phelps, Louise W. (1980). *Composition in a New Key: An Interdisciplinary Framework for Teaching.* Unpublished manuscript.

Phillips, Juliet R. (1973). Syntax and vocabulary of mothers' speech to young children: Age and sex comparisons. *Child Development.* 44, 182-85.

Pilling, Doria and Mia Kellmer Pringle. (1978). *Controversial Issues in Child Development.* N.Y.: Schocken Books.

Psathas, George and Dennis J. Arp. (1966). A thematic analysis of interviewer's statements in therapy-analogue interviews. In Stone *et al.* (ed.), 476-91.

Radel, J. (ed.). (1980). *Liebe Mutter, Liebe Tochter. Frauenbriefe aus drei Jahrhunderten.* München: Bogner & Bernhard.

Ramge, Hans. (1975). *Spracherwerb. Grundzüge der Sprachentwicklung des Kindes.* Tübingen: Max Niemeyer.

Rebelsky, Freda and Cheryl Hanks. (1971). Fathers' verbal interaction with infants in the first three months of life. *Child Development.* 42, 63-8.

Redlinger, Wendy. (1976). Mothers' speech to children in bilingual Mexican-American homes. In Betty L. Dubois and Isabel Crouch (eds.). 119-30.

Remick, Helen. (1971). *The Maternal Environment of Linguistic Development.* Unpublished dissertation, Univ. of California, Davis.

Retherford, Kristine S., Bonnie C. Schwartz and Robin S. Chapman. (1981). Semantic roles and residual grammatical categories in mothers' and children's speech: Who tunes into whom? *Journal of Child Language.* 8, 583-608.

Rheingold, Joseph C. (1964). *The Fear of Being a Woman.* N.Y.: Grune & Stratton.

Rich, Adrienne. (1977). *Of Woman born.* N.Y.: Bantam.

Richards, Martin P. M. (1974). First steps in becoming social. In M. P. M. Richards (ed.). 83-97.

Richards, Martin P. M. (ed.). (1974). *The Integration of a Child into a Social World.* Cambridge: Cambridge Univ. Press.

Richards, Martin P. M. (1977). Interaction and the concept of development: The biological and the social revisited. In M. Lewis and L. Rosenblum (eds.). 187-206.

Ringler, Norma. (1978). A longitudinal study of mothers' language. In N. Waterson and C. Snow (eds.). 151-58.

Ritsert, Jürgen. (1972). *Inhaltsanalyse und Ideologiekritik*. Frankfurt/M.: Fischer Athenäum.

Robinson, W. and S. Rackstraw. (1973). Variationen bei Antworten von Müttern auf Fragen von Kindern. In D. Kochan (ed.). *Sprache und kommunikative Kompetenz*. Stuttgart: Klett. 33-64.

Rogers-Millar, L. Edna and Frank E. Millar III. (1979). Domineeringness and dominance: A transactional view. *Human Communication Research*. 5(3), 238-46.

Romaine, Suzanne. (1978). Postvocalic /r/ in Scottish English: Sound change in progress. In P. Trudgill (ed.). 144-57.

Rondal, Jean A. (1980). Fathers' and mothers' speech in early language development. *Journal of Child Language*. 7, 353-69.

Rose, A. M. (ed.). (1962). *Human Behavior and Social Processes*. London: Routledge & Kegan Paul.

Rothbart, M. K. and Eleanor Maccoby. (1966). Parents' differential reaction to sons and daughters. *Journal of Personality and Social Psychology*. 4, 237-43.

Rubin, Jeffrey Z., Frank J. Provenzano and Zella Luria. (1974). The eye of the beholder: Parents' views on sex of newborn. *American Journal of Orthopsychiatry*. 44, 512-19.

Rūķe-Draviņa, Velta. (1976). Gibt es Universalien in der Ammensprache? In Gaberell Drachman (ed.). *Akten des 1. Salzburger Kolloquiums über Kindersprache. Salzburger Beiträge zur Linguistik, 2.* Tübingen: Günter Narr. 3-16.

Ryan, Joanna. (1974). Early language development: Towards a communicational analysis. In M. P. Richards (ed.). 185-213.

Sachs, Lothar. (1969). *Statistische Auswertungsmethoden*. Berlin: Springer.

Scanzoni, John. (1975). *Sex Roles, Life Styles and Childbearing: Changing Patterns in Marriage and the Family*. N.Y.: Free Press.

Schachter, Frances F., with Ruth E. Marquis, Ellen Shore, Carole L. Bundy and June H. McNair. (1979). *Everyday Mother Talk to Toddlers: Early Intervention*. N.Y.: Academic Press.

Schaffer, H. Rudolph and Charles K. Crook. (1979). Maternal control techniques in a directed play situation. *Child Development*. 50, 989-96.

Schank, Gerd. (1979). Zum Problem der Natürlichkeit von Gesprächen in der Konversationsanalyse. In J. Dittmann (ed.). 73-93.

Schank, Roger and Robert Abelson. (1977). *Scripts, Plans, Goals and Understanding*. Hillsdale, N.J.: Erlbaum.

Scharmann, Dora L. and Theodor Scharmann. (1979). Die Vaterrolle im Sozialisations- und Entwicklungsprozess des Kindes. Theoretische Ansätze und empirische Materialien. In F. Neidhardt (ed.). 270-316.

Schatzman, Leonard and Anselm Strauss. (1955). Social class and modes of communication. *American Journal of Sociology*. 60,329,ff.

Schieffelin, Bambi B. (1979). Getting it together: An ethnographic approach to the study of the development of communicative competence. In E. Ochs and B. Schieffelin (eds.). 73-108.

Schiefelbusch, R.L. and O.B. Bricker (eds.). (1981). *Early Language: Acquisition and Intervention*. Baltimore Md.: Univ. Park Press.

Schmalohr, Erich. (1979). "Mutter"-Entbehrung in der Frühsozialisation. In F. Neidhardt (ed.). 188-229.

Serbin, L., D. O'Leary, R. Kent, and I. Tonick. (1973). A comparison of teacher response to the pre-academic and problem behavior of boys and girls. *Child Development*. 44, 796-804.

Shatz, Marilyn and Rochel Gelman. (1977). Beyond syntax: The influence of conversational constraints on speech modifications. In C. Snow and C. Ferguson (eds.). 189-98.

Shaughnessy, Mina P. (1977). *Errors and Expectations: A Guide for the Teacher of Basic Writing*. N.Y.: Oxford Univ. Press.

Shipley, Elizabeth S., Carlotta S. Smith and Lila R. Gleitman. (1969). A study in the acquisition of Language: Free responses to commands. *Language*. 45, 322-42.

Shugar, Grace W. (1978). Text analysis as an approach to the study of early linguistic operations. In N. Waterson and C. Snow (eds.). 227-51.

Slater, Philip E. (1970). *The Pursuit of Loneliness: American Culture at the Breaking Point*. Boston: Beacon Press.

Slobin, Dan I. (1973). Cognitive prerequisites for the development of grammar. In C. Ferguson and D. I. Slobin (eds.). 175-208.

Smith, Phillip M. (1980). Judging masculine and feminine social identities from content-controlled speech. In H. Giles *et al.* (eds.). 121-26.

Smitherman, Geneva. (1980). Personal communication.

Snow, Catherine E. (1972). Mother's speech to children learning language. *Child Development*. 43, 549-65.

Snow, Catherine E. (1977a). Mothers' speech research: From input to interaction. In C. Snow and C. Ferguson (eds.). 31-49.

Snow, Catherine E. (1977b). The development of conversation between mothers and babies. *Journal of Child Language*. 4, 1-22.

Snow, Catherine E. (1979). The role of social interaction in language acquisition. In Schmalohr, E. (ed.) (1979). *Minnesota Symposia on Child Development*. Vol 12. Hillsdale, N.J.: Larence Earlbaum. 157-82.

Snow, Catherine E. and Charles A. Ferguson (eds.). (1977). *Talking to Children: Language Input and Acquisition*. Cambridge: Cambridge Univ. Press.

Soeffner, Hans-Georg. (ed.). (1979). *Interpretative Verfahren in den Sozial- und Textwissenschaften*. Stuttgart: Metzler.

Speier, Matthew. (1970). The everyday world of the child. In J. Douglas (ed.). *Understanding Everyday Life*. Chicago: Aldine. 188-217.

Spelke, E., P. Zelazo, J. Kagan, and M. Kotelchuck. (1973). Father interaction and separation protest. *Developmental Psychology*. 9, 83-90.

Spitz, René A. (1970). *Nein und Ja. Die Ursprünge der menschlichen Kommunikation*. Stuttgart: Klett.

Steger, Hugo. (1971). *Soziolinguistik. Grundlagen, Aufgaben und Ergebnisse für das Deutsche*. Sprache und Gesellschaft. Band XIII. Düsseldorf: Schwann.

Stone, P. J., D. C. Dunphy, M. S. Smith, and D. M. Ogilvie (eds.). (1966). *The General Inquirer: A Computer Approach to Content Analysis in the Behavioral Sciences*. Cambridge: M.I.T. Press.

Stone, P. J., D. C. Dunphy, M. S. Smith, and D. M. Ogilvie. (1968). *User's Manual for the General Inquirer*. Cambridge: M.I.T. Press.

Stoneman, Zolinda and Gene H. Brody. (1981). Two's company, three makes a difference: An examination of mothers' and fathers' speech to their young children. *Child Development*. 52, 705-07.

Sudnow, David (ed.). (1972). *Studies in Social Interaction*. N.Y.: Macmillan.

Sutton-Smith, Brian and B. G. Rosenberg. (1970). *The Sibling*. N.Y.: Holt, Rinehart & Winston, Inc.

Swacher, Marjorie. (1975). The sex of the speaker as a sociolinguistic variable. In B. Thorne and N. Henley (eds.). *Language and Sex: Difference and Dominance*. Rowley, Mass.: Newbury House. 76-83.

Sylvester-Bradley, B. and C. Trevarthen. (1978). Baby talk as an adaptation to the infant's communication. In N. Waterson and C. Snow (eds.). 75-92.

Tannen, Deborah. (1979). What's in a frame? Surface evidence for underlying expectations. In R. Freedle (ed.). 137-81.

Tanz, Christine. (1980). *Studies in the Acquisition of Deictic Terms*. Cambridge: Cambridge Univ. Press.

Tauber, Margaret. (1979). Sex differences in parent-child interaction styles during a free-play session. *Child Development*. 50, 981-88.

Taylor, S. E. and J. Crocken. (1979). Schematic bases of social information processing. In E. G. Higgins, P. Herman, and M. P. Zanza (eds.). *The Ontario Symposium in Personality and Social Psychology*. Vol. I. Hillsdale, N.J.

Thoman, Evelyn B. (1981). Affective communication as the prelude and context for language learning. In R. Schiefelbusch and D. Bricker (eds.). 183-200.

Thorne, Barrie. (1981). Gender . . . how is it best conceptualized? In L. Richardson and V. Taylor (eds.). *Issues in Sex, Gender and Society*. Lexington, Mass.: D. C. Heath.

Tibbetts, Sylvia-Lee. (1975a). Sex-role stereotyping in the lower grades: Part of the solution. *Journal of Vocational Behavior*. 6,255-61.

Tibbetts, Sylvia-Lee. (1975b). Children's Literature: A feminist perspective. *California Journal of Educational Research*. 26,1-5.

Trudgill, Peter (ed.). (1978). *Sociolinguistic Patterns in British English*. London: Arnold.

Tucker, G. Richard and Wallace E. Lambert. (1969). White and Negro listeners' reactions to various American-English dialects. *Social Forces*. 47, 463-68.

Tulkin, Steven R. and Jerome Kagan. (1972). Mother-child interaction in the first year of life. *Child Development*. 43, 31-41.

Tulving, Endel. (1972). Episodic and semantic memory. In E. Tulving and W. Donaldson (eds.). *The Organization of Memory*. N.Y.: Academic Press. 382-404.

van den Broeck, Johan. (1977). Class differences in syntactic complexity in the Flemish town of Maaseik. *Language in Society*. 6,149-81.

Volterra, Virginia and Traute Taeschner. (1978). The acquisition and development of language by bilingual children. *Journal of Child Language*. 5, 311-26.

Vreogh, Karen. (1968). Masculinity and femininity in the preschool years.

*Child Development.* 39,1253-7.

Vygotsky, Lev. (1962). *Thought and Language.* Ed. and trans., Eugenia Hanfmann and Gertrude Vakas. Cambridge, Mass.: M.I.T.

Wagner, Angelika, Heide Frasch, and Elke Lamberti. (1978). *Mann-Frau. Rollenklischees im Unterricht.* Wien: Urban & Schwarzenberg.

Wales, Kathleen. (1978). Further notes on personal reference in colloquial English. *UEA Papers in Linguistics.* 7, 1-10.

Ward, Martha C. (1971). *Them Children: A Study in Language Learning.* N.Y.: Holt, Rinehart & Winston.

Waterson, Natalie and Catherine Snow (eds.). (1978). *The Development of Communication.* Chichester, N.Y.: John Wiley & Sons.

Weaver, John D. (1980). *Los Angeles: The Enormous Village. 1781-1981.* Santa Barbara, Ca: Capra Press.

Weist, Richard M. and Betty Kruppe. (1977). Parent and sibling comprehension of children's speech. *Journal of Psycholinguistic Research.* 6, 49-58.

Weisz, John R. (1980). Autonomy, control, and other reasons why "Mom Is the Greatest": A content analysis of children's Mother's Day letters. *Child Development.* 51,801-07.

Wells, G. (1980). Adjustments in adult-child conversation: Some effects of interaction. In H. Giles, W. P. Robinson and P. Smith (eds.). 41-48.

Werlich, Egon. (1975). *Typologie der Texte.* Heidelberg: UTB.

Weydt, Harald (ed.). (1979). *Die Partikeln der deutschen Sprache.* Berlin: de Gruyter.

Williams, Frederick. (1973). Some research notes on dialect attitudes and stereotypes. In R. W. Shuy and R. W. Fasold (eds.). *Language Attitudes: Current Trends and Prospects.* Washington, D.C.: Georgetown Univ. Press. 113-28.

Wills, Dorothy D. (1977). Participant deixis in English and baby talk. In C. Snow and C. Ferguson (eds.). 271-95.

Winnicott, D. W. (1953). Transitional objects and transitional phenomena: A study of the first not-me possession. *International Journal of Psycho-Analysis.* 34, 89-97.

Winterowd, W. Ross. (1979). Brain, rhetoric and style. In D. McQuade (ed.). *Linguistics, Stylistics, and the Teaching of Composition.* Akron, Ohio: L&S Books. 151-81.

Wittgenstein, Ludwig. (1967). *Philosophische Untersuchungen.* Frankfurt/ M.: Fischer.

Wodak-Leodolter, Ruth and Wolfgang Dressler. (1978). Phonological varia-

tion in colloquial Viennese. *Michigan Germanic Studies*. IV(1),30-66.
Wodak-Leodolter, Ruth. (1980). Probleme der soziolinguistichen Feldforschung am Beispiel der Analyse spontansprachlicher Texte. *Linguistiche Studien Reihe A* 72/II,50-75.
Wodak, Ruth. (1981a). *Das Wort in der Gruppe. Linguistische Studien zur therapeutischen Kommunikation*. Wien: Verl. d. Österr. Akademie d. Wissenschaften. (Published in English: 1986, *Language Behavior in Therapy Groups*. L.A.: Univ. of California Press).
Wodak, Ruth. (1981b). Die Beziehung zwischen Mutter und Tochter: eine sozio- und psycholinguistische Studie zur Variation auf der Textebene. *Folia Linguistica*, 38-86.
Wodak, Ruth. (1981c). Gastarbeiterdeutsch: Probleme des Zweitspracherwerbs für Gastarbeiterkinder. *Die Sprache*. 129-40.
Wodak, Ruth. (1981d). How do I put my problem? Problem presentation in therapy and interview. *Text*. 1-2, 191-213.
Wodak, Ruth. (1981e). Women relate, men report. *Journal of Pragmatics*. 5,261-85.
Wodak, Ruth. (1981f). Geschlechtsspezifische Strategien in einer therapeutischen Gruppe. Aspekte einer sozio- und psycho- linguistischen Untersuchung. In: Autorinnengruppe Uni Wien. 232-52.
Wodak, Ruth. (1983). Arguments in favor of a socio-psycholinguistic theory of textplanning: Sex-specific language behavior revisited. In H. Pohl, (ed.). *Papers of the 10th Austrian Linguistics Meeting*. Klagenfurter Linguistische Beiträge. 313-50.
Wodak, Ruth. (1984). (1984). *Hilflose Nähe? - Mütter und Töchter erzählen*. Wien: Deuticke.
Wodak, Ruth and Sylvia Moosmüller. (1981). Sprechen Töchter anders als ihre Mütter? Eine sozio-und psycholinguistische Studie zum Wienerdeutschen. *Wiener Linguistische Gazette*. 26. 87-110.
Wunderlich, Dieter. (1976). *Sprechakttheorie*. Frankfurt/M: Suhrkamp.
Wunderlich, Dieter. (1979). Was ist das fur ein Sprechakt? In G. Grewendorf (ed.). 275-324.
Yarrow, Leon J. (1963). Research in dimensions of early maternal care. *Merrill-Palmer Quarterly*. 9, 101-14.

# INDEX OF AUTHORS & NAMES

Beaugrande, R.A. de   18ff
Bergmann, A.   49
Bernard, J.   3, 13, 35
Blos, P.   11, 89

Cherry, L.J.   42ff
Chodorow, N.   3, 7f, 10, 14, 25, 45f
Cicourel, A.   25, 53, 148
Cohler, B.   11, 46, 50, 147

Dally, A.   3, 11
van Dijk, T.A.   18f., 85
Dressler, W.U.   17ff., 24, 69

Ervin-Tripp, S.   27, 29, 32, 38, 69

Filstead, W.J.   53, 151
Freud, S.   7f., 23, 58, 91, 151
Friday, N.   3, 32
Friedrichs, J. 62, 114

Goffman, E.   33
Grunebaum,   11, 46, 50, 153
Gumperz, J.   17, 28, 36

Habermas, J.   53, 55

Klann-Delius, G.   15ff., 24, 47
Kramarae, Ch.   17, 79
Labov, W.   40, 69, 71, 111, 142, 144
Leodolter, R.   (see Wodak, R.)
Lynn, D.B.   14f., 51, 61, 91, 152
Maccoby, E.E.   33, 36f., 43f., 49
Marie Antoinette   1f.
Maria Theresa   1f.
Mitchell, J.   7
Moeller-Gambarov, M.   3

Ochs, E.   21, 39, 51
Oevermann, U.   17, 55, 63, 78

Phelps, L.   85

Snow, C.E.   26ff., 36
Stone, P.J.   55f.
Sudnow, D.   53

Wodak, R.   16, 18, 24, 40, 54, 56, 63, 69, 85, 145
Wunderlich, D.   55

# INDEX OF SUBJECTS

adjective   75, 102f, 152, 157,161
affect   (see feelings)
affectivity   (see feelings)
ambivalence   (see feelings)
bisexuality   10,23
caretaker   13, 15, 25f., 28ff., 34, 37, 39 (see also Motherese)
   influence of—   25f., 33f., 43
   — in the afternoon   23, 64, 123, 153f,171
   — register   26ff.
   — stays in   29
   —talk   25ff., 32, 39f., 51f.
case studies   53f., 69, 153ff
   American—   128ff., 155, 158, 162, 165, 169, 175, 180, 184
   Austrian—   127ff., 153, 157, 161, 164, 167, 172, 178, 182
   comparison of—   60, 63, 113, 121, 156, 160, 163, 167, 171, 177, 181, 187
   methodology of—   61
   qualitative —   60, 63, 155ff.
categories   54, 56, 67, 71
   definition of—   71ff.
   — for essay analysis   68, 72ff.
   — for Gießen-Test analysis   199ff.
   — for interview analysis   68
   — for mothertypes (clusters)   125ff.

class   16ff., 22f., 27, 36, 39f., 44, 47, 50, 58, 61, 65ff., 78
   — & culture   14, 44ff., 58, 65, 134
   — & ethnicity   14f., 40, 52, 60, 65ff., 69, 72, 92, 132
   notion of—   24, 58, 63, 65f., 68
   — & mothertype   80, 157, 173
   — & relationship   146
   — & school   59, 64, 66f., 108
   — & sex 16f., 45
cliché   (see ideology)
conflict   2f., 54, 61, 81, 83, 89
   — between mothers and daughters   2, 11, 14, 22f., 90
   — between mothers and sons   2, 11
   generation —   3, 123
   role —   12
   value   —90, 126
content analysis   54ff., 71, 89
control   14, 34, 38
   — and mothertype   124
   — as variable (Gießen-Test)   119
   direct —   35
   indirect —   35ff., 41
culture   1, 22, 25, 40, 44f., 57, 80, 87, 132, 150
   — and city development   57f.
   — and family structures   91, 147
   — and ideology   57f.

— and schools   21, 57, 65
Austrian —   57, 60, 63
differences between -s   15, 22,
  50, 57, 60, 65, 68, 77, 92, 98,
  107, 148
historical background of —
  57f.
US —   57f., 60, 148, 157

development   4, 31,35f., 40, 46
— and culture   60
disturbed —   155
female —   4, 6, 9, 11, 25, 60,
  120
male —   7
discrimination against women   13,
  124ff., 158, 161
dominance   124

education   58, 66f., 108
educational style   35, 69, 78, 82,
  89, 121, 138, 153
— and ethnicity   35, 39, 82
liberal —   69, 82, 126, 148, 157,
  168
— and mothertype   125ff.
— and relationship   146
repressive —   69, 79, 153, 160f,
  164, 181, 184, 185
— and sex   35, 41, 162
— and social class   17, 35, 82
essay   21, 60, 62, 64, 66ff., 71f.
analysis of -s   54, 76, 100, 120
analytic —   72ff., 93 (non-re-
  flective)
comparison of -s   103
correlation with —   120
crosscultural comparison of -s
  87, 107

reflective   72f., 93f., 103, 181f
— text   68
topic of —   59, 66, 75, 78, 96, 98
family   124ff., 50, 59, 61, 91, 147
change of -structure   148
function of —   109
— network   30f., 120, 123, 127,
  148f.
— structure   17, 58ff., 62, 87,
  120, 148f, 150
—type   61, 147
feelings (emotions, affectivity   8,
  15f., 29, 33, 35f., 48ff., 54, 65,
  74, 78f., 83, 93, 98, 103, 123,
  145, 156
admiration   7, 83, 91
affectivity   83, 90
aggression   15
ambivalence   3, 7ff., 23, 75ff.,
  79f., 83f., 90f., 99, 102, 105,
  122, 126, 128, 141, 145, 153f.,
  157, 161f.
— and dialogue   78
fear   16, 91
guilt   7, 11, 16, 26, 29, 35, 37,
  46f., 82, 84, 91, 161f, 164, 179
hate   7, 83f., 91, 161f, 182
— in essays   83f., 93
jealousy   2, 83f., 88, 91, 122,
  157f, 177, 179
love   2, 7f., 16, 26, 29, 35, 46,
  84, 91
feminism   4, 98
— and psychoanalysis   7
crosscultural comparison of feminist movement   58
influence of —   13, 110, 154
fieldwork   60, 64, 115ff.

crosscultural differences in —
   59f.
   ethnical dilemma in —   61
   methodology of —   59, 61f., 113
   observer paradox in —   61
participant observation in —   61
   problems in —   59,62
guilt   (see feelings)
hermeneutics   (see interpretation)
hypotheses   59
   — of crosscultural comparison
      59
   — of essay analysis   59
   — of whole study 22f., 53, 59
identity   9, 30, 50
   — development   7, 11, 14, 23,
      33
   — sex-specific   4, 8f., 38, 50
ideology   22, 120f., 146ff, 150
   — and clichés   96, 98, 149
   cliché   74, 77, 94ff., 102ff., 147,
      149, 162, 170
   cultural —   96, 98, 147f
   — on motherhood   91, 96, 149,
      170
individuation   5, 9, 11, 45, 93
   — and separation   3, 8f., 45
interpretation   55, 73
   hermeneutic   — 54f.
   multilevel —   56
interview   54, 59, 62, 67, 88
   — analysis (qualitative)   113ff.,
      120, 142ff.
   — analysis (quantitative)   113,
      115

crosscultural comparison of -s
   127, 132
   — with daughters   5, 59f., 62,
      115, 117, 153, 155
   — with mothers   5, 59f., 116,
      120, 122, 141
love   (see feelings)
marriage (partnership)   1, 8, 11,
   183
   wish to marry   128, 137, 153
masochism   11, 123, 125, 150, 156
memory
   episodic —   72, 74f., 94, 141
   semantic —   72, 74f., 94, 141
methodology
   methodological considerations
      53, 56, 114
   qualitative —   53
   quantitative —   53
mood   119
   and family relationship   124
   and mothertype   124
   — and satisfaction   124
mother   12, 27, 29f., 32ff., 44ff.,
   59f., 62, 66, 71f., 88, 121
   — ideology   1f., 12
   — love   30, 137
   — myth   13, 153
   relationship to —   7f., 10ff., 68,
      83, 145
   relationship to grandmother —
      30, 179, 185
   — role   10, 12ff., 30, 80, 88ff.,
      103, 153, 162, 172
   —type   60, 113, 115, 121, 126
   —typology   121, 123, 125
motherese (caretaker talk)   4, 15,

25ff., 29f., 38, 41, 45, 120, 151f
cultural differences in — 25
function of — 29, 41
sexspecific — 32, 149
particle 75, 79, 83, 95, 99, 103,
145, 153, 157, 161, 164, 167, 175,
182f
penis envy (anxiety) 8, 23, 50
phonology 18
pre-oedipal phase 4, 7, 9
primary person 7, 10, 26, 34,
36ff., 39, 123
profession 12
— in conflict with other roles
12f, 122
— of father 66
— of mother 64, 66, 122
satisfaction with — 125
— of women 13, 23, 66, 130
puberty 59, 156
rationalization 8, 12, 81f., 91,
147, 168, 179
— as textual strategy 84
reality 5, 25, 41, 120
analytic view of — 40, 50, 89, 94
reflective (Gestalt) view of —
40, 50, 94
regression 31, 156 (see also relationship to researcher)
— as female strategy 91
— as textual strategy 84
relationship 1, 4f., 7f., 12, 14ff.,
22, 26, 30f., 34ff., 45f., 58ff., 69,
77f., 87, 89, 92, 100, 120, 145,
146, 150
— to mother 7, 10f., 30, 50, 59,
68, 71ff., 82f., 90f., 103, 122f.,
131, 139ff., 155, 161, 176

— to father 11, 38, 122, 130,
155, 161f, 183, 169, 173, 179
— to daughter 23, 122ff., 131,
145, 147, 153f, 168, 182
— to sister, brother 138
— to researcher 84, 91f.
rivalry 2, 83, 90, 168, 170fm 173
role 16, 19, 38, 44, 46, 54
— conflict 14, 122, 168
cultural — 12f., 45
daughter — 3, 7, 23
mother — 8, 10, 12ff., 23, 30,
35, 38, 41, 45f., 59, 80, 88, 153f,
179
parental — 13, 26, 30, 37f., 52
sexspecific — 3, 4, 7ff., 13f., 38,
45, 49f., 59, 88, 145, 150
social — 4, 25, 41, 48
sanction 14, 82
— and punishment 89, 121, 138
inconsistent — 82
— in family 121, 138
nonverbal — 14, 82
verbally explained — 82, 138
satisfaction 154
— with life 124, 126f., 156f
— with profession 125
— with womens' role 123f.,
127, 146, 156f
school 10, 21, 35, 40, 58f., 62,
65f., 68, 96
— and profession 109, 130, 133
classpecific — 65f.
crosscultural comparison of —s
65, 108
ethnic — 60, 67
fieldwork in —s 59, 64, 66
halfday — 64, 122

— type 63f., 66f
whole day — 123, 178
self 119, 124, 156
— assessment 54, 59, 62, 81, 89,
113ff., 120, 153, 155
— image 80f., 89, 103
semiotics 19, 78, 95, 99, 103
separation 2f., 5, 7ff., 22, 32, 38,
45f., 51, 83, 90, 93, 122, 146ff.
sociopsychological 18
— parameters 72, 76, 87
— textvariation 69, 87, 120
— theory of textplanning 19,
22f., 41, 93, 100, 110
strategy 38
super ego 1,5
symbiosis 2, 5, 10f., 30ff., 41,
45f., 50, 52, 90, 105
— tic relationship 41

taboo 2, 62, 75, 79, 89, 91f., 120f,
138, 145, 149
tanzlied 2, 11, 38
test 121
psychological — 115
Gießen — 59f., 113, 115, 119ff.,
123, 125, 156, 161, 163, 167,
171, 177, 181, 187
text 18f., 30, 55, 79, 153
— and frame 20ff.
— and schema 19ff., 72

— and writing 5, 21, 73, 77
— categories 72, 83
— class 5
— coherence 73ff., 79, 95,
102f., 145, 147
— cohesion 73, 104
cultural — 5
— length 55, 77, 98
macro — 18, 95
— planning 18
— and script 20ff.
sexspecific — 5, 15
—type 18f., 72, 93, 95, 141, 145
179
transference 7, 70
— between researcher and infor-
mant 84, 91
— in everyday life 123
— in therapy 69f.

variables 13f., 40, 42
clusters of — 125, 150
personality — 125, 150
psychological — 22f., 87, 110
sociological — 22f., 87, 110
text — 93ff.
variation 15f., 23f., 40, 54, 68f.
sociopsychological —17f., 41,
52, 69, 78f., 87ff., 145
textual — 22, 68
verbalization 14, 16, 18ff., 41, 99

In the BENJAMINS PAPERBACKS series the following volumes have been published thus far:

1. MEY, Jacob: *Whose Language: A Study in Linguistic Pragmatics*. Amsterdam, 1985.
2. COLLINGE, N.E.: *The Laws of Indo-European*. Amsterdam, 1985.
3. WODAK, Ruth & Muriel SCHULZ: *The Language of Love and Guilt. Mother-daughter relationships from a cross-cultural perspective*. Amsterdam, 1986.
4. LUELSDORFF, Philip: Constraints on Error Variables in Grammar: Bilingual Misspelling Orthographies. Amsterdam, 1986.
5. COWAN, William & Jaromira RAKUŠAN: *Source book for Linguistics*. Philadelphia/Amsterdam, 1985.